DOCTRINE AND COVENANTS 2025

Come, Follow Me—
For Home and Church

Living, Learning, and Teaching the Gospel of Jesus Christ

Published by
The Church of Jesus Christ of Latter-day Saints
Salt Lake City, Utah

Published by The Church of Jesus Christ of Latter-day Saints

© 2024 by Intellectual Reserve, Inc.
All rights reserved.
Version: 1/23
PD80032147
Printed in the United States of America

Comments and corrections are appreciated. Please send them, including errors, to ComeFollowMe@ChurchofJesusChrist.org.

Table of Contents

Conversion Is Our Goal

The aim of all gospel learning and teaching is to deepen our conversion and help us become more like Jesus Christ. For this reason, when we study the gospel, we're not just looking for new information; we want to become a "new creature" (2 Corinthians 5:17). This means relying on Heavenly Father and Jesus Christ to help us change our hearts, our views, our actions, and our very natures.

But the kind of gospel learning that strengthens our faith and leads to the miracle of conversion doesn't happen all at once. It extends beyond a classroom into an individual's heart and home. It requires consistent, daily efforts to understand and live the gospel. True conversion requires the influence of the Holy Ghost.

The Holy Ghost guides us to the truth and bears witness of that truth (see John 16:13). He enlightens our minds, quickens our understandings, and touches our hearts with revelation from God, the source of all truth. The Holy Ghost purifies our hearts. He inspires in us a desire to live by truth, and He whispers to us ways to do this. Truly, "the Holy Ghost . . . shall teach [us] all things" (John 14:26).

For these reasons, in our efforts to live, learn, and teach the gospel, we should first and foremost seek the companionship of the Spirit. This goal should govern our choices and guide our thoughts and actions. We should seek after whatever invites the influence of the Spirit and reject whatever drives that influence away—for we know that if we can be worthy of the presence of the Holy Ghost, we can also be worthy to live in the presence of Heavenly Father and His Son, Jesus Christ.

Using *Come, Follow Me—For Home and Church*

Who Is This Resource For?

This resource is for anyone who wants to study the Doctrine and Covenants—individually, as a family, and in Church classes. If you haven't studied the scriptures regularly in the past, this resource can help you get started. If you already have a good habit of scripture study, this resource can help you have more meaningful experiences.

Individuals and Families at Home

The ideal place to learn the gospel is at home. Your teachers at church can support you, and you can get encouragement from other ward members. But to survive spiritually, each of us needs daily nourishment from "the good word of God" (Moroni 6:4; see also Russell M. Nelson, "Opening Remarks," *Ensign* or *Liahona*, Nov. 2018, 6–8).

Use this resource in any way that is helpful to you. The outlines highlight some eternal truths found in the Doctrine and Covenants. They also suggest ideas and activities to help you study the scriptures individually, with family members, or with friends. As you study, follow the Spirit's guidance to find eternal truths that are meaningful to you. Look for God's messages for you, and follow the promptings you receive.

Teachers and Learners at Church

If you teach a Primary class, a youth or adult Sunday School class, an Aaronic Priesthood quorum, or a Young Women class, you are encouraged to use the outlines in this resource as you prepare to teach. *Come, Follow Me—For Home and Church* is the curriculum for your Sunday class. The learning ideas in this resource are designed for learning at home and at church. As you prepare to teach, start by having your own experiences in the scriptures. Your most important preparation will occur as you search the scriptures and seek personal inspiration from the Holy Ghost. You could also study with the needs of the people you teach in mind. Look for eternal truths. *Come, Follow Me* can help you identify some of these truths and learn how the scriptures can be applied in your life.

Keep in mind that learning the gospel, at its best, is home centered and Church supported. In other words, your main responsibility is to support the people you teach in their efforts to learn and live the gospel at home. Don't worry about having unique content to provide for them in class. Instead, give them opportunities to share their experiences, thoughts, and questions about the scripture passages they've read at home. Invite them to share the eternal truths they have found. This is more important than covering a certain amount of material.

Youth and Adult Sunday School Classes

One main reason we gather in Sunday School classes is to support and encourage one another as we strive to know and follow Jesus Christ. A simple way to do this is to ask a question like "What has the Holy Ghost taught you this week as you studied the scriptures with *Come, Follow Me*?" Answers to this question could lead to meaningful discussions that build faith in Jesus Christ and His gospel.

Then you could invite discussion based on the study suggestions in *Come, Follow Me*. For instance, a study idea might suggest searching Doctrine and Covenants 19:15–20, looking for how the Savior described His suffering. You might ask class members to share how they felt as they read His description and talk about how this affects the way they think about Him. Or you could spend some time studying these verses as a class.

Aaronic Priesthood Quorums and Young Women Classes

When Aaronic Priesthood quorums and Young Women classes meet on Sundays, their purpose is somewhat different from a Sunday School class. In addition to helping each other learn the gospel of Jesus Christ, these groups also meet to counsel together about accomplishing the work of salvation and exaltation (see *General Handbook: Serving in The Church of Jesus Christ of Latter-day Saints*, 1.2), as directed by their class or quorum presidency.

For this reason, each quorum or class meeting should begin with a member of the quorum or class presidency leading a discussion about their efforts. For example, they could counsel together about their efforts to live the gospel, minister to people in need, share the gospel, or participate in temple and family history work.

After this time for counseling together, an instructor leads the class or quorum in learning the gospel together. Adult leaders or members of the class or quorum can be assigned to teach. The class or quorum presidency, consulting with adult leaders, makes these assignments.

People assigned to teach should prepare by using the learning suggestions in the weekly outline of *Come, Follow Me*. In each outline, this icon 📖 indicates an activity that is especially relevant to youth and aligned with what they are learning in seminary. However, any of the suggestions in the outline could be used as a learning activity for youth.

For a sample agenda for quorum and class meetings, see appendix D.

Primary

Your preparation to teach Primary begins as you study the scriptures personally and with your family. As you do, be open to spiritual impressions and insights from the Holy Ghost about the children in your Primary class. Be prayerful. The Spirit can inspire you with ideas to help them learn the gospel of Jesus Christ.

As you prepare to teach, you might gain additional inspiration by exploring the teaching ideas in this resource. Each outline in *Come, Follow Me—For Home and Church* has a section titled "Ideas for Teaching Children." Think of these ideas as suggestions to spark your inspiration.

You know the children in your Primary class—and you will get to know them even better as you interact with them in class. God knows them too, and He will inspire you with the best ways to teach and bless them.

Children in your class may have already done some of the activities in *Come, Follow Me* with their families. That's OK. Repetition is good. Consider inviting the children to share with each other what they learned at home. You should also plan ways for children to participate even if they aren't learning at home. Children learn gospel truths more effectively when these truths are taught repeatedly through a variety of activities. If you find that a learning activity is effective for the children, consider repeating it, especially if you are teaching younger children.

In months that have five Sundays, Primary teachers are encouraged to replace the scheduled *Come, Follow Me* outline on the fifth Sunday with one or more of the learning activities in "Appendix B: For Primary—Preparing Children for a Lifetime on God's Covenant Path."

Ideas to Improve Learning at Home and at Church

As you study the Savior's gospel at home and at church, consider the following questions:

- How can you invite the Spirit into your study?

- How can you focus on the Savior in your study?

- How can you take advantage of everyday learning moments?

- How can you encourage family and class members to study the scriptures on their own and share what they are learning?

Here are some simple ways to enhance your study of the word of God.

Pray for inspiration

The scriptures are the word of God, so ask Him for help to understand them.

Look for truths about Jesus Christ

All things testify of Christ (see 2 Nephi 11:4; Moses 6:63), so consider noting or marking verses that testify of the Savior, deepen your love for Him, and teach how to follow Him. Sometimes truths about the Savior and His gospel are stated directly, and sometimes they are implied through an example or story. Ask yourself, "What eternal truths are taught in these verses? What do these truths teach me about the Savior?"

Listen to the Spirit

Pay attention to your thoughts and feelings, even if they are unrelated to what you are reading. These impressions may be what your Heavenly Father wants you to learn.

Record your impressions

There are many ways to record the impressions that come as you study. For example, you may find that certain words and phrases in the scriptures impress you; you could mark them and record your thoughts as a note in your scriptures. You could also keep a journal of the insights, feelings, and impressions you receive.

Share what you're learning with others

Discussing insights from your personal study is a good way to teach others, and it also helps strengthen your understanding of what you have read. Share what you're learning with family members and friends (in person or digitally), and invite them to do the same.

Relate the scriptures to your life

Consider how the stories and teachings you are reading apply to your life. For example, you could ask yourself, "What experiences have I had that are similar to what I am reading?"

Ask questions as you study

As you study the scriptures, questions may come to mind. These questions might relate to what you are reading or to your life in general. Ponder these questions and look for answers as you continue studying the scriptures.

Use scripture study helps

To gain additional insights into the verses you read, use the footnotes, the Topical Guide, the Bible Dictionary, the Guide to the Scriptures, and other study helps.

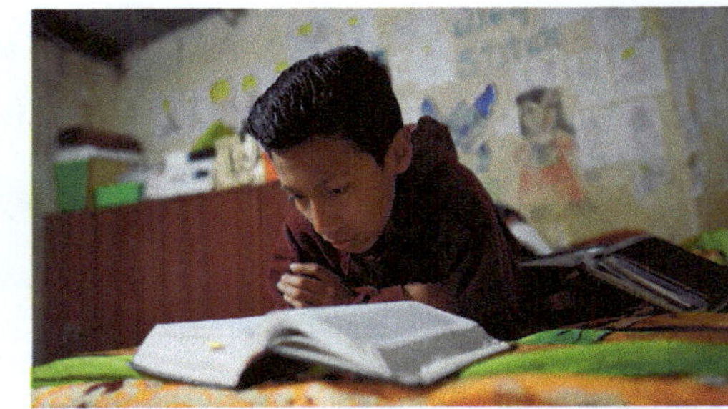

Consider the context of the scriptures

You can find meaningful insights about a scripture passage as you consider its context, including the circumstances or setting it came from. For example, knowing the background and beliefs of the people God spoke to can help you better understand the intent of His words. You can learn about them in *Saints*, *Revelations in Context*, the section headings in the Doctrine and Covenants, and other resources.

Study the words of latter-day prophets and apostles

Read what latter-day prophets and apostles have taught about the principles you find in the scriptures.

Live by what you learn

Scripture study should not only inspire us but also lead us to change the way we live. Listen to what the Spirit prompts you to do as you read, and then act on these promptings.

Use music

Suggested hymns and children's songs are found throughout *Come, Follow Me.* Use sacred music to invite the Spirit and to deepen your faith and testimony of gospel truths.

Memorize scriptures

Select a scripture passage that is meaningful to you, your family, or your class, and memorize it by repeating it daily or by playing a memorization game.

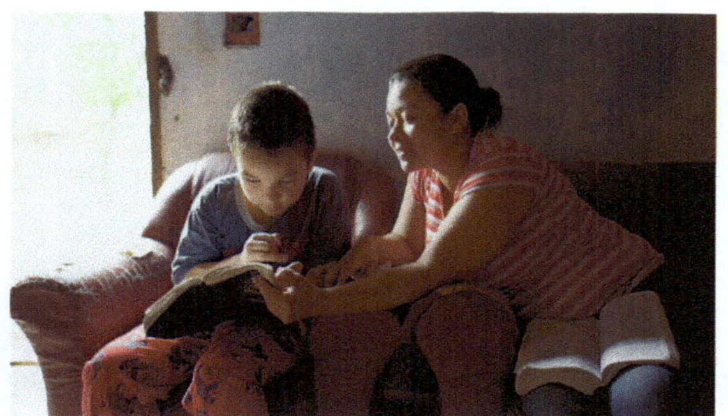

Share object lessons

Find objects that relate to the chapters and verses that you are reading. Consider how each object relates to the teachings in the scriptures.

Draw, find, or take a picture

Read a few verses, and then draw something that relates to what you read. Or you could look for a picture in the *Gospel Art Book* or elsewhere in the Gospel Library. You could also take a picture that illustrates what you learned.

Dramatize a story

After reading a story, invite family or class members to act it out. Afterward, talk about how the story relates to the things that you are experiencing.

Be flexible at home

If you have family members who aren't willing to participate in family scripture study, look for other ways to connect with them. For example, could you share eternal truth naturally in your conversations or share a meaningful scripture in a way that doesn't seem preachy or overbearing? Scripture study doesn't have to look the same in every family. Some children may respond better to studying the scriptures one on one. Be prayerful and follow the promptings of the Spirit.

Teacher council meetings for parents. If you would like additional help in your efforts to teach your children, find out if your ward is holding teacher council meetings for parents (see *General Handbook*, 17.4). These meetings are an opportunity for parents to counsel and learn together about how to improve their teaching. They can discuss the principles in *Teaching in the Savior's Way*, the ideas on these pages for improving family scripture study, and the learning and teaching suggestions found throughout *Come, Follow Me.*

The Restoration of the Fulness of the Gospel of Jesus Christ

How do you commemorate the 200th anniversary of an event that changed the world? That's the question the First Presidency and Quorum of the Twelve Apostles pondered as April 2020 approached, marking 200 years since Joseph Smith's First Vision. "We wondered if a monument should be erected," President Russell M. Nelson recalled. "But as we considered the unique historic and international impact of that First Vision, we felt impressed to create a monument not of granite or stone but of words . . . , not to be carved in 'tables of stone' but rather to be etched in the 'fleshy tables' of our hearts [2 Corinthians 3:3]" ("Hear Him," *Ensign* or *Liahona*, May 2020, 90).

The monument of words they created is titled "The Restoration of the Fulness of the Gospel of Jesus Christ: A Bicentennial Proclamation to the World." It's a monument not just to the First Vision but also to everything Jesus Christ has done—and is still doing—since then. The Restoration of His gospel started when one person turned to God and heard Him. It continues that same way: one heart, one sacred experience at a time—including yours.

 Ideas for Learning at Home and at Church

"God loves His children in every nation of the world."

In your opinion, why would a proclamation about the Restoration begin with a statement about God's love? As you study the proclamation, look for expressions of God's love for "His children in every nation of the world." How has the Restoration of the gospel helped you feel His love?

See also Gerrit W. Gong, "All Nations, Kindreds, and Tongues," *Ensign* or *Liahona*, Nov. 2020, 38–41.

The Restoration began with an answer to a question.

It could be said that the Savior started the Restoration of His gospel by responding to a question. What message do you feel the Restoration proclamation has for a person with questions about God, the gospel, or "the salvation of his [or her] soul"? You might also study Joseph

Detail from *The Desires of My Heart*, by Walter Rane

Smith—History 1:5–20 to see what you can learn from Joseph Smith about finding answers to gospel questions.

See also Topics and Questions, "Seeking Answers," Gospel Library.

📖 Jesus Christ has restored His Church.

What do you know about "Christ's New Testament Church," which the Savior restored through Joseph Smith? Consider studying these scriptures and listing some features of His Church:

- Matthew 16:15–19

  Keys

- Mark 16:15–18

  Blessing - preach the Gospel, baptized

- Luke 6:12–13

  12 disciples - called by God

- Acts 4:34–35

  tithing

- 1 Corinthians 15:29

  baptized for the dead

- Ephesians 4:11–15

  truth in love Christ - prophet and teachers

Next, you could match the scriptures above with those below, which describe how Jesus Christ restored those features of His Church through Joseph Smith:

- Doctrine and Covenants 18:37–38; 107:23–24

  luke 6:12-13

- Doctrine and Covenants 51:3; 70:14

  Act 4:34-35

- Doctrine and Covenants 84:64–72

  Mark 16:15-18

- Doctrine and Covenants 110:11–16

  Matthew 16:15-19

- Doctrine and Covenants 124:31, 36

  1 Corinthians 15-29

- Articles of Faith 1:6

  Ephesians 4:11-15

Why are you grateful for the Restoration of the gospel of Jesus Christ?

Elder Jeffrey R. Holland and his wife once tried to imagine how they would have felt living before the Church was restored. "What do we wish we had?" they asked themselves. Read about their experiences in "A Perfect Brightness of Hope" (*Ensign* or *Liahona*, May 2020, 81–82). How has the Restoration helped fulfill your spiritual hopes?

See also Topics and Questions, "Apostasy and the Restoration of the Gospel," Gospel Library.

"The promised Restoration goes forward."

Have you ever thought of yourself as part of the Restoration of the gospel? Consider these words from President Dieter F. Uchtdorf: "Sometimes we think of the Restoration of the gospel as something that is complete, already behind us. . . . In reality, the Restoration is an ongoing process; we are living in it right now" ("Are You Sleeping through the Restoration?," *Ensign* or *Liahona*, May 2014, 59).

As you prepare to study how the gospel was restored in the 1800s, you might start by pondering how it was restored in your life. Read the Restoration proclamation with questions like these in mind: How have I come to know that this is true? How do I participate in the Restoration today?

"The heavens are open."

What does the phrase "the heavens are open" mean to you? What evidence do you see—in the Restoration proclamation, in the Church today, in the scriptures, and in your life—that the heavens truly are open?

You might also include "The Morning Breaks" (*Hymns*, no. 1) as part of your study. What do you find in this hymn that adds to your understanding of the phrase "the heavens are open"?

See also Quentin L. Cook, "The Blessing of Continuing Revelation to Prophets and Personal Revelation to Guide Our Lives," *Ensign* or *Liahona*, May 2020, 96–100.

Learn together. President Nelson invited us to "study [the Restoration proclamation] privately and with [our] family members and friends" ("Hear Him," 92). Consider how you might include others in your study.

For more ideas, see this month's issues of the *Liahona* and *For the Strength of Youth* magazines.

 ## Ideas for Teaching Children

"We solemnly proclaim."

- As you read parts of the Restoration proclamation with your children (or watch the video of President Nelson reading it), help them find sentences that begin with phrases like "we proclaim," "we declare," or "we testify." What truths are our prophets and apostles declaring? Perhaps you and your children could share your own testimonies of some of these same truths.

"Joseph Smith . . . had questions."

- It might be interesting to your children to explore some of the questions Joseph Smith had that led to the Restoration of the Savior's gospel. Help them find some examples in Joseph Smith—History 1:10, 29, 68. How are we blessed today because God answered Joseph Smith's questions?

- You might also give your children a chance to talk about questions they have. What do we learn from Joseph Smith about how to find answers? (see Joseph Smith—History 1:8–17; see also verses 3 and 4 of "This Is My Beloved Son," *Children's Songbook*, 76).

"Heavenly messengers came to instruct Joseph."

- Who were the "heavenly messengers [who] came to instruct Joseph"? Your children might enjoy looking for pictures of them in the *Gospel Art Book* (see nos. 91, 93, 94, 95). How did each of these messengers help "re-establish the Church of Jesus Christ"? The scriptures suggested in this week's activity page can help your children answer this question.

Jesus Christ has restored His Church.

- How might you help your children understand what it means for the Savior's Church to be restored? Maybe they could build a simple tower with blocks or cups and "restore," or rebuild, it. Or, if your children have ever had to replace something because it was lost or damaged, you could compare that experience to the Savior restoring His Church. Help them find specific things mentioned in the Restoration proclamation that the Savior restored.

"The heavens are open."

- To illustrate what the phrase "the heavens are open" means, maybe you could share a message with your children, first behind a closed door and then through an open door. Let them take turns sharing a message too. What messages does Jesus Christ have for us? What experiences have helped us know that the heavens are open to us?

For more ideas, see this month's issue of the *Friend* magazine.

THE RESTORATION OF THE FULNESS OF THE GOSPEL OF JESUS CHRIST

A BICENTENNIAL PROCLAMATION TO THE WORLD

THE FIRST PRESIDENCY AND COUNCIL OF THE TWELVE APOSTLES OF THE CHURCH OF JESUS CHRIST OF LATTER-DAY SAINTS

We solemnly proclaim that God loves His children in every nation of the world. God the Father has given us the divine birth, the incomparable life, and the infinite atoning sacrifice of His Beloved Son, Jesus Christ. By the power of the Father, Jesus rose again and gained the victory over death. He is our Savior, our Exemplar, and our Redeemer.

Two hundred years ago, on a beautiful spring morning in 1820, young Joseph Smith, seeking to know which church to join, went into the woods to pray near his home in upstate New York, USA. He had questions regarding the salvation of his soul and trusted that God would direct him.

In humility, we declare that in answer to his prayer, God the Father and His Son, Jesus Christ, appeared to Joseph and inaugurated the "restitution of all things" (Acts 3:21) as foretold in the Bible. In this vision, he learned that following the death of the original Apostles, Christ's New Testament Church was lost from the earth. Joseph would be instrumental in its return.

We affirm that under the direction of the Father and the Son, heavenly messengers came to instruct Joseph and re-establish the Church of Jesus Christ. The resurrected John the Baptist restored the authority to baptize by immersion for the remission of sins. Three of the original twelve Apostles—Peter, James, and John—restored the apostleship and keys of priesthood authority. Others came as well, including Elijah, who restored the authority to join families together forever in eternal relationships that transcend death.

We further witness that Joseph Smith was given the gift and power of God to translate an ancient record: the Book of Mormon—Another Testament of Jesus Christ. Pages of this sacred text include an account of the personal ministry of Jesus Christ among people in the Western Hemisphere soon after His Resurrection. It teaches of life's purpose and explains the doctrine of Christ, which is central to that purpose. As a companion scripture to the Bible, the Book of Mormon testifies that all human beings are sons and daughters of a loving Father in Heaven, that He has a divine plan for our lives, and that His Son, Jesus Christ, speaks today as well as in days of old.

We declare that The Church of Jesus Christ of Latter-day Saints, organized on April 6, 1830, is Christ's New Testament Church restored. This Church is anchored in the perfect life of its chief cornerstone, Jesus Christ, and in His infinite Atonement and literal Resurrection. Jesus Christ has once again called Apostles and has given them priesthood authority. He invites all of us to come unto Him and His Church, to receive the Holy Ghost, the ordinances of salvation, and to gain enduring joy.

Two hundred years have now elapsed since this Restoration was initiated by God the Father and His Beloved Son, Jesus Christ. Millions throughout the world have embraced a knowledge of these prophesied events.

We gladly declare that the promised Restoration goes forward through continuing revelation. The earth will never again be the same, as God will "gather together in one all things in Christ" (Ephesians 1:10).

With reverence and gratitude, we as His Apostles invite all to know—as we do—that the heavens are open. We affirm that God is making known His will for His beloved sons and daughters. We testify that those who prayerfully study the message of the Restoration and act in faith will be blessed to gain their own witness of its divinity and of its purpose to prepare the world for the promised Second Coming of our Lord and Savior, Jesus Christ.

This proclamation was read by President Russell M. Nelson as part of his message at the 190th Annual General Conference, April 5, 2020, in Salt Lake City, Utah.

"The heavens are open."

Read these scriptures to learn about some of the angels who appeared to Joseph Smith to help restore the Savior's gospel. Then match the scriptures with the pictures below.

1. Doctrine and Covenants 27:12
2. Doctrine and Covenants 110:13–16
3. Joseph Smith—History 1:33
4. Joseph Smith—History 1:72

Doctrine and Covenants 1

In November 1831, the restored Church of Jesus Christ was just a year and a half old. Though growing, it was still a little-known group of believers living in relatively small towns, led by a prophet in his mid-twenties. But God considered these believers to be His servants and His messengers, and He wanted the revelations He had given them to be published to the world.

Doctrine and Covenants section 1 is the Lord's preface, or introduction, to these revelations. It clearly shows that even though the membership of the Church was small, there was nothing small about the message God wanted His Saints to share. It is a "voice of warning" for all "the inhabitants of the earth," teaching them to repent and establish God's "everlasting covenant" (verses 4, 8, 22). The servants carrying this message are "the weak and the simple." But humble servants are just what God calls for—then and now—to bring His Church "out of obscurity and out of darkness" (verses 23, 30).

 Ideas for Learning at Home and at Church

DOCTRINE AND COVENANTS 1

"Hearken, O ye people."

A preface introduces a book. It identifies the book's themes and purposes and helps readers prepare to read. As you read section 1—the Lord's "preface" to the Doctrine and Covenants (verse 6)—look for the themes and purposes the Lord gave for His revelations. What do you learn that will help you in your study of the Doctrine and Covenants this year? For example, you might ponder what it means to "hear the voice of the Lord" in these revelations (verse 14) or to "search these commandments" (verse 37).

See also the introduction to the Doctrine and Covenants.

DOCTRINE AND COVENANTS 1:4–6, 23–24, 37–39

The Lord speaks through His servants, including latter-day prophets.

Section 1 begins and ends with the Lord's declaration that He speaks through His chosen servants (see verses 4–6, 23–24, 38). Write down what you learn from this revelation about:

- The Lord and His voice. *everyone to hear*

- Why prophets are needed in our day. *God word*

What do you feel impressed to do as a result of what you find?

When have you heard the Lord's voice through the voice of His servants? (see verse 38). *God work through people*

You could also imagine that a friend who doesn't know about living prophets is reading section 1 with you. What questions might your friend have? Which verses would you want to discuss with your friend to help him or her understand how you feel about having prophets in our day?

You might be interested to know that when a council of elders met in 1831 to talk about publishing Joseph Smith's revelations, some people opposed the idea. They were embarrassed by Joseph's weakness in writing, and they worried that publishing the revelations might cause more problems for the Saints (see *Saints*, 1:140–43). If you had been a member of this council, how would you have addressed these concerns? What insights do you find in section 1 that might have helped? (see, for example, verses 6, 24, 38).

Consider including a hymn like "Come, Listen to a Prophet's Voice" (*Hymns*, no. 21) in your study and worship. Look for phrases in the hymn that teach the same principles as verses in section 1.

See also Topics and Questions, "Prophets," Gospel Library.

The Lord speaks to us through His servants, the prophets.

DOCTRINE AND COVENANTS 1:12–30, 34–36

The Restoration helps me face the challenges of the latter days.

In Doctrine and Covenants section 1, the Lord explains why He restored His gospel. See how many reasons you can list as you read verses 12–23. In your experience, how are the Lord's purposes for the Restoration being accomplished?

The Lord knew that our day would have serious challenges (see verse 17). What do you find in verses 17–30, 34–36 that helps you feel peace and confidence despite these challenges?

See also Russell M. Nelson, "Embrace the Future with Faith," *Ensign* or *Liahona*, Nov. 2020, 73–76.

DOCTRINE AND COVENANTS 1:19–28

The Lord uses "the weak and the simple" to accomplish His work.

As you read Doctrine and Covenants 1:19–28, you might ponder what it means to be a servant of the Lord. What characteristics does the Lord want His servants to have? What is the Lord accomplishing through His servants? How are the prophecies in these verses being fulfilled throughout the world and in your life?

> **Look for Jesus Christ.** The purpose of the scriptures is to testify of the Savior and His gospel. As you read Doctrine and Covenants 1, consider marking or noting verses that teach you something about Jesus Christ.

> For more ideas, see this month's issues of the *Liahona* and *For the Strength of Youth* magazines.

 # Ideas for Teaching Children

DOCTRINE AND COVENANTS 1:4, 37–39

Through His prophets, the Lord warns me of spiritual danger.

- To start a discussion about warnings from the Lord, you could talk about warnings we receive from other people about dangers we cannot see. Some examples might include a slippery floor, a coming storm, or an approaching car. Maybe you and your children could look at examples of warning signs and compare these warnings to the warnings the Lord gives us. According to Doctrine and Covenants 1:4, 37–39, how does the Lord warn us? What has He warned us about recently? Perhaps you could watch or read parts of recent general conference messages and look for examples of God's "voice of warning."

- Sing together a song about prophets, such as the last verse of "Follow the Prophet" (*Children's Songbook*, 111). Share your testimony that the prophet speaks the word of God.

DOCTRINE AND COVENANTS 1:17

The Restoration helps me face the challenges of the latter days.

- To encourage discussion about Doctrine and Covenants 1:17, you and your children could imagine you are preparing for a trip. What would you pack? If you knew ahead of time that it would rain or that your car or bus would get a flat tire, how would that affect the way you prepared for the trip? Read together verse 17, and talk about what the Lord knew would happen to us. How did He prepare for it? (If necessary, explain that a "calamity" is a disaster or terrible thing.) How do God's commandments help us deal with the challenges of our time?

DOCTRINE AND COVENANTS 1:17, 29

The Lord called Joseph Smith to be a prophet.

- To learn about the role of Joseph Smith in restoring the Savior's gospel, you and your children could look at a picture of the Savior and a picture of Joseph Smith (see the pictures in this outline) and talk about what the Savior gave us through Joseph Smith. Your children could look for examples in Doctrine and Covenants 1:17, 29. Tell your children how you know that God "called upon my servant Joseph Smith, Jun., and spake unto him from heaven" (verse 17).

© 1998 David Lindsley

DOCTRINE AND COVENANTS 1:30

The Church of Jesus Christ of Latter-day Saints is the Lord's "true and living church."

- What does it mean to say that the Church is "true and living"? To get your children thinking about this question, perhaps you could show them living and nonliving things—such as a live plant and a dead plant. How do we know something is living? Then you could read Doctrine and Covenants 1:30 and talk about what it might mean for the Church to be "true and living."

For more ideas, see this month's issue of the *Friend* magazine.

Beside Still Waters, by Simon Dewey

Through His prophets, the Lord warns us of spiritual danger (Doctrine and Covenants 1:4)

Complete the maze by using the warning signs to avoid going the wrong way.
Write in the space something from Doctrine and Covenants 1
that the Lord warned us about through the Prophet Joseph Smith.

Joseph Smith—History 1:1–26

You might say the Doctrine and Covenants is a book of answers to prayers: many of the sacred revelations in this book came in response to questions. The question that began it all—the one that sparked the latter-day outpouring of revelation—was asked by a 14-year-old boy. A "war of words and tumult of opinions" (Joseph Smith—History 1:10) had left Joseph Smith confused about religion and his relationship with God. Perhaps you can relate to that. We find many conflicting ideas and persuasive voices in our day. When we want to sort through these messages and find truth, we can do what Joseph did. We can ask questions, study the scriptures, ponder, and ultimately ask God. In response to Joseph's prayer, a pillar of light descended from heaven. God the Father and Jesus Christ appeared and answered his questions. Joseph's testimony of that miraculous experience boldly declares that anyone "who [lacks] wisdom might ask of God, and obtain" (Joseph Smith—History 1:26). We can all receive, if not a heavenly vision, at least a clearer vision, illuminated by heavenly light.

 Ideas for Learning at Home and at Church

JOSEPH SMITH—HISTORY 1:1–26

Joseph Smith is the Prophet of the Restoration.

The purpose of Joseph Smith's history was to put us "in possession of the facts" because the truth about Joseph has often been distorted (Joseph Smith—History 1:1). As you read Joseph Smith—History 1:1–26, what strengthens your testimony of his divine calling?

See also *Saints*, 1:3–19.

JOSEPH SMITH—HISTORY 1:5–25

How can I receive answers to my prayers?

Have you ever "lacked wisdom" or felt confused about a decision you needed to make? (Joseph Smith—History 1:13). The experience Joseph Smith had in 1820 can serve as a good pattern for your own personal revelation. For example, as you search Joseph Smith—History 1:5–25, look for experiences you can relate to. What do you learn about:

- How Joseph prepared for a sacred experience in prayer? (see verses 8, 11, 14–15).

- The role of scripture study in seeking revelation? (see verses 11–12).

- What to do when you face opposition? (see verses 15–16, 21–26).

- Accepting and acting on answers you receive? (see verses 18–25).

Invite sharing. Searching the scriptures invites impressions from the Holy Ghost. Sharing these impressions can invite the Holy Ghost to bear witness to others, as well as to the individual who is sharing.

What additional insights can you gain from President Henry B. Eyring's article "The First Vision: A Pattern for Personal Revelation"? (*Ensign* or *Liahona*, Feb. 2020, 12–17).

You might also look for other examples in the scriptures of people communicating with God. Images in the *Gospel Art Book* or other *Come, Follow Me* books could give you ideas. Try answering the questions listed previously for each example you find. What experiences have you had receiving answers to prayer? What can you do to help others have good experiences as well?

See also Russell M. Nelson, "Hear Him," *Ensign* or *Liahona*, May 2020, 88–92; Topics and Questions, "Personal Revelation," Gospel Library.

JOSEPH SMITH—HISTORY 1:15–20

Joseph Smith saw God the Father and His Son, Jesus Christ.

Joseph Smith trusted that God would answer his prayer, but he didn't anticipate how that answer would change his life—and the world. As you read about Joseph's experience, ponder how the results of the First Vision have changed your life.

For example, the First Vision revealed several truths about God the Father and His Son, Jesus Christ, that were different from what many people in Joseph's day believed. As you read Joseph Smith—History 1:15–20, consider writing down different ways to complete a statement like this one: "Because the First Vision happened, I know that . . ."

What feelings do you have as you ponder Joseph's experience and everything that came of it?

See also "Ask of God: Joseph Smith's First Vision" (video), Gospel Library; "Joseph Smith's First Prayer," *Hymns*, no. 26.

Detail from *If Any of You Lack Wisdom*, by Walter Rane

JOSEPH SMITH—HISTORY 1:21–26

I can remain true to what I know, even if others reject me.

After his remarkable First Vision, Joseph Smith naturally wanted to share his experience with others. The opposition he faced surprised him. As you read his account, what inspires you to remain true to your testimony? What other examples—from the scriptures, an ancestor, or people you know—give you courage to stay true to the spiritual experiences you have had?

See also Gary E. Stevenson, "Nourishing and Bearing Your Testimony," *Liahona*, Nov. 2022, 111–14.

For more ideas, see this month's issues of the *Liahona* and *For the Strength of Youth* magazines.

Ideas for Teaching Children

JOSEPH SMITH—HISTORY 1:3–14

Joseph Smith was prepared to be a prophet of God.

- Learning about Joseph Smith's youth could help your children relate to him as they learn from his experiences. Maybe they could hold a picture of Joseph Smith and share what they know about him. If needed, you might add some facts about him from Joseph Smith—History 1:3–14 (see also "Chapter 1: Joseph Smith and His Family," in *Doctrine and Covenants Stories*, 6–8, or the corresponding video in Gospel Library). What did Joseph experience that helped prepare him to become a prophet? What might God be preparing us to do?

Detail from *Joseph Smith's First Vision*, by Greg Olsen

JOSEPH SMITH—HISTORY 1:10–13

God can answer my questions through the scriptures.

- Consider showing your children a variety of books, including the scriptures. Help them think of questions these books can answer. Then you could read together Joseph Smith—History 1:10–11 to find out what questions Joseph Smith had and what answers he found in the scriptures.

- Your children might be able to find words in verse 12 that describe how reading James 1:5 affected Joseph. Then you could share experiences with each other in which a passage of scripture had a powerful influence on you. You could also sing together a song about reading the scriptures, such as "Search, Ponder, and Pray" (*Children's Songbook*, 109). What does the song teach about why we read the scriptures?

Heavenly Father hears and answers my prayers.

- To start a discussion about how we communicate with Heavenly Father, perhaps you and your children could ask each other questions using various communication methods, like a text message, a phone call, or a handwritten note. How do we ask questions to Heavenly Father? How do we show Him that we love and honor Him in our prayers? Read together Joseph Smith—History 1:16–19 and discuss how Heavenly Father answered Joseph Smith's prayer. You and your children could then share experiences when you asked God for help and received an answer.

Joseph Smith saw Heavenly Father and His Son, Jesus Christ.

- Young children might enjoy standing with outstretched arms pretending to be trees in the Sacred Grove while you tell them about the First Vision. Ask the children to sway as if being blown by the wind while you talk about Joseph praying. Then ask them to stand very still and quiet when you tell them Heavenly Father and Jesus appeared to Joseph.

- Older children might enjoy using one or more of the pictures in this outline to tell you what they know about the First Vision. Encourage them to refer to Joseph Smith—History 1:14–17 and to share their thoughts and feelings about Joseph's experience (see also "Chapter 2: Joseph Smith's First Vision," in *Doctrine and Covenants Stories*, 9–12, or the corresponding video in Gospel Library).

For more ideas, see this month's issue of the *Friend* magazine.

Truth Restored, by Leon Parson

Use the pictures to tell the story of the First Vision. Cut out the picture of Heavenly Father and Jesus Christ, and attach a craft stick to the back of the picture. Cut the dotted line on the picture of Joseph Smith, and insert the picture of Heavenly Father and Jesus Christ as if They are coming down from heaven.

Attach a craft stick to the back of the picture.

Joseph Smith saw Heavenly Father and His Son, Jesus Christ (Joseph Smith—History 1:17–19).

Detail from He Called Me by Name, by Michael Malm

Doctrine and Covenants 2; Joseph Smith—History 1:27–65

It had been three years since God the Father and His Son, Jesus Christ, appeared to Joseph Smith in the grove, and Joseph hadn't received any additional revelations since then. He began to wonder whether the Lord was displeased with him. Like all of us, he had made mistakes, and he felt condemned by them. Yet God still had a work for him to do. And the work Joseph was called to do is connected to what God asks of us. Joseph would bring forth the Book of Mormon; we are invited to share its message. Joseph would receive priesthood keys to turn the hearts of the children to their fathers; we can now receive ordinances for our ancestors in temples. Joseph was told of prophecies that would soon be fulfilled; we are called to help fulfill these prophecies. As we take part in God's work, we can expect to face opposition and even persecution, just as the Prophet did. But we can also have faith that the Lord will make us instruments in His hands, just as He did for Joseph.

See also *Saints*, 1:20–48.

  # Ideas for Learning at Home and at Church

JOSEPH SMITH—HISTORY 1:27–33

📖 God has a work for me to do.

It's one thing to believe that God had a work for Joseph Smith to do—we can look back on his life and clearly see what he accomplished. But have you ever considered that God has a work for you too? As you read Joseph Smith—History 1:27–33, think about what that work might be. How does it contribute to the ongoing Restoration of the Savior's gospel?

Elder Gary E. Stevenson taught: "As we come unto Christ and help others do the same, we participate in God's work of salvation and exaltation, which focuses on divinely appointed responsibilities. . . . These responsibilities are simple, inspirational, motivating, and doable. Here they are:

- Living the gospel of Jesus Christ

- Caring for those in need

- Inviting all to receive the gospel

- Uniting families for eternity" ("Simply Beautiful—Beautifully Simple," *Liahona*, Nov. 2021, 47).

Ponder the experiences you've had participating in each of these divinely appointed responsibilities. What would the Savior have you do next? There is a Topics and Questions page for each of these responsibilities (see "Our Role in God's Work of Salvation and Exaltation," Gospel Library). You might explore these pages to help you answer this question.

You may sometimes feel like the Lord can't use you because of mistakes you've made. What do you learn from Joseph Smith's experience in Joseph Smith—History 1:28–29? How can you know your "standing before [God]"?

Ask questions that encourage meaningful discussion. Questions that have more than one right answer invite learners to respond based on their personal thoughts, feelings, and experiences. The questions in this outline are examples of this.

See also "Youth Responsibility in the Work of Salvation" (video), ChurchofJesusChrist.org; "The Work of Salvation and Exaltation," *General Handbook*, 1.2.

JOSEPH SMITH—HISTORY 1:34–47

By restoring His gospel, the Savior fulfilled ancient prophecies.

When Moroni appeared to Joseph Smith, he quoted several Old and New Testament prophecies, such as Isaiah 11; Acts 3:22–23; and Joel 2:28–32. As you read Joseph Smith—History 1:34–47, think about why these prophecies might have been important for Joseph to know. Why are they important for you to know?

You could also read what Elder David A. Bednar taught about Moroni's first visit to Joseph Smith in "With the Power of God in Great Glory" (*Liahona*, Nov. 2021, 28).

See also "An Angel from on High," *Hymns*, no. 13.

Hill Cumorah, by Al Rounds

JOSEPH SMITH—HISTORY 1:48–60

God will prepare me to work in His kingdom.

Joseph was only 17 years old when he first saw the gold plates. They weren't entrusted to his care, however, until four years later. Read Joseph Smith—History 1:48–60, looking for what happened in Joseph's life during that time. How do you think these events prepared him for the work God called him to do? What experiences have you had that have prepared you to serve God and others? What are you currently experiencing that can help you prepare for future service?

DOCTRINE AND COVENANTS 2

The Lord sent Elijah to turn my heart to my ancestors.

What do words like "plant," "hearts," and "turn" in this section teach you about the mission of Elijah and the blessings of the priesthood keys he restored? How have you felt your heart turn toward your ancestors? Think of ways you can experience such feelings more often. Seeking your ancestors and performing ordinances for them in the temple is one way (see FamilySearch. org). What others can you think of?

See also Doctrine and Covenants 110:13–16; Gerrit W. Gong, "Happy and Forever," *Liahona*, Nov. 2022, 83–86.

For more ideas, see this month's issues of the *Liahona* and *For the Strength of Youth* magazines.

 # Ideas for Teaching Children

JOSEPH SMITH—HISTORY 1:28–29

I can repent and be forgiven.

- We all sometimes feel "condemned for [our] weakness and imperfections," as Joseph Smith did. You and your children could study Joseph Smith—History 1:29 together, looking for what Joseph did when he felt that way. What can we learn from his example that can help us when we make mistakes? Why is it important to know that Joseph was called by God even though he was not perfect?

JOSEPH SMITH—HISTORY 1:27–54

Heavenly Father called Joseph Smith to help Him do His work.

- Your children might have fun pretending to be Joseph Smith as you tell the account of Moroni's visits in Joseph Smith—History 1:27–54 or "Chapter 3: The Angel Moroni and the Gold Plates" (in *Doctrine and Covenants Stories*, 13–17, or the corresponding video in Gospel Library). For example, they could fold their arms like they are praying or pretend to climb the Hill Cumorah, and so on. Then you could ask them to talk about what God called Joseph Smith to do and how we are blessed as a result. For example, how have we been blessed because Joseph Smith translated the Book of Mormon? How has his work helped us come closer to Heavenly Father and Jesus Christ?

DOCTRINE AND COVENANTS 2

Heavenly Father wants families to be sealed in the temple.

- Perhaps you and your children would enjoy looking at some pictures of your family, possibly including a picture of your family at a temple (or see *Gospel Art Book*, no. 120). You could then read Doctrine and Covenants 2 and share with each other your thoughts about why we have temples and why Heavenly Father wants families to be together forever. Consider singing together "Families Can Be Together Forever" (*Children's Songbook*, 188). What does this song say we can do to be with our family forever?

Palmyra New York Temple

DOCTRINE AND COVENANTS 2

Learning about my ancestors can bring me joy.

- Children can become excited about and feel the joy of family history. To help them, you could share stories or pictures of your ancestors. Talk with your children about what life was like for their ancestors when they were children. Your children could also enjoy some of the family history activities on FamilySearch.org/discovery.

For more ideas, see this month's issue of the *Friend* magazine.

Joseph Receives the Plates, by Gary E. Smith

"The hearts of the children shall turn to their fathers"
(Doctrine and Covenants 2:2; Joseph Smith—History 1:39).

Draw a picture of yourself in the frame on the trunk of the tree, and draw members of your family in the other frames. Share your family tree with someone, and tell them why you are thankful for your family.

Doctrine and Covenants 3–5

During his first few years as the Lord's prophet, Joseph Smith didn't yet know everything about the "marvelous work" he had been called to do. But one thing his early experiences taught him was that to do God's work, his eye must be "single to the glory of God" (Doctrine and Covenants 4:1, 5). For example, if the Lord counseled him to do something he wasn't sure he wanted to do, he needed to follow the Lord's counsel. And even if he had "many revelations, and . . . power to do many mighty works," if he felt that what he wanted was more important than God's will, he "must fall" (Doctrine and Covenants 3:4). But Joseph learned something else just as important about doing God's work: "God is merciful," and if Joseph sincerely repented, he was "still chosen" (verse 10). God's work is, after all, a work of redemption. And that work "cannot be frustrated" (verse 1).

 Ideas for Learning at Home and at Church

DOCTRINE AND COVENANTS 3:1–16

I can trust God.

Early in Joseph Smith's ministry, good friends were hard to find—especially friends like Martin Harris, a respected, prosperous man who made great sacrifices to support Joseph's work. So when Martin asked for permission to show the first 116 manuscript pages of the Book of Mormon translation to his wife, Joseph naturally wanted to honor his request, even though the Lord had warned against it. Tragically, the pages were lost while in Martin's possession, and Joseph and Martin were sharply chastised by the Lord (see *Saints*, 1:51–53).

As you read Doctrine and Covenants 3:1–15, ponder what the Lord wants you to learn from their experience. For example, what do you learn about:

- God's work? (see verses 1–3, 16).
- The consequences of fearing man rather than trusting God? (see verses 4–8).
- The blessings that come from remaining faithful? (see verse 8).
- The way the Lord both corrected and encouraged Joseph? (see verses 9–16).

In his message "Which Way Do You Face?," Elder Lynn G. Robbins gives many scriptural examples of people who feared God and people who gave in to pressure from others (*Ensign* or *Liahona*, Nov. 2014, 9–11). Consider reading these examples in the scriptures he refers to. What do you learn from these accounts? What experiences have you had where you trusted the Lord when faced with pressure to do something different? What were the results of your actions?

See also Dale G. Renlund, "A Framework for Personal Revelation," *Liahona*, Nov. 2022, 16–19; "The Contributions of Martin Harris," in *Revelations in Context* (2016), 1–9; Topics and Questions, "Seeking Truth and Avoiding Deception," Gospel Library; "How Gentle God's Commands," *Hymns*, no. 125.

DOCTRINE AND COVENANTS 4

I can serve God with all my heart, might, mind, and strength.

Section 4 is often applied to full-time missionaries. However, it's interesting to note that this revelation was given to Joseph Smith Sr., who wasn't being called on a mission but still had "desires to serve God" (verse 3).

One way to read this section is to imagine it as a job description for someone who wants to help with the Lord's work. What is the Lord looking for? What benefits does He offer?

What do you learn about serving the Lord from this revelation?

President Russell M. Nelson called the gathering of Israel "the *greatest* challenge, the *greatest* cause, and the *greatest* work on earth" ("Hope of Israel" [worldwide youth devotional, June 3, 2018], Gospel Library). What do you find in his address that inspires you to participate in this work?

Everyone who has a desire to serve God is called to the work.

DOCTRINE AND COVENANTS 5

Through the Holy Ghost, I can gain a witness of the Book of Mormon.

In March 1829, Martin Harris's wife, Lucy, filed a claim in court that Joseph Smith was deceiving people by pretending to translate gold plates (see *Saints*, 1:56–58). So Martin asked Joseph for more evidence that the gold plates were real. Doctrine and Covenants 5 is a revelation in response to Martin's request. What do you learn from this section about the following:

- What the Lord says would happen if the gold plates were displayed for the world to see (see Doctrine and Covenants 5:7). Why do you think that's the case?

- The role of witnesses in the work of the Lord (see verses 11–15; see also 2 Corinthians 13:1).

- How to gain a testimony of the Book of Mormon for yourself (see verses 16, 24; see also Moroni 10:3–5).

DOCTRINE AND COVENANTS 5:1–10

Jesus Christ gave us His word through Joseph Smith.

What does Doctrine and Covenants 5:1–10 teach you about Joseph Smith's role in our day—and in your life? (See also 2 Nephi 3:6–24.)

For more ideas, see this month's issues of the *Liahona* and *For the Strength of Youth* magazines.

 Ideas for Teaching Children

DOCTRINE AND COVENANTS 3:5–10; 5:21–22

I can choose the right when others try to get me to do wrong.

- To start a discussion about learning to trust Heavenly Father, you might want to review the story of the lost manuscript pages (see *Doctrine and Covenants Stories*, 18–21). You could then role-play with your children situations when they might be tempted to do something they know isn't right. What words or phrases in Doctrine and Covenants 3:5–8; 5:21–22 could help them during these situations?

DOCTRINE AND COVENANTS 4

The Lord invites me to help with His work.

- Each verse in Doctrine and Covenants 4 contains precious truths that can help your children learn about serving God. Here are some ideas to help them discover these truths:

  - You could read together Doctrine and Covenants 4:1 and show pictures that depict God's "marvelous" latter-day work (such as missionaries, temples, and the Book of Mormon).

  - Your children could think of actions or draw pictures depicting the phrase "serve him with all your heart, might, mind and strength" (Doctrine and Covenants 4:2).

  - You could look together at tools that are used to work in a field. How do these tools help us? Then your children could find things in Doctrine and Covenants 4:5–6 that are like tools for doing God's work.

  - Older children could search Doctrine and Covenants 4 on their own and make a list of things they learn about what it means to serve God.

  - You could sing together a song about missionary work, such as "I Want to Be a Missionary Now" (*Children's Songbook*, 168).

I can help with God's work by serving others.

Adapt activities to accommodate people with disabilities. Small adaptations to activities can ensure that everyone has an opportunity to learn. For instance, if an activity suggests showing a picture, you could sing a song instead to include people with visual impairments.

DOCTRINE AND COVENANTS 5:1–7, 11, 16, 23–24

I can be a witness that the Book of Mormon is true.

- To teach your children about witnesses, you could ask them to imagine that a friend told them they saw a cat walking on its front legs. Would they believe it? What if another friend said the same thing? Talk about what a "witness" is and why witnesses are important. You could then help your children search Doctrine and Covenants 5:1–3, 7, 11 for answers to questions like these:

  - What did Martin Harris want to know?

  - Who could Joseph Smith show the gold plates to?

  - Why would seeing the plates probably not convince someone the Book of Mormon is true?

  - What can we do to be witnesses of the Book of Mormon? (see Doctrine and Covenants 5:16; Moroni 10:3–5).

For more ideas, see this month's issue of the *Friend* magazine.

Devastating Weight of 116 Pages, by Kwani Povi Winder

The Lord invites me to help with His work (Doctrine and Covenants 4).

Write ways that you can help the Lord do His work now and as you grow. Color the pictures, and cut them out on the solid lines. Cut the slit on the dotted line. Insert the legs from the back, and slide them up and down to make the children grow.

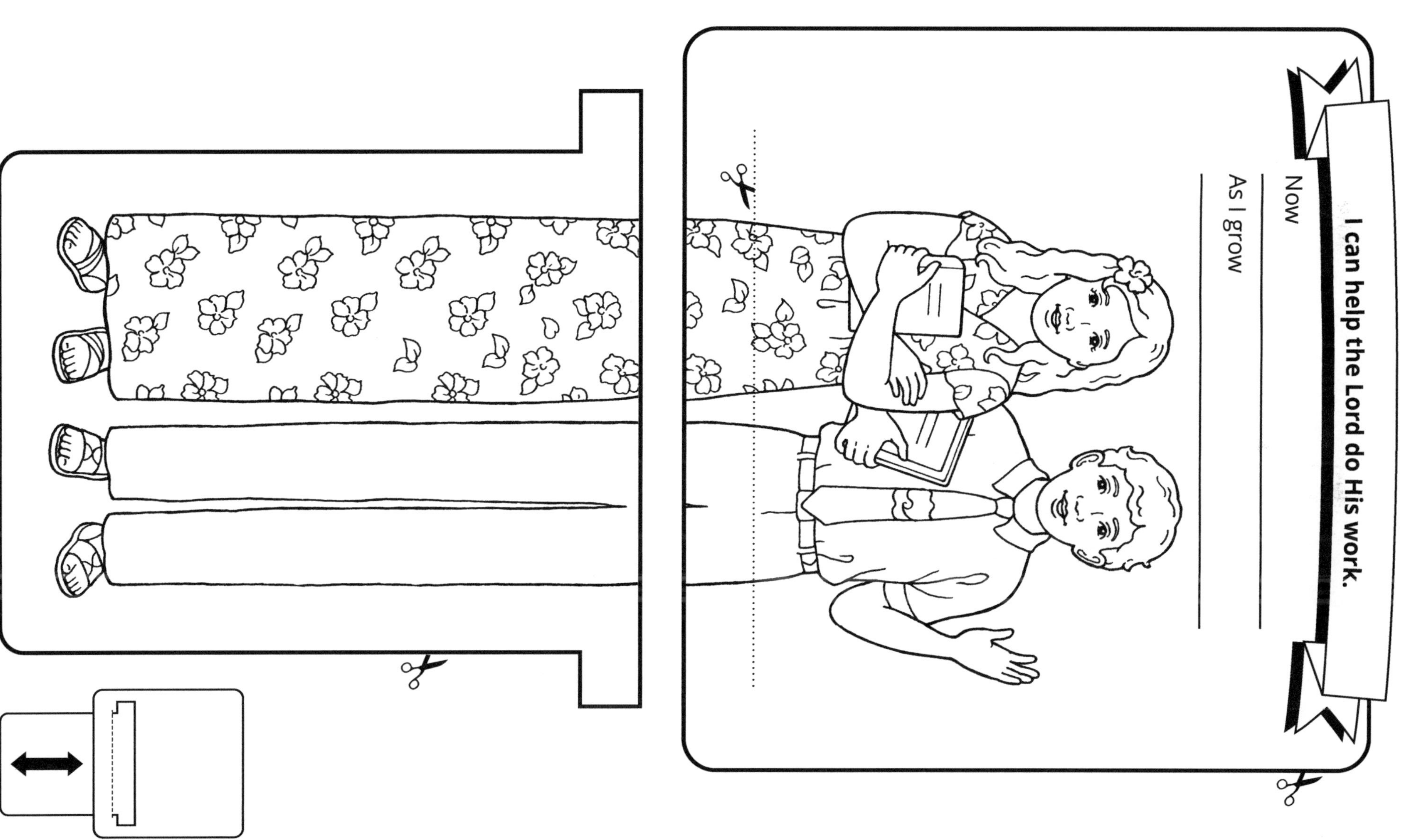

Doctrine and Covenants 6–9

In the fall of 1828, a young schoolteacher named Oliver Cowdery took a teaching job in Manchester, New York, and stayed with the family of Lucy and Joseph Smith Sr. Oliver had heard about their son Joseph and his remarkable experiences, and Oliver, who considered himself a seeker of truth, wanted to know more. The Smiths described visits from angels, an ancient record, and the gift to translate by the power of God. Oliver was fascinated. Could it be true? Lucy and Joseph Sr. gave him advice that applies to anyone seeking truth: pray and ask the Lord.

Oliver did, and the Lord answered, speaking "peace to [his] mind" (Doctrine and Covenants 6:23). Revelation, Oliver discovered, isn't just for prophets like Joseph Smith. It's for anyone who wants it and seeks it diligently. Oliver still had a lot to learn, but he knew enough to take his next step. He knew the Lord was doing something important through Joseph Smith, and Oliver wanted to be part of it.

See also *Saints*, 1:58–64; "Days of Harmony" (video), Gospel Library.

 Ideas for Learning at Home and at Church

DOCTRINE AND COVENANTS 6; 8–9

Heavenly Father speaks to me through the Holy Ghost.

In the spring of 1829, Oliver Cowdery volunteered to be Joseph Smith's scribe as he continued to translate the Book of Mormon. The experience thrilled him, and he wondered if he could also receive revelation and the gift to translate. His first try, though, didn't go well.

If you've ever struggled to receive or understand revelation, maybe you can relate to Oliver's experience—and learn from it. As you read Doctrine and Covenants 6, 8, and 9, notice what the Lord taught Oliver about personal revelation. For example:

- What do Doctrine and Covenants 6:5–7; 8:1; 9:7–8 suggest about what the Lord requires of you before He will reveal His will?

- What do you learn from Doctrine and Covenants 6:14–17, 22–24; 8:2–3; 9:7–9 about the different ways revelation might come? How can you recognize it?

- What else do you learn about revelation from these sections?

Oliver's experiences might cause you to "cast your mind" on moments when you've felt that the Lord was speaking to you (Doctrine and Covenants 6:22). Have you ever recorded your thoughts or feelings about these experiences? If so, consider reading what you wrote. If not, take some time to write down what you remember. Consider how you can continue to draw strength from these experiences. For some ideas, see Elder Neil L. Andersen's message "Spiritually Defining Memories" (*Ensign* or *Liahona*, May 2020, 18–22).

Several Church leaders have shared their experiences with revelation in the "Hear Him" video collection. After watching one or more of these videos, you might feel inspired to record your own experiences, sharing how the Lord has spoken to you.

See also Topics and Questions, "Personal Revelation," Gospel Library; "Oliver Cowdery's Gift," in *Revelations in Context*, 15–19.

DOCTRINE AND COVENANTS 6:18–21, 29–37

Look unto Christ in every thought.

The Lord knew Joseph Smith would experience "difficult circumstances" in coming years (Doctrine and Covenants 6:18). He knows what trials are in your future too. What do you find in His counsel to Joseph and Oliver in Doctrine and Covenants 6:18–21, 29–37 that helps you trust Him?

What do you feel it means to "look unto [Christ] in every thought"? (verse 36). How can you do this more consistently—during good times and "difficult circumstances"? Consider this counsel from President Russell M. Nelson: "It is mentally rigorous to strive to look unto Him in *every* thought. But when we do, our doubts and fears flee" ("Drawing the Power of Jesus Christ into Our Lives," *Ensign* or *Liahona*, May 2017, 41).

See also Neil L. Andersen, "My Mind Caught Hold upon This Thought of Jesus Christ," *Liahona*, May 2023, 91–94.

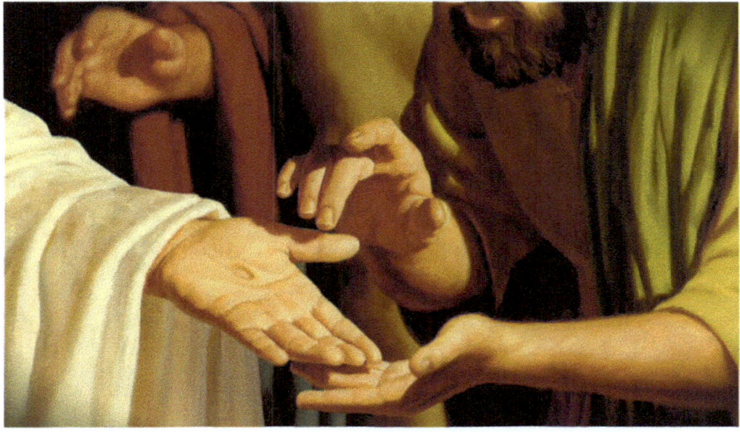

Detail of *Behold My Hand*, by Jeffrey Ward

DOCTRINE AND COVENANTS 6:29–37

"Fear not to do good."

Why do we sometimes "fear . . . to do good"? (verse 33). What do you find in Doctrine and Covenants 6:29–37 that gives you courage to do good? Consider singing or listening to a hymn that inspires you to have courage in Christ, such as "Let Us All Press On" (*Hymns*, no. 243).

DOCTRINE AND COVENANTS 6–7; 9:3, 7–14

"Even as you desire of me so it shall be."

Notice how many times words like "desire" or "desires" appear in sections 6 and 7. What do you learn from these sections about the importance God places on your desires? Ask yourself the Lord's question in Doctrine and Covenants 7:1: "What desirest thou?"

One of Oliver Cowdery's righteous desires—to translate as Joseph Smith did—was not fulfilled. As you read Doctrine and Covenants 9:3, 7–14, what impressions do you receive that might help you when your righteous desires go unfulfilled for now?

See also Doctrine and Covenants 11:8; Dallin H. Oaks, "Desire," *Ensign* or *Liahona*, May 2011, 42–45.

For more ideas, see this month's issues of the *Liahona* and *For the Strength of Youth* magazines.

 # Ideas for Teaching Children

DOCTRINE AND COVENANTS 6:5, 15–16, 22–23; 8:2; 9:7–9

Heavenly Father speaks to me through the Holy Ghost.

- The truths Oliver Cowdery learned about personal revelation can help your children as they develop their ability to recognize the Holy Ghost. You could use "Chapter 5: Joseph Smith and Oliver Cowdery" (in *Doctrine and Covenants Stories*, 22–25, or the corresponding video in Gospel Library) to teach them about Oliver and what he learned. Share with each other your favorite parts of the story. As you do, emphasize things the Lord taught Oliver about how to hear God's voice, and read relevant verses, such as Doctrine and Covenants 6:23 or 9:7–9.

Oliver Cowdery learned about revelation while helping Joseph Smith translate the Book of Mormon.

- You could also invite your children to touch their heads and their chests as you read the words "mind" and "heart" in Doctrine and Covenants 8:2. Tell your children, from your experiences, what it's like when the Holy Ghost speaks to your mind and heart. Help them find answers to the question "How does the Holy Ghost speak to us?" in these verses: Doctrine and Covenants 6:15–16, 22–23; 8:2; 9:7–9.

Use stories. Stories help children understand gospel principles because they demonstrate how other people live these principles. As you teach, find ways to include stories—from the scriptures, from Church history, or from your own life—that illustrate the principles in the scriptures.

DOCTRINE AND COVENANTS 6:34

Because of Jesus Christ, I can "fear not."

- The Lord told Joseph and Oliver, "Fear not, little flock" (Doctrine and Covenants 6:34). You might invite your children to repeat that phrase with you several times. They might also enjoy pretending to be a flock of frightened sheep. What might sheep be afraid of? Then you and your children could look at a picture of the Savior as a shepherd (there's one at the end of this outline) and talk about how He watches over us like a shepherd watches over His sheep.

- Consider playing or singing a song about finding courage in Christ, such as "Dare to Do Right" (*Children's Songbook*, 158) or "Let Us All Press On" (*Hymns*, no. 243). What does the song teach about how the Savior helps us not be afraid?

DOCTRINE AND COVENANTS 6:36

I can look to Jesus Christ in every thought.

- After reading together Doctrine and Covenants 6:36, you and your children could make drawings to help you remember to "look unto [Jesus Christ] in every thought." Share with each other your drawings, and help your children think of places they could put them so they will see them often.

For more ideas, see this month's issue of the *Friend* magazine.

The Lord Is My Shepherd, by Yongsung Kim

Because of Jesus Christ, I can "fear not" (Doctrine and Covenants 6:34).

Make a necklace to help remind you that Jesus Christ can help you when you are afraid. Color and cut out the sheep and the heart. Glue the heart to the sheep, and tape a string to the back so you can wear it around your neck.

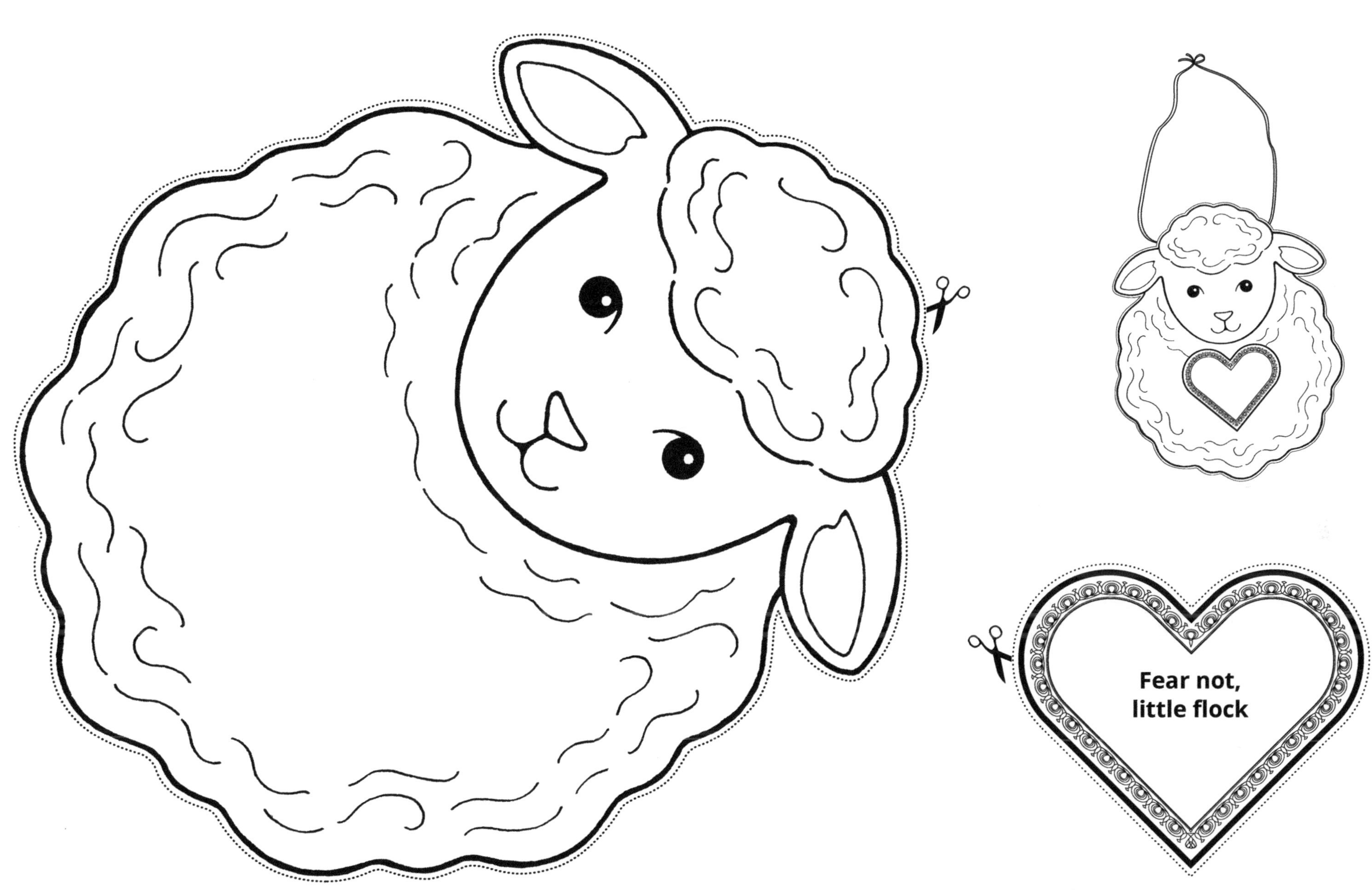

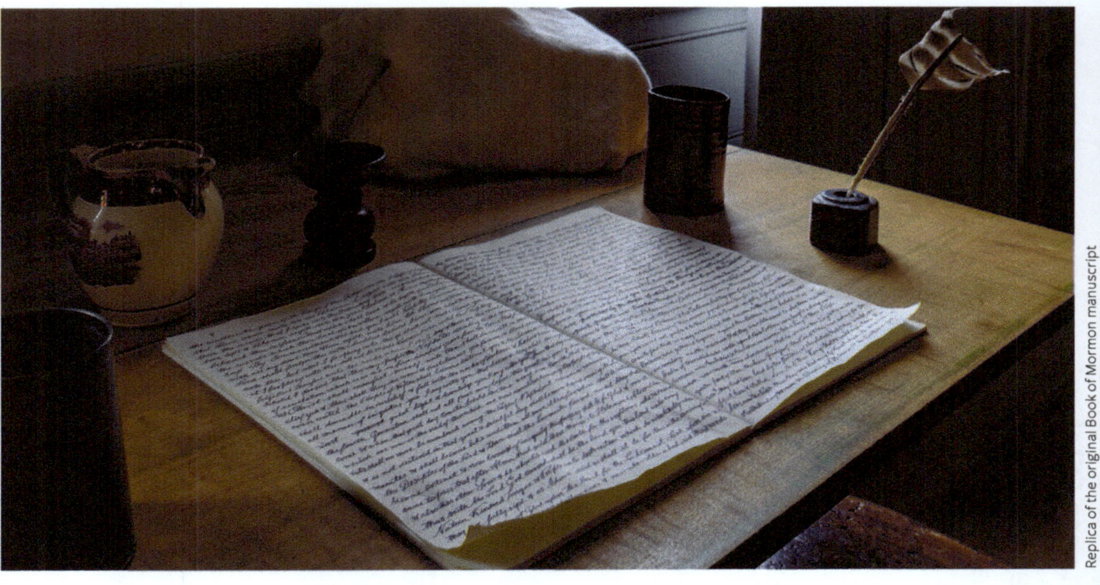

Replica of the original Book of Mormon manuscript

Doctrine and Covenants 10–11

As the translation of the Book of Mormon continued, a question came up: What should Joseph Smith and Oliver Cowdery do about those lost pages of the translation? It might make sense to retranslate that portion, but the Lord saw something they could not: their enemies were planning to alter the words on those pages to cast doubt on Joseph's inspired work. God had a plan to avoid that problem and keep the work moving forward. Thousands of years earlier, God inspired Nephi to write a second record that covered the same time period "for a wise purpose in Him" (1 Nephi 9:5).

"My wisdom," the Lord said to Joseph, "is greater than the cunning of the devil" (Doctrine and Covenants 10:43). That's a reassuring message in a day like ours, when the adversary is intensifying his efforts to weaken faith. Like Joseph, we can be "faithful and continue on" in the work God has called us to do (verse 3). Then we will find that He has already provided a way so that "the gates of hell shall not prevail" against us (verse 69).

See *Saints*, 1:51–61.

 Ideas for Learning at Home and at Church

DOCTRINE AND COVENANTS 10:1–33

God "will not suffer that Satan shall accomplish his evil design."

Satan would prefer that we forget he exists—or that we at least fail to recognize his attempts to influence us (see 2 Nephi 28:22–23). But the Lord's words in Doctrine and Covenants 10 confirm that Satan is real—and he actively opposes the work of the Lord. In verses 1–33, identify what God knew about Satan's efforts (see also verses 62–63). You could also ask the Lord to help you see how Satan may be tempting you. As you read section 10, ponder how the Savior can help you resist Satan's efforts.

DOCTRINE AND COVENANTS 10:34–52

The Lord's "wisdom is greater than the cunning of the devil."

Nephi didn't know why he was inspired to make two sets of records of his people. And Mormon didn't know why he was inspired to include the second set with the gold plates. But both prophets trusted that God had "a wise purpose" (1 Nephi 9:5; Words of Mormon 1:7). Today we know at least part of that purpose: to replace the 116 lost pages of the Book of Mormon. What do you think the Lord wants you to learn from all this? Ponder that question as you read Doctrine and Covenants 10:34–52. You might also make a list of truths you learn about the Lord from these verses. How do these truths affect your relationship with Him? What impresses you about the Lord's wisdom and foresight in preparing for the loss of the 116 pages?

You might also feel inspired to look for evidence of His wisdom and foresight in your life. Read the accounts in Elder Ronald A. Rasband's message "By Divine Design"—they might bring examples to your mind (*Ensign* or *Liahona*, Nov. 2017, 55–57). Consider writing them down as they come to you. How has the Lord been working in your life? For example, what "coincidences" has He prepared? What foundations has He laid for your blessings? When has He led you to minister to someone in need?

See also Romans 8:28; Doctrine and Covenants 90:24; Topics and Questions, "Plan of Salvation," Gospel Library.

Detail from *Mormon Abridging the Plates*, by Tom Lovell

DOCTRINE AND COVENANTS 11

"Put your trust in [the Lord's] Spirit."

Joseph's older brother Hyrum was eager to know the Lord's will for him, so he asked Joseph to seek a revelation on his behalf. The Prophet was happy to do so, but at least one message in that revelation (Doctrine and Covenants 11) is that Hyrum could also seek revelation for himself. And so can "all who have good desires, and have thrust in their sickle to reap" (verse 27). As you read section 11, what do you feel the Lord is teaching you about personal revelation? How does this relate to what He taught Oliver Cowdery in sections 6–9? What other messages does He have for you?

See also "Let the Holy Spirit Guide," *Hymns*, no. 143.

Invite learners to ask questions. Questions often lead to revelation. If you are teaching your family or a Church class, encourage them to ask questions, and help them find answers in the scriptures. For example, if they have questions about personal revelation, look together for answers in Doctrine and Covenants 11:12–14.

DOCTRINE AND COVENANTS 11:15–26

As I seek to "obtain [God's] word," I will receive His Spirit and power.

Even before the Book of Mormon had been translated, Hyrum Smith was anxious to assist in the work of the Restoration. As you read the Lord's response to his desires, consider what it means to you to "obtain [God's] word" (verse 21). How does obtaining God's word help you serve Him with power?

For more ideas, see this month's issues of the *Liahona* and *For the Strength of Youth* magazines.

Ideas for Teaching Children

DOCTRINE AND COVENANTS 10:5

As I pray always, I receive strength from God.

- To introduce this verse to your children, you could ask them about things they "always" do. What does the Lord say we should always do in Doctrine and Covenants 10:5? Why does He want us to do this?

- How can you help your children remember to pray always? Maybe they could collect a few small, smooth stones and paint on them "Doctrine and Covenants 10:5" or "Pray Always." They could put their stones in various places where they want to be reminded to pray, like near their bed, with their schoolbooks, or where they eat meals. According to Doctrine and Covenants 10:5, how does God bless us when we pray? Your children could find additional answers in a song like "A Child's Prayer" (*Children's Songbook*, 13).

DOCTRINE AND COVENANTS 11:12–13

The Holy Ghost leads me to do good.

- Children can learn to recognize when the Spirit is speaking to them. To help them, you could hide a light bulb or flashlight and a picture of a happy face somewhere in the room; then ask your children to find these items. Read Doctrine and Covenants 11:13, and help your children identify words that relate to the items they found. What do these words teach about how the Holy Ghost helps us?

- Sharing your own spiritual experiences can help your children recognize the Holy Ghost's influence in their lives. As you share, ask them to share their experiences too. You could also read together Doctrine and Covenants 11:12–13, looking for how we can recognize when the Holy Ghost is guiding us. Testify that Heavenly Father wants to guide us through the Holy Ghost.

DOCTRINE AND COVENANTS 11:21, 26

I need to know the gospel so I can help others find the truth.

- Just like Hyrum Smith, your children will probably have many opportunities to share the gospel with others. You could read together Doctrine and Covenants 11:21, 26 and ask your children to find what the Lord told Hyrum he needed to do so he could teach the gospel. What does it mean to "obtain" God's word? How can we do this? How do we "treasure up" God's word in our hearts? Perhaps your children could role-play sharing something about Jesus Christ or the Book of Mormon with others.

For more ideas, see this month's issue of the *Friend*.

Joseph and Hyrum Smith, by Ken Corbett

I can pray always (Doctrine and Covenants 10:5).

Color the picture, and cut out the figure on the solid lines. Fold the figure on the dotted lines
to make a booklet to remind you what it means to "pray always."

Doctrine and Covenants 12–17; Joseph Smith—History 1:66–75

Most people around the world have probably never heard of Harmony, Pennsylvania. The Lord often chooses humble places for the most significant events in His kingdom. In a wooded area near Harmony on May 15, 1829, John the Baptist appeared to Joseph Smith and Oliver Cowdery. He placed his hands on their heads and conferred the Aaronic Priesthood upon them, calling them "my fellow servants" (Doctrine and Covenants 13:1).

John the Baptist was the trusted servant of God who baptized the Savior and prepared the way for His coming (see Matthew 3:1–6, 13–17). To these two young men in their twenties, it must have been humbling, perhaps even overwhelming, to be called John's fellow servants. At the time, Joseph and Oliver were relatively unknown, much as Harmony was. But service in God's work has always been about *how* we serve, not about who notices. However small or unseen your contribution may seem at times, you too are a fellow servant in the Lord's "great and marvelous work" (Doctrine and Covenants 14:1).

 Ideas for Learning at Home and at Church

I can participate in God's "great and marvelous work."

Joseph Knight and David Whitmer both wanted to know how they could help in the work of the Lord. As you read the Lord's answer to them (Doctrine and Covenants 12; 14), think about what it means to you "to bring forth and establish the cause of Zion" (12:6; see also 14:6). What principles and Christlike attributes do you find in these sections that can help you do this?

See also "The Knight and Whitmer Families," in *Revelations in Context*, 20–24.

DOCTRINE AND COVENANTS 13

Jesus Christ sent John the Baptist to restore the Aaronic Priesthood.

John the Baptist called Joseph Smith and Oliver Cowdery his "fellow servants." What do you think it means to be a fellow servant with John the Baptist? (see Matthew 3:13–17; Luke 1:13–17; 3:2–20).

As you read what John the Baptist said about the Aaronic Priesthood in section 13, ponder how the keys of this priesthood help accomplish John's mission to prepare the way of the Lord. For example:

- What is "the ministering of angels"? (see 2 Nephi 32:2–3; Moroni 7:29–32; Guide to the Scriptures, "Angels," Gospel Library).

- What is "the gospel of repentance"? (see Doctrine and Covenants 84:26–27; Dale G. Renlund, "The Priesthood and the Savior's Atoning Power," *Ensign* or *Liahona*, Nov. 2017, 64–67).

How do the ordinances of the Aaronic Priesthood (such as baptism and the sacrament) help prepare the way for you to receive the Savior in your life?

JOSEPH SMITH—HISTORY 1:66–75

📖 Ordinances give me access to God's power.

Have you ever wondered what it would have been like to be with Joseph Smith and Oliver Cowdery for the major events of the Restoration? As you read Joseph Smith—History 1:66–75, including the note at the end of verse 71, you might understand at least some of what they felt. What impresses you

Joseph Smith Baptizes Oliver Cowdery, by Del Parson

about their words? Note, in particular, the blessings they received because they received the priesthood and were baptized. What blessings has the Savior given you through priesthood ordinances?

To learn more, consider creating a table with the headings *Ordinances* and *Blessings*. Then you could search scriptures like these to list ordinances and the blessings that come from them: John 14:26; Acts 2:38; Doctrine and Covenants 84:19–22; 131:1–4; Joseph Smith—History 1:73–74. What other blessings would you add to the list? How have the ordinances you've received brought the Savior's power into your life?

See also David A. Bednar, "With the Power of God in Great Glory," *Liahona*, Nov. 2021, 28–30; *Saints*, 1:65–68; "God of Power, God of Right," *Hymns*, no. 20; Topics and Questions, "Covenants and Ordinances," Gospel Library.

DOCTRINE AND COVENANTS 15–16

Bringing souls unto Christ is of great worth.

Have you ever wondered, as John and Peter Whitmer did, what "would be of the most worth" in your life? (Doctrine and Covenants 15:4; 16:4). As you read Doctrine and Covenants 15–16, ponder why bringing souls to Christ is of such great worth. What are you doing to "bring souls" unto Christ?

See also *Saints*, 1:68–71.

DOCTRINE AND COVENANTS 17

The Lord uses witnesses to establish His word.

What is a witness? Why does the Lord use witnesses in His work? (see 2 Corinthians 13:1). Ponder these questions as you read God's words to the Three Witnesses in Doctrine and Covenants 17. (See also "The Testimony of Three Witnesses" in the Book of Mormon.) How do witnesses help bring about God's "righteous purposes"? (verse 4).

What can you bear witness of?

See also *Saints*, 1:73–75; "A Day for the Eternities" (video), Gospel Library.

For more ideas, see this month's issues of the *Liahona* and *For the Strength of Youth* magazines.

Ideas for Teaching Children

DOCTRINE AND COVENANTS 13; JOSEPH SMITH—HISTORY 1:68–74

John the Baptist restored the Aaronic Priesthood.

- The artwork in this outline could help your children visualize the restoration of the Aaronic Priesthood (see also "Chapter 6: Joseph and Oliver Are Given the Priesthood," in *Doctrine and Covenants Stories*, 26–27, or the corresponding video in Gospel Library). Would they enjoy drawing a picture of the event based on what you read with them in Joseph Smith—History 1:68–74?

- You could also show a picture of John the Baptist while you read together Matthew 3:13–17; Joseph Smith—History 1:68–70. Why was it important that the Lord sent John the Baptist to give Joseph Smith the priesthood authority to baptize?

Preparing your children for a lifetime on God's covenant path. For more ideas to help your children learn about priesthood power, authority, and keys, see appendix A or appendix B.

Illustration of Jesus being baptized, by Dan Burr

DOCTRINE AND COVENANTS 13

Heavenly Father blesses me through the Aaronic Priesthood.

- To prompt a discussion about the keys mentioned in Doctrine and Covenants 13, you and your children could look at a set of keys and talk about what keys allow us to do. Maybe you could help them find the word *keys* in section 13. What other words or phrases in Doctrine and Covenants 13 describe the blessings of the Aaronic Priesthood? Your children could also identify ways Heavenly Father blesses us through the priesthood in the video "Blessings of the Priesthood" (Gospel Library).

DOCTRINE AND COVENANTS 15:4–6; 16:4–6

Helping others come to Jesus Christ is "of the most worth."

- John and Peter Whitmer wanted to know what would be of the most worth to them (see Doctrine and Covenants 15:4; 16:4). Maybe you and your children could talk about things that are worth a lot to you. As you read Doctrine and Covenants 15:6 or 16:6, ask your children to raise their hands when they hear what the Lord said is "of the most worth."

- What does it mean to "bring souls unto [Jesus Christ]"? Help your children make a list of ideas, such as being friends to others, sharing the scriptures with a friend, or praying for someone in need. Your children could look for pictures of these things in Church magazines or the *Gospel Art Book*. Or they could draw their own pictures. Invite them to pick something from their list that they will do. You could also sing together the fourth verse of "I Feel My Savior's Love" (*Children's Songbook*, 74–75).

DOCTRINE AND COVENANTS 17

I can be a witness of the Book of Mormon.

- "Chapter 7: Witnesses See the Gold Plates" (in *Doctrine and Covenants Stories*, 31–33, or the corresponding video in Gospel Library) can help your children learn about the Three Witnesses. After reading Doctrine and Covenants 17:5–6, tell your children how you know the Book of Mormon is true. How can we be witnesses of the Book of Mormon?

For more ideas, see this month's issue of the *Friend* magazine.

Upon You My Fellow Servants, by Linda Curley Christensen

Because John the Baptist gave Joseph Smith and Oliver Cowdery the Aaronic Priesthood, we can receive many blessings, including being baptized, partaking of the sacrament, and being watched over and strengthened (see Doctrine and Covenants 20:46–47, 53–55). Color the picture and draw in the empty circle a picture of yourself receiving one of these blessings.

Doctrine and Covenants 18

There are many different ways to try to measure a person's worth. Talent, education, wealth, and physical appearance can all affect how we evaluate each other—and ourselves. But in God's eyes, our worth is a much simpler matter, and it is stated clearly in Doctrine and Covenants 18: "Remember the worth of souls is great in the sight of God" (verse 10). This simple truth explains so much of what God does and why He does it. Why did He instruct Joseph Smith and Oliver Cowdery to establish the Church of Jesus Christ in our day? (see verses 1–5). Because the worth of souls is great. Why does He "command all men everywhere to repent" and send Apostles to preach repentance? (verse 9). Because the worth of souls is great. And why did Jesus Christ suffer "death in the flesh" and "the pain of all men"? (verse 11). Because the worth of souls is great. If even one of these souls chooses to accept the Savior's gift, He rejoices, for "great is his joy in the soul that repenteth" (verse 13).

 Ideas for Learning at Home and at Church

"Build up my church."

In section 18, the Lord gave Oliver Cowdery instructions to help lay the foundation of the Church of Jesus Christ. What do you notice about the counsel He gave—especially in verses 1–5? You might consider how this same counsel applies to you as you "build up" your faith in Christ. For example:

- What have you "desired to know" of the Lord? (verse 1).

- What does it mean to you to "rely upon the things which are written"? (verse 3). How has the Spirit "manifested unto you" that these things are true? (verse 2; see also Doctrine and Covenants 6:22–24).

- How do you build your life on "the foundation of [the Savior's] gospel and [His] rock"? (verse 5).

Ask questions. The Doctrine and Covenants is evidence that questions lead to revelation. As you study the scriptures, record questions that you have. Then ponder and pray to seek answers.

DOCTRINE AND COVENANTS 18:10–13

"The worth of souls is great in the sight of God."

How do we determine the worth of something? For example, why is one item at a market more expensive than another? As you read section 18 this week, especially verses 10–13, you might contrast how people often determine value with what makes a soul valuable in God's eyes. Consider substituting your name in place of the words "soul," "souls," and "all men." How could these verses help someone who questions his or her worth?

Here are some other passages that teach about the worth of a soul: Luke 15:1–10; John 3:16–17; 2 Nephi 26:24–28; Moses 1:39. Based on these passages, how would you summarize the way God feels about you? You might also search President Dieter F. Uchtdorf's message "You Matter to Him" (*Ensign* or *Liahona*, Nov. 2011, 19–22) to find words and phrases that help you know about your worth to God.

How does God show you that you are of great worth to Him? How does this affect the way you feel about yourself and others?

See also Joy D. Jones, "Value beyond Measure," *Ensign* or *Liahona*, Nov. 2017, 13–15; Topics and Questions, "Children of God," Gospel Library.

DOCTRINE AND COVENANTS 18:11–16

The Lord rejoices when I repent.

Notice how often words like *repent* and *repentance* are used throughout Doctrine and Covenants 18. Ponder what you learn from these words each time they are used. Consider especially verses 11–16. How do these verses affect how you feel about repentance—your own repentance and the duty to invite other people to repent and improve? Here's one way to record what you learn: list several ways you would complete the sentence "Repentance is ____."

See also Alma 36:18–21; Guide to the Scriptures, "Repentance," Gospel Library; Dale G. Renlund, "Repentance: A Joyful Choice," *Ensign* or *Liahona*, Nov. 2016, 121–24.

DOCTRINE AND COVENANTS 18:14–16

Joy comes from helping others come unto Christ.

As you read verses 14–16, ponder what it means to "cry repentance"—and why it brings such joy. What are some ways you've found to help others come unto the Savior and receive forgiveness? How have other people done that for you?

Detail from *The Prodigal Son*, by Clark Kelley Price

See also Craig C. Christensen, "There Can Be Nothing So Exquisite and Sweet as Was My Joy," *Liahona*, May 2023, 45–47.

I can hear the Lord's voice in the scriptures.

If someone asked you what the voice of the Lord is like, what would you say? Think about this question as you read Doctrine and Covenants 18:34–36. What have you learned about the voice of the Lord from reading Doctrine and Covenants? What can you do to hear His voice more clearly?

See also "As I Search the Holy Scriptures," *Hymns*, no. 277.

For more ideas, see this month's issues of the *Liahona* and *For the Strength of Youth* magazines.

 # Ideas for Teaching Children

DOCTRINE AND COVENANTS 18:10–13

Each of us is of great worth to God.

- As you and your children read Doctrine and Covenants 18:10–13, consider substituting each other's names in place of the words "soul," "souls," and "all men." You could then talk about how these verses help us understand how Heavenly Father feels about each of us.

- You could also ask your children about things that people consider valuable. Or you might show them something that is valuable to you. How do we treat things that are valuable to us? Then let them take turns looking in a mirror. As they do, tell each child that they are a child of God and they are of great worth. How can we show others that "the worth of [their] souls is great" in our sight?

- To emphasize that all people are of great worth to Heavenly Father, your children could look at the picture at the end of this outline while you read Doctrine and Covenants 18:10–13. Singing together a song like "Every Star Is Different" (*Children's Songbook*, 142–43) could help reinforce this point.

Detail from *Worth of a Soul*, by Liz Lemon Swindle

DOCTRINE AND COVENANTS 18:13–16

Sharing the gospel brings great joy.

- To inspire your children to share the gospel of Jesus Christ, you could talk with each other about experiences when you found something that you wanted to share with your friends or family. Why did you want to share it, and how did sharing it make you feel? Then you could read Doctrine and Covenants 18:13, 16. What brings the Lord joy? What does He say will bring us joy? You and your children could talk about any experiences you've had sharing the joy of the Savior's gospel.

- A song about sharing the gospel, such as "I Want to Be a Missionary Now" (*Children's Songbook*, 168), can help your children think of ways they can share the gospel.

DOCTRINE AND COVENANTS 18:34–36

I can hear the Lord's voice in the scriptures.

- Your children might enjoy a game where they try to identify voices of different people, such as family members, friends, or Church leaders. How do we recognize each other's voices? How do we recognize the Lord's voice? You could read together Doctrine and Covenants 18:34–36 to discuss this question. You could also share with each other how you have heard the Lord's voice in the scriptures.

For more ideas, see this month's issue of the *Friend* magazine.

Every soul is precious to God.

I am of great worth to God (Doctrine and Covenants 18:10–12).

Write your name on the line, and draw or paste a picture of yourself in the center space.

Doctrine and Covenants 19

It took Martin and Lucy Harris years to acquire one of the finest farms in Palmyra, New York. But in 1829 it became clear that the Book of Mormon could be published only if Martin mortgaged his farm to pay the printer. Martin had a testimony of the Book of Mormon, but Lucy did not. If Martin went forward with the mortgage and the Book of Mormon did not sell well, he would lose his farm, put his marriage at risk, and damage his reputation in the community. Although our circumstances are different from Martin's, at some time or another we all face difficult questions like those he faced: What is the gospel of Jesus Christ worth to me? What am I willing to sacrifice to help build God's kingdom? Martin Harris ultimately decided that he would mortgage his farm so the first 5,000 copies of the Book of Mormon could be printed. But even this sacrifice—and any sacrifice we might make—is small compared to the sacrifice of Jesus Christ, "the greatest of all" (Doctrine and Covenants 19:18), who bled from every pore to save the repentant.

For more information about the publication of the Book of Mormon, see *Saints*, 1:76–84.

 Ideas for Learning at Home and at Church

"I, God, am endless."

Joseph Smith explained that the revelation in section 19 is "a commandment . . . to Martin Harris, given by him who is Eternal" (section heading). Look for places in verses 1–12 where the Lord emphasizes His eternal nature. Why do you think it was important for Martin Harris to know this about the Lord? Why is it important for you to know it?

Why do you think Jesus Christ is called "the beginning and the end"? (verse 1).

Jesus Christ suffered so that I can repent and come unto Him.

The New Testament describes the Savior's suffering in Gethsemane from the perspective of the people who observed it. In Doctrine and Covenants 19:15–20, Jesus Christ told about His suffering from His own perspective. As you read this sacred personal account, look for how the Savior described His suffering. Consider what each word or phrase teaches you. Why was the Savior willing to suffer? You can discover more in John 15:13; Mosiah 3:7; Alma 7:11–12; Doctrine and Covenants 18:10–13.

The feelings you have as you study the Savior's suffering might prompt questions like these: Why did the Savior have to suffer for my sins? Why do I need to repent to receive the full blessings of His sacrifice? You might find insights about these questions and others in Elder Ulisses Soares's message "Jesus Christ: The Caregiver of Our Soul" (*Liahona*, May 2021, 82–84). As you study, what impressions come to your mind? Consider recording your feelings about Jesus Christ and His sacrifice for you.

As part of your study and worship, you might look for a hymn that you can listen to or sing that expresses your gratitude to the Savior for His suffering on your behalf. "I Stand All Amazed" (*Hymns*, no. 193) is a good example.

What do you feel Heavenly Father and Jesus Christ would have you do as a result of what you have felt and studied?

See also "Jesus Christ will help you," *For the Strength of Youth: A Guide for Making Choices* (2022), 6–9; Topics and Questions, "Atonement of Jesus Christ," "Repentance," Gospel Library; D. Todd Christofferson, "The Divine Gift of Repentance," *Ensign* or *Liahona*, Nov. 2011, 38–41; "Jesus Suffers in Gethsemane" (video), Gospel Library.

DOCTRINE AND COVENANTS 19:23

Peace comes from learning of Jesus Christ and following Him.

Consider the Savior's invitation: "Learn of me." What do you learn about Jesus Christ in Doctrine and Covenants 19? Record your thoughts, and ponder how these truths about the Savior help you find peace. What does it mean to you to "walk in the meekness of [His] Spirit"?

See also Henry B. Eyring, "Finding Personal Peace," *Liahona*, May 2023, 29–31; "Peace in Christ" (video), Gospel Library.

DOCTRINE AND COVENANTS 19:26–41

God's blessings are greater than the treasures of the earth.

The Book of Mormon did not sell very well in Palmyra. As a result, Martin Harris ended up having to sell a large portion of his farm to pay the debt to the printer (see "The Contributions of Martin Harris," in *Revelations in Context*, 7–8). Ponder Martin's sacrifice—and the blessings you've received because of it—as you read Doctrine and Covenants 19:26–41. You might also think about what the Lord has asked you to sacrifice. What do you find in these verses that inspires you to make these sacrifices with "rejoicing" and "gladness"? (see also verses 15–20).

Detail from *Martin Harris Farm*, by Al Rounds

For more ideas, see this month's issues of the *Liahona* and *For the Strength of Youth* magazines.

Ideas for Teaching Children

DOCTRINE AND COVENANTS 19:16–19

Jesus Christ suffered for me.

- You can help your children feel reverence and gratitude for the Savior by reading together Doctrine and Covenants 19:16–19 or "Chapter 51: Jesus Suffers in the Garden of Gethsemane," in *New Testament Stories*, 129–32, or the corresponding video in Gospel Library. Consider pausing to make sure your children understand and to let them express their feelings. For example, in verse 16, what are "these things" Jesus suffered for us? (see Mosiah 3:7; Alma 7:11–12). What do we learn from His description of His suffering? How can we show our gratitude for what He did for us?

Help children learn from the scriptures. Some children have a hard time reading scriptures. Focusing on a single verse or phrase may help them.

- You and your children could look in *Hymns* or the *Children's Songbook* for songs that help you express your feelings about Jesus Christ (see the topic indexes in these books).

DOCTRINE AND COVENANTS 19:18–19, 24

Jesus Christ obeyed Heavenly Father, even when it was hard.

- Suffering for our sins was very difficult, but Jesus Christ was willing to do it to obey His Father and to show His love for Him and for us. You could look together at a picture of Jesus Christ suffering in Gethsemane (like those in this outline) and ask your children to tell you what they know about what is happening in the picture. You might read together Doctrine and Covenants 19:18–19, 24 to emphasize that suffering for our sins was the hardest thing anyone has ever done, but because Jesus loved His Father and us, He obeyed God's will (see also Mosiah 3:7). What difficult things does God ask us to do? How can we find courage to obey Him?

DOCTRINE AND COVENANTS 19:23

"Learn of me, and listen to my words."

- You might help your children think of simple actions that go along with phrases in Doctrine and Covenants 19:23. Read the verse several times while they do the actions. What are some ways we can learn of Christ and listen to His words?

DOCTRINE AND COVENANTS 19:38

God's blessings are greater than the treasures of the earth.

- You and your children could take turns holding a copy of the Book of Mormon and sharing what you love about it. Briefly talk about Martin Harris's sacrifice so the Book of Mormon could be printed (see *Doctrine and Covenants Stories*, 33). What did the Lord say to Martin in Doctrine and Covenants 19:38 that might have helped him be faithful and obedient? Help your children think of something they can sacrifice to obey God or help in His work.

For more ideas, see this month's issue of the *Friend* magazine.

Praying in the Garden of Gethsemane, by Hermann Clementz

Jesus Christ suffered for me (Doctrine and Covenants 19:16–19).

Draw a line to match the ways we can show gratitude for what He did for us.

Doctrine and Covenants 20–22

The Savior's work of bringing forth the Book of Mormon was now complete. But His work of Restoration had just started. In addition to restoring doctrine and priesthood authority, the Lord had made it clear through earlier revelations that He also wanted to restore a formal organization—His Church (see Doctrine and Covenants 10:53; 18:5). On April 6, 1830, more than 40 believers crowded into the Whitmer family's log home in Fayette, New York, to witness the organization of the Church of Jesus Christ.

Some people wonder why an organized Church is necessary. The answer may be found, at least in part, in the revelations connected with that first Church meeting in 1830. They describe blessings that would not have been possible if the true Church of Jesus Christ had not been "regularly organized and established" in the latter days (Doctrine and Covenants 20:1).

See also *Saints*, 1:84–86; "Build Up My Church," in *Revelations in Context*, 29–32.

 Ideas for Learning at Home and at Church

DOCTRINE AND COVENANTS 20–21

Jesus Christ has restored His Church.

Why do we have an organized Church? Perhaps the best answer is "Because Jesus Christ organized one." As you study Doctrine and Covenants 20–21, you might notice similarities between the Church He established anciently and the one He has restored today. Use the following verses to learn about the Savior's Church in ancient times: Matthew 16:15–19; John 7:16–17; Ephesians 2:19–22; 3 Nephi 11:23–26; Moroni 4–5. Use these verses to learn about the restored Church: Doctrine and Covenants 20:17–25, 60, 72–79; 21:1–2. You could record what you find in a table like this one:

	Doctrine	Ordinances	Priesthood authority	Prophets
Christ's ancient Church				
Christ's restored Church				

What do you learn from this activity about why Jesus Christ established—and restored—His Church?

See also Dallin H. Oaks, "The Need for a Church," *Liahona,* Nov. 2021, 24–26.

Invite sharing. When you invite people to share what they have been learning on their own, they will feel encouraged to continue with their personal study. What could you invite others to share?

DOCTRINE AND COVENANTS 20:37, 75–79; 22

Sacred ordinances help me become like the Savior.

When the Church was organized, the Lord taught His Saints about sacred ordinances, including baptism and the sacrament. As you read about these ordinances, ponder how they help you feel connected to the Savior. For example, how do these ordinances help you maintain your "determination to serve [Jesus Christ] to the end"? (verse 37). You might also read the sacrament prayers (verses 77, 79) and imagine that you are hearing them for the first time. What insights do you receive?

See also D. Todd Christofferson, "Why the Covenant Path," *Liahona*, May 2021, 116–19.

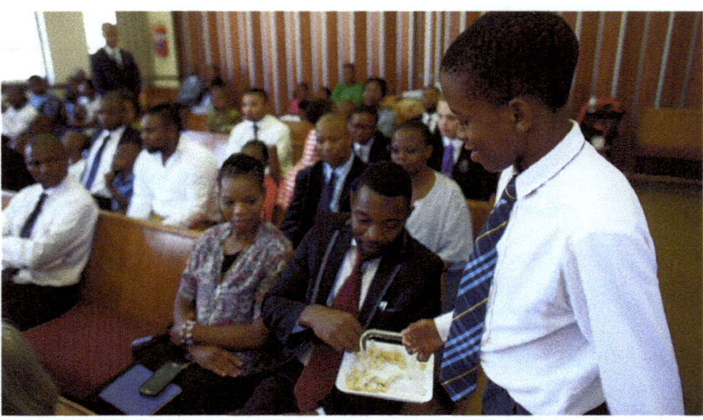

DOCTRINE AND COVENANTS 20:38–60

Priesthood service blesses Church members and their families.

Have you ever thought about why it was important to the Savior to restore the priesthood in His Church? Reading what He asks priesthood holders to do in Doctrine and Covenants 20:38–60 might give you some insights. How has the Savior blessed you and your family through the work described in these verses?

In addition to those who are ordained to the priesthood, women who are set apart to serve in the Church also exercise God's authority as they participate in His work. To learn how, see President Dallin H. Oaks's message "The Keys and Authority of the Priesthood" (*Ensign* or *Liahona,* May 2014, 49–52).

See also Topics and Questions, "Joseph Smith's Teachings about Priesthood, Temple, and Women," Gospel Library.

DOCTRINE AND COVENANTS 21

📖 Obeying God's word through His prophets will give me divine protection.

Doctrine and Covenants 21:4–9 contains invitations to follow the Lord's prophet and powerful promises for people who do. The following ideas can help you ponder these verses:

- What words in verses 4–5 describe what the Savior wants you to do with the words of His living prophet? Why do you feel "patience and faith" are needed to do this?

- Ponder the imagery the Savior uses in verse 6 to describe the blessings of following His prophet. What do think is meant by "the gates of hell"? How does the Lord "disperse the powers of darkness" for you? What does it mean for "the heavens to shake for your good"?

- What is the Lord asking you to do through the current President of the Church? How has the Lord fulfilled His promises as you have followed His counsel?

List additional insights you gain from the following sections of Elder Neil L. Andersen's message "The Prophet of God" (*Ensign* or *Liahona,* May 2018, 24–27):

- Why We Follow the Prophet:____

- A Watchman on the Tower:____

- Don't Be Surprised:____

See also "Watchman on the Tower" (video), ChurchofJesusChrist.org; Topics and Questions, "Prophets," Gospel Library; "We Listen to a Prophet's Voice," *Hymns,* no. 22.

For more ideas, see this month's issues of the *Liahona* and *For the Strength of Youth* magazines.

 Ideas for Teaching Children

DOCTRINE AND COVENANTS 20–21

The Church of Jesus Christ has been restored.

- Consider using the section heading for Doctrine and Covenants 21, chapter 9 of *Doctrine and Covenants Stories,* or the video "Organization of the Church" (ChurchofJesusChrist.org) to help your children understand what happened on the day the Church was organized.

- Perhaps your children could match pictures of Jesus Christ, someone ministering, a baptism, and the sacrament with verses in section 20 (see verses 21–23, 47, 72–74, 75–79). Use these pictures and verses to discuss the blessings we have because Jesus Christ restored His Church.

When I am baptized and confirmed, I promise to follow Jesus Christ.

- Your children might enjoy seeing a picture of a child being baptized and confirmed. They can point out how it matches the instructions in Doctrine and Covenants 20:41, 71–74. What do we learn from Doctrine and Covenants 20:37 about people who want to be baptized? You could also sing "When I Am Baptized" together (*Children's Songbook*, 103) or watch the video "The Baptism of Jesus" (Gospel Library).

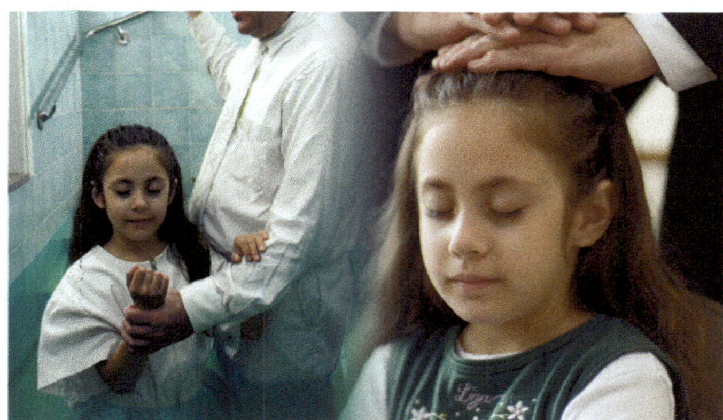

- If your children have already been baptized and confirmed, ask them about their experience. Do they have pictures they could share? Talk with them about what they are doing to follow Jesus Christ and how He is blessing them.

I can take Jesus's name upon me and always remember Him.

- Your children could look for the word "willing" in both Doctrine and Covenants 20:37 (about baptism) and verse 77 (the sacrament prayer). What does Jesus Christ want us to be willing to do? Maybe your children could look at something that has a name on it (such as a brand name or a personal name). What does the name tell us about the item? What does it mean to take Jesus Christ's name upon us?

- Consider reading together Doctrine and Covenants 20:77 and asking your children to identify the promises we make as part of the sacrament. Maybe they could take turns acting out something they can do to "always remember" the Savior and guessing what each other's actions are. According to verse 77, how are we blessed when we always remember the Savior?

Jesus blesses me as I follow His prophet.

- After discovering the invitations and promises in Doctrine and Covenants 21:4–6, your children could look at a picture of the current prophet and share something they have learned or heard from him. Share with each other ways Jesus Christ has blessed you for following His prophet.

For more ideas, see this month's issue of the *Friend* magazine.

Oliver Cowdery Ordains Joseph Smith, by Walter Rane

The Church of Jesus Christ has been restored (Doctrine and Covenants 20–21).

Color the picture of the first meeting of the restored Church on April 6, 1830. Cut out the arms and attach them with brads to the people, matching the shapes. Move the arms up and down to show the members raising their hands to organize the Church.

Doctrine and Covenants 23–26

For most people, being baptized is a reverent, peaceful experience. The baptism of Emma Smith and others, however, was disrupted by a mob who mocked them, threatened them, and forced them to flee. Later, just as Joseph was about to confirm the new members, he was arrested for upsetting the community with his preaching. In all this opposition, how could Emma find reassurance that she was doing the right thing? The same place we can all find it—through revelation from the Lord. He spoke to Emma about "the things of a better [world]"—His kingdom—and her place in it. He told her not to fear, to "lift up [her] heart and rejoice," and to "cleave unto the covenants [she had] made." And these words of encouragement and counsel are His "voice unto all" (Doctrine and Covenants 25:9–10, 13, 16).

See also *Saints*, 1:89–90, 94–97.

 Ideas for Learning at Home and at Church

DOCTRINE AND COVENANTS 24

The Savior can lift me "up out of [my] afflictions."

The revelation in Doctrine and Covenants 24 was given to "strengthen, encourage, and instruct" Joseph Smith and Oliver Cowdery during a time of trial (section heading; see also *Saints*, 1:94–96). Look for words in Doctrine and Covenants 24 that you feel would have been strengthening and encouraging to them.

What do the following scriptures suggest to you about how the Savior helps you with your challenges?

Doctrine and Covenants 24:1–3

Doctrine and Covenants 24:8

Doctrine and Covenants 121:7–8

Isaiah 40:28–31

Mosiah 24:14–15

Detail from *He Healed Many of Diverse Diseases*, by J. Kirk Richards

DOCTRINE AND COVENANTS 25

I have an important role to play in God's kingdom.

As Emma Smith watched the Restoration unfold through her husband, Joseph Smith, she might have wondered what her role might be. Look for answers God provided in Doctrine and Covenants 25. Do you find anything in this section that you feel is His "voice unto [you]"? (verse 16).

See also "An Elect Lady" (video), Gospel Library; "Thou Art an Elect Lady," in *Revelations in Context*, 33–39; Joy D. Jones, "An Especially Noble Calling," *Ensign* or *Liahona*, May 2020, 15–18.

DOCTRINE AND COVENANTS 25:5, 14

"Continue in the spirit of meekness."

What does the phrase "the spirit of meekness" mean to you? Consider searching section 25 for words and phrases that help you understand what it means to be meek. Elder David A. Bednar's message "Meek and Lowly of Heart" could also help (*Ensign* or *Liahona*, May 2018, 30–33). How is Jesus Christ an example of meekness to you? (see Matthew 11:28–30). Think about things in your life you can do "in the spirit of meekness."

DOCTRINE AND COVENANTS 25:10, 13

📖 "Lay aside the things of this world, and seek for the things of a better."

As you ponder the Lord's counsel in Doctrine and Covenants 25:10, it might help to make a list of "things of this world" He wants you to "lay aside." Then you could make a list of "things of a better [world]" He wants you to seek. You might choose at least one thing from the first list that you will lay aside and one thing from the second list that you will seek.

President Russell M. Nelson has given counsel and promises about "[putting] aside many things of this world." Look for it on page 77 of his message "Spiritual Treasures" (*Ensign* or *Liahona*, Nov. 2019). How will you follow his counsel?

As you read verse 13, think about the covenants you have made with Heavenly Father and Jesus Christ. What does it mean to "cleave unto" these covenants? How do your covenants help you "lay aside the things of this world, and seek for the things of a better"?

Here are some other scriptures that could help you discern between "the things of this world" and "the things of a better": Matthew 6:19, 21, 25–34; Luke 10:39–42; 2 Nephi 9:51.

See also Topics and Questions, "Sacrifice," Gospel Library.

Invite sharing. If you're teaching others about how to "lay aside the things of the world," consider ways to invite them to share what they are doing to follow this counsel. We can draw great strength and courage from hearing each other's insights and experiences.

DOCTRINE AND COVENANTS 25:11–12

The Lord delights in my "song of the heart."

What are some of your "song[s] of the heart"—songs that express your feelings about Heavenly Father or Jesus Christ? Consider singing or listening to a few of them. What is it about these songs that makes them special to you?

You might also ponder how these hymns are like a prayer. What do sacred music and prayer have in common? How have your sacred songs been "answered with a blessing"?

See also "Oh, What Songs of the Heart," *Hymns*, no. 286.

DOCTRINE AND COVENANTS 26:2

"All things shall be done by common consent in the church."

The phrase "common consent" in this verse refers to the act of raising our hands to show that we sustain and support a person who is receiving a calling or a priesthood ordination. How would you explain to a visitor to a Church meeting what it means when we sustain someone? What answers do you find in President Henry B. Eyring's message "The Power of Sustaining Faith"? (*Ensign* or *Liahona*, May 2019, 58–60).

For more ideas, see this month's issues of the *Liahona* and *For the Strength of Youth* magazines.

 # Ideas for Teaching Children

DOCTRINE AND COVENANTS 24:1, 8

The Savior can lift me "up out of [my] afflictions."

- To learn about some of the afflictions or challenges Joseph Smith and the early Saints faced, you could review "Chapter 11: More People Join the Church," in *Doctrine and Covenants Stories*, 46–47, or the corresponding video in Gospel Library. Then you and your children could discover what the Lord said to Joseph about his afflictions in Doctrine and Covenants 24:1, 8. You could also share with each other how the Lord helps you during difficult times.

- To learn what it means to be "patient in [our] afflictions," you and your children could re-create the experiment in the video "Continue in Patience" (Gospel Library). What does Doctrine and Covenants 24:8 teach us about patience? How does the Savior let us know that He is "with [us]" during our afflictions?

DOCTRINE AND COVENANTS 25:11–12

Jesus loves "the song of the heart."

- After reading Doctrine and Covenants 25:12, you could tell each other about your favorite hymn or Church song—your "song of the heart"—and sing them together. Share with each other why you love these songs. Why is the Lord happy when we sing these songs? How is our singing like "a prayer unto [Him]"?

DOCTRINE AND COVENANTS 25:13, 15

My covenants with Heavenly Father bring me joy.

- To understand what it means to "cleave unto the covenants" (Doctrine and Covenants 25:13), your children could take turns holding on to something as tightly as they can. Then you and your children could talk about how you "cleave" or hold on to your covenants. If needed, review with your children the covenants we make (see Mosiah 18:8–10; Doctrine and Covenants 20:37; and this week's activity page).

- To give your children context for Doctrine and Covenants 25:13, you might point out that this is something the Lord told Emma Smith soon after her baptism. Why would this be good counsel for someone who was recently baptized?

For more ideas, see this month's issue of the *Friend* magazine.

Emma's Hymns, by Liz Lemon Swindle

My covenants with Heavenly Father bring me joy (Doctrine and Covenants 25:13, 15).

To make a crown of righteousness, color the pieces below, cut them out, and attach them with tape.

CROWN OF RIGHTEOUSNESS

(Doctrine and Covenants 25:15)

Doctrine and Covenants 27–28

Revelation was still a relatively new concept for the Saints as the Restoration continued to unfold. Early Church members knew that the Prophet Joseph Smith could receive revelation for the Church. But could others? Questions like this became critical when Hiram Page, one of the Eight Witnesses of the gold plates, believed he had received revelations for the Church. Many faithful Saints believed that these revelations were from God. The Lord responded by teaching that in His Church "all things must be done in order" (Doctrine and Covenants 28:13). This meant having only one person "appointed to receive commandments and revelations" for the entire Church (Doctrine and Covenants 28:2). Others, however, could receive personal revelation for their part in the Lord's work. In fact, the Lord's words to Oliver Cowdery are a reminder to all of us: "It shall be given thee . . . what thou shalt do" (Doctrine and Covenants 28:15).

See also "All Things Must Be Done in Order," in *Revelations in Context*, 50–53.

 Ideas for Learning at Home and at Church

I take the sacrament in remembrance of Jesus Christ.

Sally Knight and Emma Smith were baptized in June 1830, but their confirmations were disrupted by a mob. Two months later, Sally and her husband, Newel, visited Emma and Joseph, and it was decided that they would now be confirmed and that the group would partake of the sacrament together. While on his way to obtain wine for the sacrament, Joseph was stopped by an angel.

Read Doctrine and Covenants 27:1–4 to find out what the angel taught him about the sacrament. What do these verses suggest about how the Savior wants you to approach the sacrament? What do you think it means to partake of it "with an eye single to [His] glory"? Ponder this—and look for other insights about the sacrament—as you read Luke 22:19–20 and 3 Nephi 18:1–11. (See also the videos "The Last Supper," "Jesus Christ Blesses Bread in Remembrance of Him," and "Jesus Christ Blesses Wine in Remembrance of Him," Gospel Library).

To learn about making the sacrament a worshipful experience, consider studying Elder D. Todd Christofferson's message "The Living Bread Which Came Down from Heaven" (*Ensign* or *Liahona*, Nov. 2017, 36–39). What did Elder Christofferson teach that can help you feel a greater connection to the Savior through the sacrament? Ponder what you can do to better prepare to partake of the emblems of the Savior's Atonement and treat them with greater reverence or purpose.

Consider singing, listening to, or reading a sacrament hymn, like "As Now We Take the Sacrament" (*Hymns*, no. 169), and recording your feelings about participating in this sacred ordinance.

Use music. Sacred music invites the Spirit to testify of gospel truths. It can help you understand and feel these truths in a memorable way. Music also helps make learning more engaging.

See also Doctrine and Covenants 20:77, 79; 59:9–13; Topics and Questions, "Sacrament," Gospel Library; "Obtaining and Retaining a Remission of Sins through Ordinances," in David A. Bednar, "Always Retain a Remission of Your Sins," *Ensign* or *Liahona*, May 2016, 60–62.

DOCTRINE AND COVENANTS 27:5–14

The Lord gives His servants priesthood keys to direct His work.

What do you know about the prophets mentioned in these verses? You could search for information about them in the Guide to the Scriptures. What blessings have been unlocked for you through the keys that these prophets held?

DOCTRINE AND COVENANTS 27:15–18

The armor of God helps me stand against evil.

President M. Russell Ballard said: "There is not one great and grand thing we can do to arm ourselves spiritually. True spiritual power lies in numerous smaller acts woven together in a fabric of spiritual fortification that protects and shields from all evil" ("Be Strong in the Lord," *Ensign*, July 2004, 8).

As you learn about the armor of God in Doctrine and Covenants 27:15–18, you could create a table like this one. What are you doing to put on each piece of the armor of God?

Piece of armor	Part of body protected	What that body part may represent
Breastplate of righteousness	Heart	My desires and affections
Helmet of salvation	Head or mind	

See also Ephesians 6:11–18; Jorge F. Zeballos, "Building a Life Resistant to the Adversary," *Liahona*, Nov. 2022, 50–52.

DOCTRINE AND COVENANTS 28

Jesus Christ directs His Church through His living prophet.

Imagine what it would be like if anyone could receive commandments and revelation for the entire Church. When Hiram Page claimed to have received such revelation, many Church members were confused. In Doctrine and Covenants 28, the Lord revealed an order for revelation in His Church. What do you learn from this section about the specific role of the President of the Church? What do you learn about how God can direct you?

See also Dale G. Renlund, "A Framework for Personal Revelation," *Liahona*, Nov. 2022, 16–19.

For more ideas, see this month's issues of the *Liahona* and *For the Strength of Youth* magazines.

 Ideas for Teaching Children

DOCTRINE AND COVENANTS 27:1–2

The sacrament helps me remember Jesus Christ.

- Children might wonder why we use water for the sacrament when Jesus used wine (see Luke 22:19–20; 3 Nephi 18:1–11). You could read Doctrine and Covenants 27:1–2 together and discuss what it means to take the sacrament "with an eye single to [God's] glory" (verse 2). What can we do to focus on the Savior while we take the sacrament?

- Perhaps having pictures, scripture verses, or song lyrics about the Savior could help your children remember Him when taking the sacrament. They might enjoy creating a booklet with some of these pictures, verses, and lyrics. They could draw their own pictures or find some in the *Friend* magazine.

Detail from *The Last Supper,* by Simon Dewey

The armor of God protects me.

- You could show your children a picture of armor like the one in this outline or on the activity page in the outline for Ephesians in *Come, Follow Me—For Primary: New Testament 2023*. As you read Doctrine and Covenants 27:15–18, help them find the pieces of armor in the picture. How can the armor of God help us "withstand the evil day"? (verse 15).

The prophet receives revelation for the Church; I can receive revelation for my life.

- If you have several children, you might invite them to play "follow the leader," but ask two or more children to be the leader at the same time. What happens when there is more than one leader? You could then learn about Hiram Page (see "Chapter 14: The Prophet and Revelations for the Church," in *Doctrine and Covenants Stories*, 56–57, or the corresponding video in Gospel Library; or the section heading for Doctrine and Covenants 28). How did Heavenly Father correct the confusion of the early Church members? How does He lead the Church today? (see Doctrine and Covenants 28:2). Share your testimony that the current prophet is called by the Lord to lead His Church in our day.

- While revelation for the Church will always be given through the prophet, we can all be guided by the Holy Ghost. You could help your children search some of the following scriptures and make a list of ways the Holy Ghost can guide us: Doctrine and Covenants 28:1, 4, 15; John 14:26; Moroni 8:26; 10:4–5. Share with each other how you have been guided by the Holy Ghost.

For more ideas, see this month's issue of the *Friend* magazine.

The Armor of God

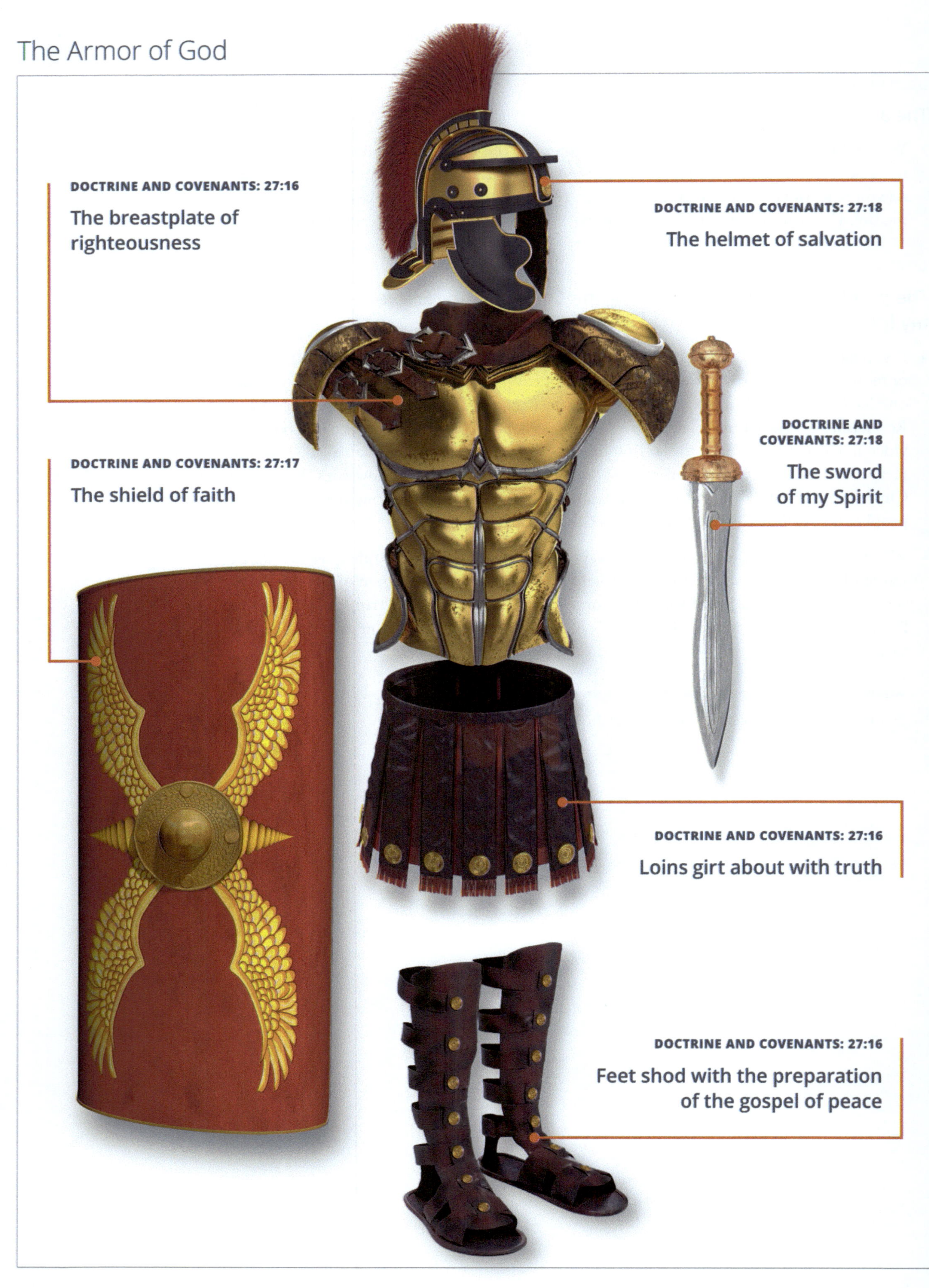

The prophet leads the Church (Doctrine and Covenants 28:2, 6–7).

Make a two-sided mobile showing that Jesus leads His Church through His prophets—in Joseph Smith's time and our day. Color the pictures, and draw a picture of the current prophet's face in the space provided. Cut out the pieces, fold them, and attach them together with paper clips or string as shown.

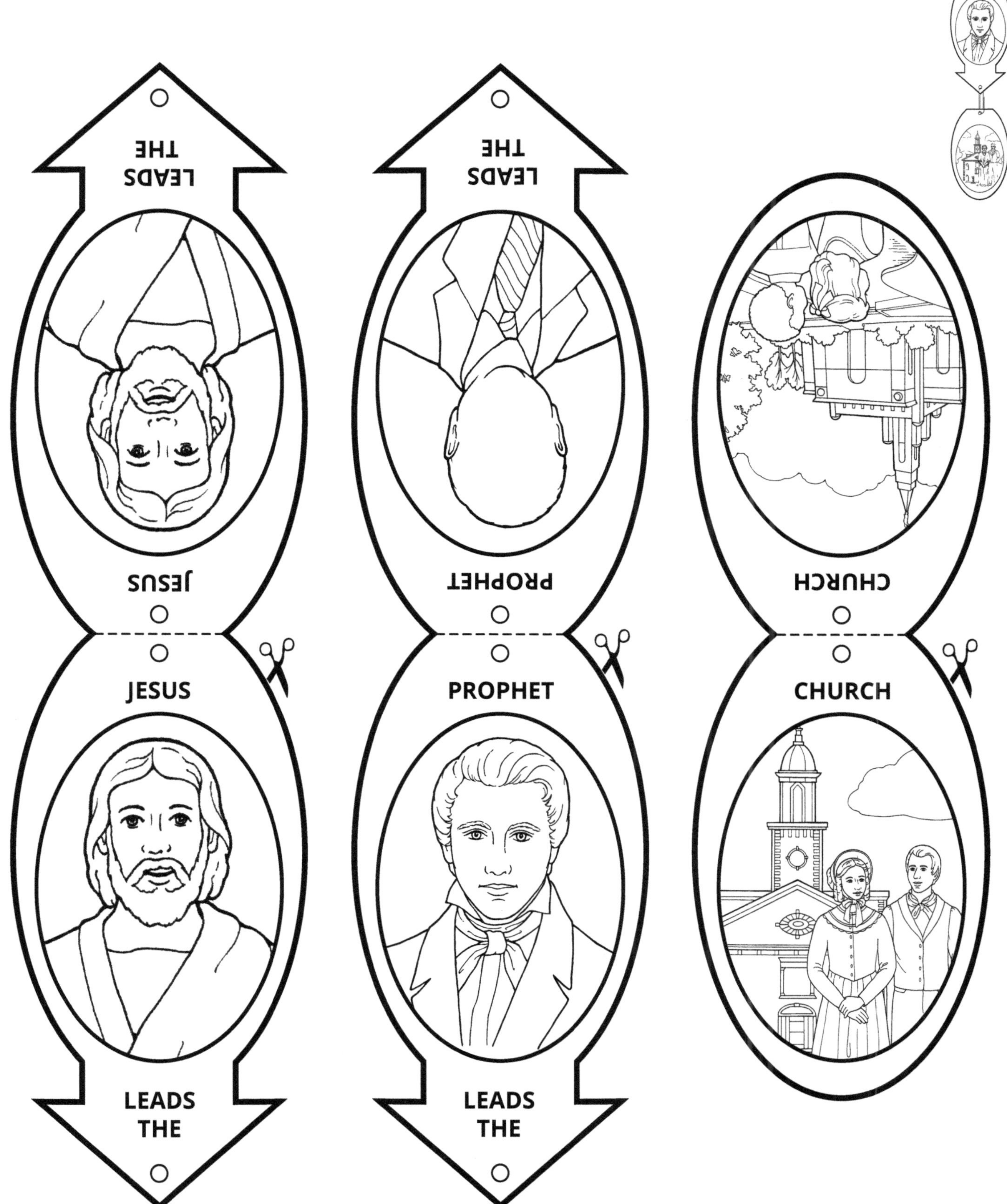

Doctrine and Covenants 29

Even though the Church of Jesus Christ had been organized in 1830, many gospel truths were still yet to be revealed, and several early Church members had questions. They had read prophecies in the Book of Mormon about the gathering of Israel and the building up of Zion (see 3 Nephi 21). How would that happen? The revelations Hiram Page claimed to receive speculated on that subject, which only increased members' curiosity (see Doctrine and Covenants 28). Other people wondered about the Fall of Adam and Eve and spiritual death. The Lord welcomed these questions in 1830, and He welcomes our questions today. "Whatsoever ye shall ask in faith," He told the Saints, "being united in prayer according to my command, ye shall receive" (Doctrine and Covenants 29:6). In fact, as the doctrinally rich revelation in Doctrine and Covenants 29 shows, the Lord sometimes responds to our questions by giving us truth and knowledge far beyond what we ask.

Ideas for Learning at Home and at Church

Heavenly Father has a plan for the salvation of His children.

Doctrine and Covenants 29 teaches many truths about God's plan for you. As you read, look for truths you learn about each of the following parts of His plan:

- Premortal life (see verses 36–37)

- Creation (see verses 31–33)

- The Fall of Adam and Eve (see verses 40–41)

- Mortal life (see verses 39, 42–45)

- The Atonement of Jesus Christ (see verses 1, 42–43, 46–50)

- The Resurrection (see verses 13, 26)

- The Final Judgment (see verses 12–13, 27–30)

What insights did you gain? If it's helpful to you, you could write them in the space provided with the images at the end of this outline. How do these truths influence your life?

See also Topics and Questions, "Plan of Salvation," Gospel Library.

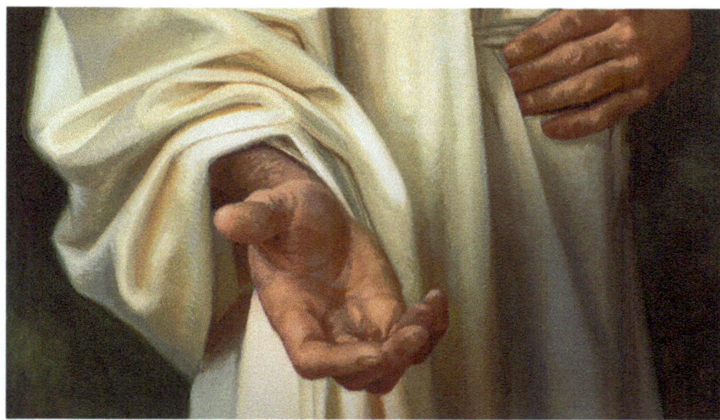

Detail from *Come Unto Me*, by Jenedy Paige

DOCTRINE AND COVENANTS 29:1–28

📖 Jesus Christ invites me to help gather His people before His Second Coming.

Jesus Christ speaks of gathering His people "as a hen gathereth her chickens under her wings" (Doctrine and Covenants 29:2). What does this comparison teach you about Jesus Christ? What additional thoughts or impressions come to you as you study the illustration of a hen and chicks in this outline? Think about how you have felt Jesus Christ gathering and protecting you.

As you read Doctrine and Covenants 29:1–11, look for insights about:

- Who will be gathered.

- What it means to "gather" to Christ.

- Why we gather to Him.

Ponder why you want other people to gather to Jesus Christ. What do you feel inspired to do to help?

You could ask yourself the same questions while watching the video "A Witness of God" (Gospel Library) or reading or listening to a hymn about gathering, such as "Israel, Israel, God Is Calling" (*Hymns*, no. 7). What do you feel the Lord is trying to teach you about His work of gathering?

President Russell M. Nelson said: "Now the gathering takes place in each nation. The Lord has decreed the establishment of Zion in each realm where He has given His Saints their birth and nationality" ("The Gathering of Scattered Israel," *Ensign* or *Liahona*, Nov. 2006, 81). How does gathering in this way help us "be prepared in all things" for the Savior's Second Coming? (verse 8; see also verses 14–28).

See also Russell M. Nelson and Wendy W. Nelson, "Hope of Israel" (worldwide youth devotional, June 3, 2018), Gospel Library; D. Todd Christofferson, "The Doctrine of Belonging," *Liahona*, Nov. 2022, 53–56; Topics and Questions, "Gathering of Israel," Gospel Library.

DOCTRINE AND COVENANTS 29:31–35

"All things unto me are spiritual."

As you study Doctrine and Covenants 29:31–35, ask yourself, "In what sense are all commandments spiritual?" You might list a few commandments and consider the spiritual truths related to each one. A review of *For the Strength of Youth: A Guide for Making Choices* could be helpful—it teaches some of the eternal truths behind several of God's commandments.

How does knowing that "all things . . . are spiritual" affect the way you look at God's commandments? Consider looking for spiritual meaning or purpose in other aspects of your life as well.

See also 2 Nephi 9:39.

Focus on Jesus Christ. "Every gospel topic [is] an opportunity to teach and learn about Jesus Christ" (*Teaching in the Savior's Way*, 6). What do you learn about His attributes, His roles, and His example as you read Doctrine and Covenants 29?

DOCTRINE AND COVENANTS 29:36–50

Jesus Christ redeems us from the Fall.

How could you use Doctrine and Covenants 29:36–50 to explain why we need redemption through Jesus Christ?

The Fall of Adam and Eve brought death and sin into the world, but it also prepared the way for redemption and joy through Christ. With that thought in mind, read verses 39–43 and note words and phrases that bring you joy. What impresses you about what Adam and Eve said about the Fall in Moses 5:10–12?

See also "Why We Need a Savior" (video), Gospel Library.

For more ideas, see this month's issues of the *Liahona* and *For the Strength of Youth* magazines.

 Ideas for Teaching Children

DOCTRINE AND COVENANTS 29

Heavenly Father has a plan for the salvation of His children.

- To start a conversation about Heavenly Father's plan for us, you and your children could talk about a time when you made a plan, such as for a trip or for accomplishing a task. You could also share examples of plans, such as a calendar with activities written on it or instructions to make something. Why are plans useful? You could then talk about what Heavenly Father wants to accomplish and how His plan helps us accomplish it.

- You could use the images at the end of this outline to help your children find verses in Doctrine and Covenants 29 that teach about different parts of Heavenly Father's plan. You could also cut out the images and ask your children to put them in the correct order. Why are we thankful to know that Heavenly Father has a plan for us? How does knowing about it influence our everyday lives?

DOCTRINE AND COVENANTS 29:1–2, 7–8

Jesus Christ is gathering His people before He comes again.

- The illustration below of a hen gathering her chicks or the video "Chicks and Hens" (ChurchofJesusChrist.org) could help your children visualize the analogy in Doctrine and

Covenants 29:1–2. Then you could read these verses together and talk with each other about how a hen protects her chicks and how that's similar to what the Savior can do for us.

I Would Gather Thee, by Liz Lemon Swindle

- What would inspire your children to want to help the Savior gather His people? Maybe they'd like to hear the experience of someone who "gathered" to Him by joining His Church. For example, who introduced your family to the Church? How have we been blessed by accepting the Savior's call to gather to Him? How can we help others gather to Him? (See "A Message for Children from President Russell M. Nelson" [video], ChurchofJesusChrist.org.)

DOCTRINE AND COVENANTS 29:11

Jesus Christ will come again.

- A picture of the Savior's Second Coming (such as *Gospel Art Book*, no. 66) or a song about it (such as "When He Comes Again," *Children's Songbook*, 82–83) could help you and your children discuss Doctrine and Covenants 29:11. Help your children notice phrases in the scripture that relate to something in the picture or song. Share with each other how you feel about Jesus Christ coming to earth again.

For more ideas, see this month's issue of the *Friend* magazine.

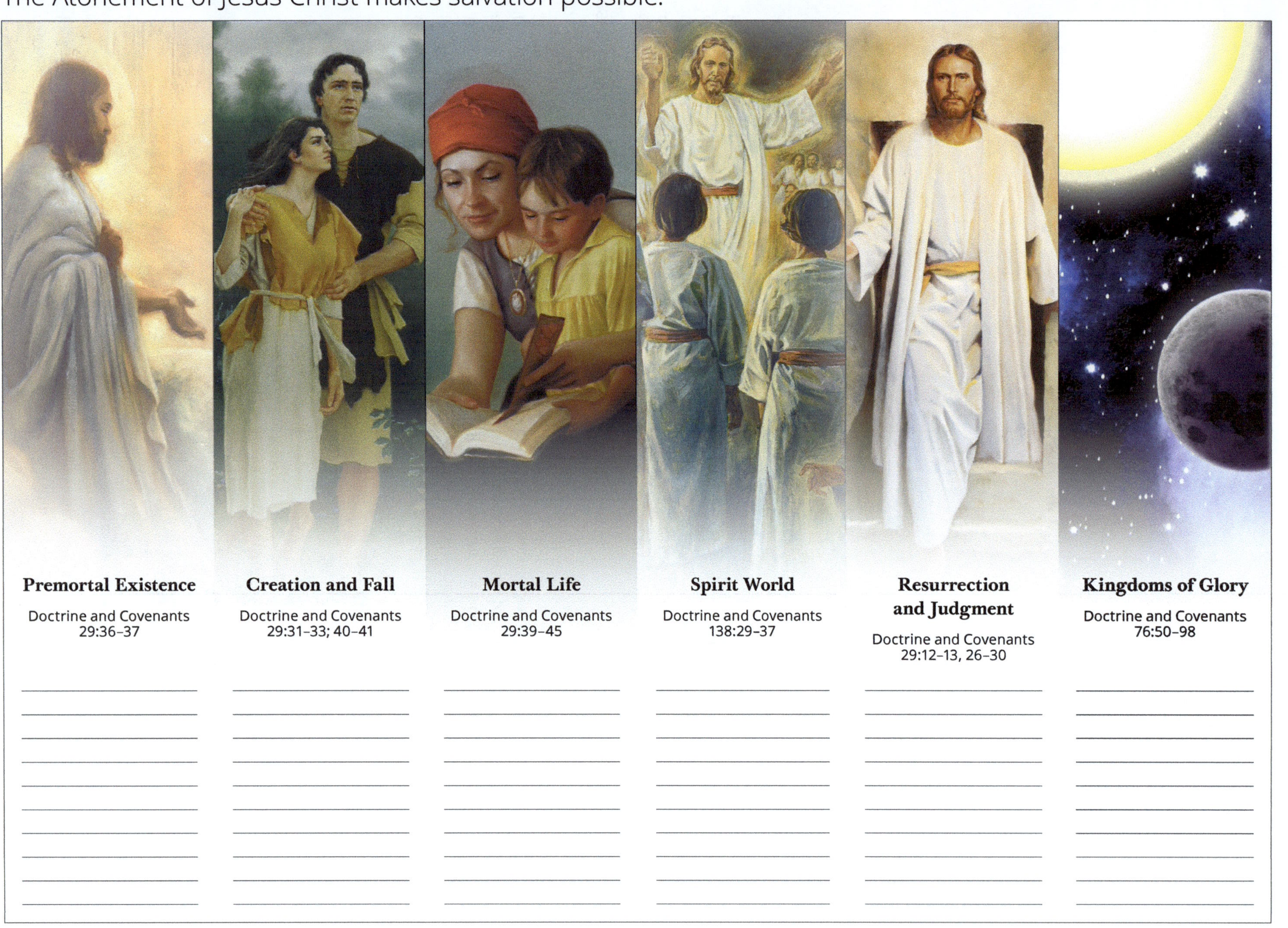

| **Premortal Existence** | **Creation and Fall** | **Mortal Life** | **Spirit World** | **Resurrection and Judgment** | **Kingdoms of Glory** |
| Doctrine and Covenants 29:36–37 | Doctrine and Covenants 29:31–33; 40–41 | Doctrine and Covenants 29:39–45 | Doctrine and Covenants 138:29–37 | Doctrine and Covenants 29:12–13, 26–30 | Doctrine and Covenants 76:50–98 |

Jesus Christ is gathering His people before He comes again (Doctrine and Covenants 29:1–2, 7–8).

Color the picture. Draw yourself in the frame gathering to Jesus Christ with the other people.

Doctrine and Covenants 30–36

Parley P. Pratt had been a member of the Church for about a month when he was called "into the wilderness" to preach the gospel (Doctrine and Covenants 32:2). Thomas B. Marsh had been a member for even less time than that when he was told, "The hour of your mission is come" (Doctrine and Covenants 31:3). Orson Pratt, Edward Partridge, and many others had likewise barely been baptized when their mission calls came. Perhaps there's a lesson in this pattern for us today: if you know enough to accept the restored gospel by baptism, you know enough to share it with others. Of course, we always want to increase our gospel knowledge, but God has never hesitated to call upon the "unlearned" to preach His gospel (Doctrine and Covenants 35:13). In fact, He invites all of us, "Open your mouth to declare my gospel" (Doctrine and Covenants 30:5). And we do that best not through our own wisdom and experience but "by the power of [the] Spirit" (Doctrine and Covenants 35:13).

See also "The Faith and Fall of Thomas Marsh," "Ezra Thayer: From Skeptic to Believer," "Orson Pratt's Call to Serve," in *Revelations in Context*, 54–69.

 Ideas for Learning at Home and at Church

DOCTRINE AND COVENANTS 30–36

I am called to be a witness of Jesus Christ.

Whether or not you have a formal calling as a missionary, you can be a witness of Jesus Christ "at all times, and in all things, and in all places" (Mosiah 18:9). As you study Doctrine and Covenants 30–36, record what you learn about your opportunities to share the gospel. You could make a list of things the Lord asks of you and another list of promises the Lord makes as you share the gospel (for example, see Doctrine and Covenants 30:8; 31:3–5; 32:1, 5; 35:13–15, 24). You could also look for principles that can help you share the gospel. What do you find that inspires you to "declare glad tidings of great joy"? (Doctrine and Covenants 31:3).

Elder Gary E. Stevenson taught that proclaiming the gospel "can be accomplished through simple, easily understandable principles taught to each of us from childhood: love, share, and invite" ("Love, Share, Invite," *Liahona*, May 2022, 85). Consider studying his message while thinking about your acquaintances, friends, and family. What ideas come to you about how

you can share with them "what [you] love about the gospel of Jesus Christ"? In what ways can you invite them to "come and see," "come and serve," and "come and belong"? As you sing or listen to "I'll Go Where You Want Me to Go" (*Hymns*, no. 270) or a related hymn, you might ask yourself, "What does the Lord want me to say and be in order to share His gospel?"

See also Marcos A. Aidukaitis, "Lift Up Your Heart and Rejoice," *Liahona*, May 2022, 40–43; Topics and Questions, "Inviting All to Receive the Gospel of Jesus Christ," "Ministering as the Savior Does," Gospel Library; "Inviting All to Come unto Christ: Sharing the Gospel" (video), Gospel Library.

DOCTRINE AND COVENANTS 31:1–2, 5–6, 9, 13

The Lord can help me with my family relationships.

Families in the 1830s struggled with many of the same issues that families face today. What guidance and promises did the Lord give to Thomas B. Marsh about his family in Doctrine and Covenants 31? (see especially verses 1–2, 5–6, 9, 13). How can His words help you in your family relationships?

For more information about Thomas B. Marsh, see *Saints*, 1:79–80, 119–20.

DOCTRINE AND COVENANTS 32–33; 35

The Lord prepares me for the work He wants me to do.

Studying the lives of the people addressed in Doctrine and Covenants 32–33; 35 could help you recognize how the Lord is preparing you for His work. For example, you could read about the relationship between Parley P. Pratt and Sidney Rigdon in "Voices of the Restoration: Early Converts." How did this relationship bless God's children? (see Doctrine and Covenants 35).

What evidence do you see that the Lord's hand was in the lives of these early Church members? Who has the Lord placed in your life to help you come to Christ? How is He preparing you to bless others through your faithfulness, love, or invitation?

See also "A Mission to the Lamanites," in *Revelations in Context*, 45–49.

DOCTRINE AND COVENANTS 33:12–18

If I build my life on the Savior's gospel, I will not fall.

Doctrine and Covenants 33 was addressed to Northrop Sweet and Ezra Thayer, two new members of the Church. Northrop left the Church soon after this revelation was given. Ezra served faithfully for some time, but he also eventually fell away. Reading about them in this section might prompt you to consider how firmly you are built "upon [the] rock" (verse 13) of the gospel. What truths in these verses can help you remain faithful to the Savior?

See also Helaman 5:12.

For more ideas, see this month's issues of the *Liahona* and *For the Strength of Youth* magazines.

Ideas for Teaching Children

DOCTRINE AND COVENANTS 30:1–2

I should focus more on the things of God than the things of the earth.

- It may be fun for your children to try to do two tasks at once, such as reciting the words to a favorite song while writing down the names of all their family members. Why is it difficult to do two things at once? You could then read Doctrine and Covenants 30:1–2 together. What are some "things of the earth" that can distract us from remembering Jesus Christ and His gospel? How can we keep our focus on Him?

DOCTRINE AND COVENANTS 33:2–3, 6–10

I can share the gospel of Jesus Christ.

- To help your children understand Doctrine and Covenants 33:8–10, you could invite them to try to say a phrase with their mouths closed while you or your other children guess what they are saying. Read verses 8–10 and ask them to open

There are many ways to share the gospel.

their mouths each time the phrase "open your mouths" is repeated. Why does Heavenly Father want us to open our mouths and share the gospel with others? What can we tell our family and friends about the Savior or His gospel? You could also sing a song about sharing the gospel, such as "We'll Bring the World His Truth" (*Children's Songbook*, 172–73).

- Consider sharing experiences you've had related to the principles or promises in Doctrine and Covenants 30–34. What did you learn or feel about your Savior and His work as you served Him?

Testify of promised blessings. When you invite children to live a gospel principle, you can share the promises that God has made to people who live that principle. For example, you can bear testimony of the blessings that He gives to us when we open our mouths and share the gospel.

DOCTRINE AND COVENANTS 33:12–13

I can build my life on the gospel of Jesus Christ.

- You could take your children outside to see the foundation of their home or Church building and ask them to describe it. Why does a building need a strong, solid foundation? Read with them Doctrine and Covenants 33:12–13, and share with each other your feelings about why the Lord wants us to build our lives on His gospel. Why is "rock" a good word to describe the gospel? How can we build our lives on the rock of the gospel? (see also Matthew 7:24–29).

For more ideas, see this month's issue of the *Friend* magazine.

Go into the Wilderness, by Robert T. Barrett

I can share the gospel of Jesus Christ (Doctrine and Covenants 33:2–3, 6–10).

Find items to use as game pieces, like different coins. Write the numbers 1–6 on separate pieces of paper, and put them in a container. Take turns drawing out a piece of paper and moving your game piece the number of spaces drawn. If you land on a spot with a heart, move forward one extra space.

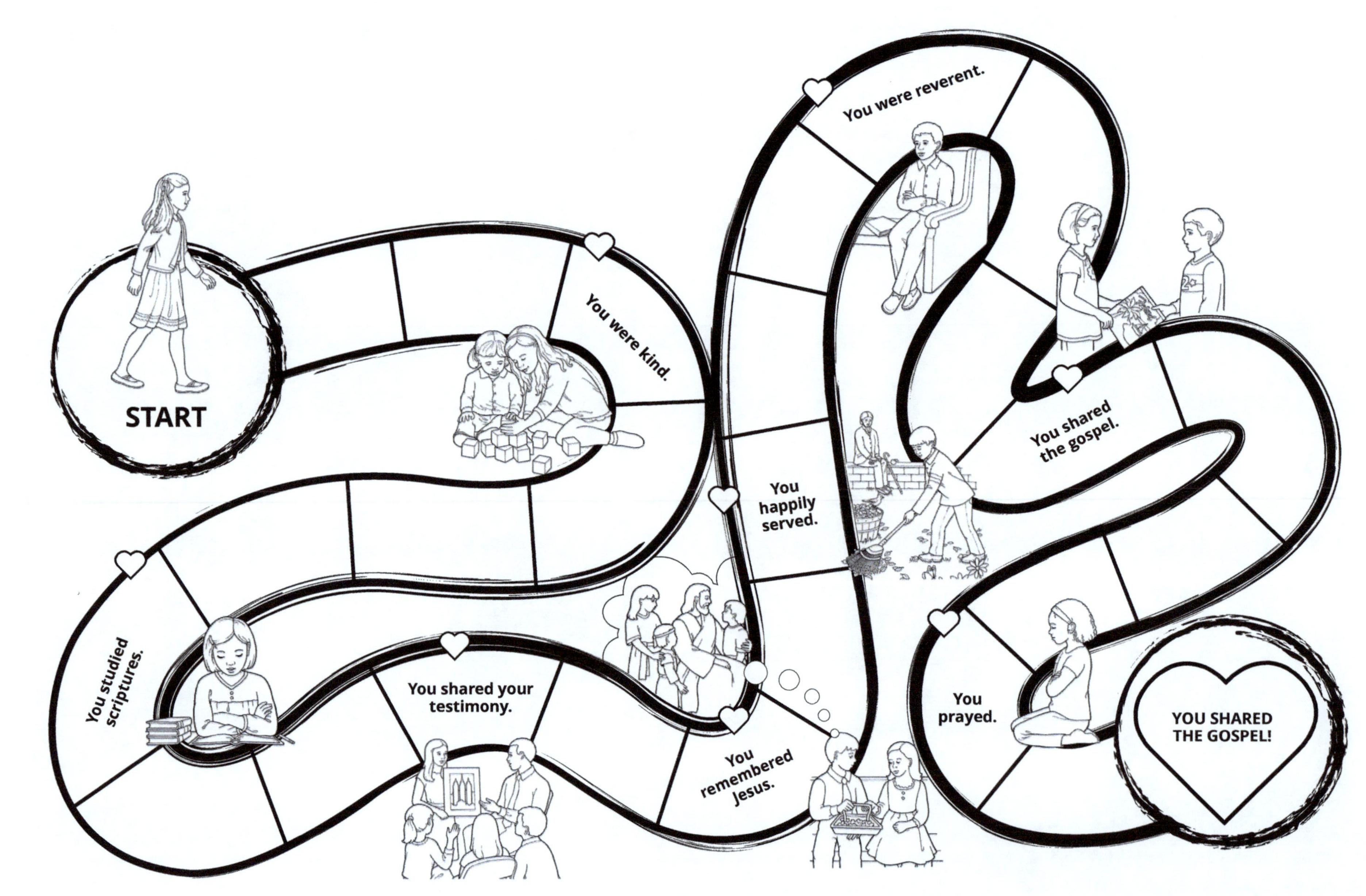

Easter

April 3, 1836, was Easter Sunday. After helping administer the sacrament to Saints in the newly dedicated Kirtland Temple, Joseph Smith and Oliver Cowdery found a quiet place behind a veil and bowed in silent prayer. Then, on this sacred day when Christians everywhere were commemorating the Resurrection of Jesus Christ, the risen Savior Himself appeared in His temple, declaring, "I am he who liveth, I am he who was slain" (Doctrine and Covenants 110:4).

What does it mean to say that Jesus Christ is "he who liveth"? It doesn't just mean that He rose from the tomb and appeared to His disciples in Galilee. It means that He lives today. He speaks through prophets today. He leads His Church today. He heals wounded souls and broken hearts today. So we can echo the words of Joseph Smith's powerful testimony: "After the many testimonies which have been given of him, this is the testimony . . . which we give of him: That he lives!" (Doctrine and Covenants 76:22). We can hear His voice in these revelations, witness His hand in our lives, and feel "the joy this sentence gives: 'I know that my Redeemer lives!'" (*Hymns*, no. 136).

  Ideas for Learning at Home and at Church

Jesus Christ lives.

Most of us have not seen Jesus Christ as the Prophet Joseph Smith did. But we can know, as he did, that the Savior lives, that He knows our successes and struggles, and that He will help us in times of need. Consider your own testimony of the living Christ as you ponder the questions below and study the accompanying resources.

- Who is Jesus Christ? Why do we worship Him? (see "The Living Christ: The Testimony of the Apostles").

- What does the Spirit teach me about the experiences of Joseph Smith and others who saw the Savior? How do their testimonies strengthen mine? (see Doctrine and Covenants 76:11–14, 20–24; 110:1–10; Joseph Smith—History 1:17).

- What do I learn about the Savior's mission and divinity from His own words? (see Doctrine and Covenants 29:5; 38:7).

- How can the Savior help me today? (see Isaiah 53:3–5; Hebrews 2:17–18; Mosiah 3:7; Alma 7:11–13; 36:3; Ether 12:27; Moses 5:10–12).

Power comes from memorization. Elder Richard G. Scott explained: "Great power can come from memorizing scriptures. To memorize a scripture is to forge a new friendship. It is like discovering a new individual who can help in time of need, give inspiration and comfort, and be a source of motivation for needed change" ("The Power of Scripture," *Ensign*, Nov. 2011, 6). If you find a scripture about the Savior that's especially meaningful to you—perhaps one that could give you comfort in a time of need—consider memorizing it.

In the video "My Spiritual Goal," a young woman decides to memorize "The Living Christ" (Gospel Library). What impresses you about her experience? What do you feel inspired to do to receive the truths in "The Living Christ" in your heart and mind?

To learn more about how the Savior blesses us today, you could study, listen to, or sing "I Know That My Redeemer Lives" (*Hymns*, no. 136). It could be inspiring to look for truths in this hymn that are also taught in Doctrine and Covenants 6:34; 84:77; 98:18; 138:23.

See also Topics and Questions, "Jesus Christ," Gospel Library.

Because of Jesus Christ, I will be resurrected.

Joseph Smith knew how it feels to mourn the death of loved ones, including his father and two of his brothers. Joseph and Emma buried six of their children, each younger than two years old. From the revelations God gave, Joseph and Emma gained an eternal perspective.

Look for truths about death and God's eternal plan in Doctrine and Covenants 29:26–27; 42:45–46; 63:49; 88:14–17, 27–31; 93:33–34. How do these truths affect the way you view death? How do they affect the way you live?

See also 1 Corinthians 15; *Teachings of Presidents of the Church: Joseph Smith* (2007), 174–76; Easter.ChurchofJesusChrist.org.

Jesus Christ accomplished a "perfect atonement" for me.

One way to focus on the Savior at Easter time is to study revelations in the Doctrine and Covenants that teach about His atoning sacrifice. Some can be found in Doctrine and Covenants 18:10–13; 19:16–19; 45:3–5; 76:69–70. Consider making a list of truths that you find in these verses. To deepen your study, you could add to your list by searching Luke 22:39–44; 1 John 1:7; 2 Nephi 2:6–9; Mosiah 3:5–13, 17–18; Moroni 10:32–33.

Here are some questions that could guide your study:

- What is the Atonement of Jesus Christ?

- Why did Jesus Christ choose to suffer and die for us?

- What must I do to receive the blessings of His sacrifice?

- How do I feel about Jesus Christ after reading these verses?

See also Guide to the Scriptures, "Atonement," Gospel Library; "The Savior Suffers in Gethsemane" (video), Gospel Library.

For more ideas, see this month's issues of the *Liahona* and *For the Strength of Youth* magazines.

Ideas for Teaching Children

Because of Jesus Christ, I will be resurrected.

- To teach your children about resurrection, you could start by showing them pictures of the death and Resurrection of the Savior. Let your children share what they know about these events. You could also sing a song like "Did Jesus Really Live Again?" (*Children's Songbook*, 64).

- Consider an object lesson that could help your children understand what happens when we die (our spirits and bodies separate) and when we are resurrected (our spirits and bodies come back together, and our bodies are perfect and immortal). For example, what happens when we remove the battery from a flashlight or the ink container from a pen? What happens when they are reunited? (See Alma 11:44–45.)

- Do your children know someone who has passed away? Let them share a little about these individuals, and then read together Doctrine and Covenants 138:17. Talk with each other about how it feels to know that our loved ones will be resurrected and have bodies again.

- If you have older children, you might invite them to look for phrases that capture the message of Easter in the following passages: Doctrine and Covenants 63:49; 88:14–17, 27; 138:11, 14–17. They could do the same with the video "Because He Lives" (Gospel Library). How can we share this message with others?

The Prophet Joseph Smith saw Jesus Christ.

- You and your children might be interested to read about three different times Jesus Christ appeared to Joseph Smith and others, as recorded in Joseph Smith—History 1:14–17; Doctrine and Covenants 76:11–24; 110:1–10. Your children could also look at pictures of these events in this week's activity page. What do we learn about Jesus Christ from each of these experiences? Why is it a blessing to know that Joseph Smith and others saw the risen Savior?

Because of Jesus Christ, I can be forgiven of my sins.

- The truths Joseph Smith learned about forgiveness through Christ can give your children hope that they can be forgiven of their mistakes and sins. Consider inviting your children to create a table with headings like these: *What the Savior did for me* and *What I must do to receive His forgiveness*. Help your children search the following passages to find things that belong under these headings: Doctrine and Covenants 18:10–13; 19:16–19; 45:3–5; 58:42–43. Share with each other your joy and gratitude for what the Savior did for us.

- You could also watch the video "The Shiny Bicycle" with your children (Gospel Library) and share experiences when you felt the Savior's forgiveness as you repented.

For more ideas, see this month's issue of the *Friend* magazine.

Christ and Mary at the Tomb, by Joseph Brickey

The Prophet Joseph Smith saw Jesus Christ (Doctrine and Covenants 76:11–24; 110:1–7; Joseph Smith—History 1:17).
Color the pictures of different times when Joseph Smith saw Jesus Christ. Cut out the pictures and the other puzzle pieces.
Match the pictures with the correct pieces, and read the related scripture verses.

Doctrine and Covenants 37–40

To the early Saints, the Church was more than a place to hear some preaching on Sunday. The revelations used words like *cause*, *kingdom*, *Zion*, and, quite often, *work*. That may have been part of what attracted people to the restored Church. As much as they loved the doctrine, many also wanted something holy they could dedicate their lives to. Even so, obeying the Lord's 1830 command to gather in Ohio was not easy. For many, it meant leaving comfortable homes for an unfamiliar frontier (see "Voices of the Restoration: Gathering to Ohio," Gospel Library). Today we can see clearly what those Saints could see only with the eye of faith: the Lord had great blessings waiting for them in Ohio.

The need to gather to Ohio has long since passed, but Saints today still unite around the same cause: to "bring forth Zion" (Doctrine and Covenants 39:13). Like those early Saints, we are invited to forsake "the cares of the world" (Doctrine and Covenants 40:2) and trust the Lord's promise: "You shall receive . . . a blessing so great as you never have known" (Doctrine and Covenants 39:10).

See also *Saints*, 1:109–11.

 Ideas for Learning at Home and at Church

God gathers us to bless us.

Members of the Church in Fayette, New York, had to make difficult sacrifices to move to Ohio (more than 250 miles away) in the winter of 1831. As you read about the Lord's command in Doctrine and Covenants 37:3–4, you might think about sacrifices the Lord has asked of you. Then, as you study Doctrine and Covenants 38:1–33, look for truths about the Savior that give you faith to follow His counsel. What do you learn from verses 11–33 about the blessings of gathering as followers of Jesus Christ?

"Hear my voice and follow me."

How can you make Jesus Christ your "lawgiver"? How does following His laws make you "a free people"?

See also 2 Nephi 2:26–27.

If I am prepared, I don't need to be afraid.

When have you experienced the principle the Lord revealed in Doctrine and Covenants 38:30: "If ye are prepared ye shall not fear"? As you study section 38, notice how the Lord prepares His Saints so they can face the future with courage. How does He want you to prepare for challenges so that you don't need to be afraid?

See also David A. Bednar, "We Will Prove Them Herewith," *Ensign* or *Liahona*, Nov. 2020, 8–11.

God wants us to "be one."

The Saints who gathered in Ohio came from a variety of circumstances. The same is likely true of people in your ward. But the Lord commands His people to "be one" (verse 27). How can we accomplish this kind of unity? What ideas come to mind as you read Doctrine and Covenants 38:24–27? Why do we need to be united in order to be God's people?

Reading these verses could also inspire you to think about your relationships—for example, with family members, ward members, and quorum or class members. What might be keeping you from being united in Christ? How can the Savior help you "be one"? The videos "A Friend to All" or "Love in Our Hearts" (Gospel Library) could help you answer these questions. You might also find ideas in Elder Dale G. Renlund's message "The Peace of Christ Abolishes Enmity," *Liahona*, Nov. 2021, 83–85.

How could you help these groups be more unified? For example, consider sending or texting a kind note to members of your quorum, class, or family. Who do you feel inspired to reach out to?

What inspires you about the Savior's example in Ephesians 2:14, 18–22; 2 Nephi 26:24–28?

See also Quentin L. Cook, "Hearts Knit in Righteousness and Unity," *Ensign* or *Liahona*, Nov. 2020, 18–21; "Love One Another," *Hymns*, no. 308; Topics and Questions, "Belonging in the Church of Jesus Christ," Gospel Library.

DOCTRINE AND COVENANTS 38:39; 39–40

Heavenly Father wants to give me the riches of eternity.

In your opinion, what's the difference between "the riches of the earth" and "the riches of eternity"? (Doctrine and Covenants 38:39). What experiences have taught you to value the riches of eternity?

Keep this in mind as you read about James Covel in sections 39–40 (including the historical background in the section headings). Consider how his experience might apply to you. For example, think of times when your "heart . . . was right before [God]" (Doctrine and Covenants 40:1). How were you blessed for your faithfulness? Also think of what "cares of the world" you face. How might they prevent you from receiving God's word "with gladness"? (Doctrine and Covenants 39:9; 40:2). What do you find in these sections that inspires you to be more consistently obedient to God?

See also Matthew 13:3–23.

Applying the scriptures to your life. "One way you can help learners see the relevance of [the scriptures] is by asking questions like 'How can this help you with something you are experiencing now?' 'Why is it important for you to know this?' 'What difference can this make in your life?'" (*Teaching in the Savior's Way*, 23). The questions in this activity about Doctrine and Covenants 39–40 are other examples of questions that can help us apply these revelations to our lives.

For more ideas, see this month's issues of the *Liahona* and *For the Strength of Youth* magazines.

# Ideas for Teaching Children

DOCTRINE AND COVENANTS 37; 38:31–33

God gathers us to bless us.

- The map and the activity page at the end of this outline could help your children understand what God commanded in Doctrine and Covenants 37:3. Maybe you can help them find the places mentioned in these revelations. You could also help them find a phrase from Doctrine and Covenants 38:31–33 that describes why God wants His people to gather together.

DOCTRINE AND COVENANTS 38:24–27

God wants us to "be one."

- As you read Doctrine and Covenants 38:24–25 with your children, talk about what it means to esteem your brother or sister as yourself (see also Matthew 7:12). Help them repeat the scripture, replacing "his brother" with each other's names.

- To teach your children what it means to "be one" (Doctrine and Covenants 38:27), you could help them draw a large number *1* and decorate it with names and drawings or pictures of each person in your family or class. Next to the *1*, you could write things you will do to be more united.

- Consider sharing an object lesson that illustrates how things can be combined or united to become one, such as pieces of cloth that make one quilt or ingredients that make one loaf of bread. What do these examples teach us about becoming one as God's people?

DOCTRINE AND COVENANTS 38:30

If I am prepared, I don't need to be afraid.

- As you read together Doctrine and Covenants 38:30, you and your children could talk about recent experiences that required preparation. Then you could ask your children about things Heavenly Father wants us to prepare for. Share with your children an experience in which being prepared helped you not be fearful. You could also watch together the video "Men's Hearts Shall Fail Them" (Gospel Library).

DOCTRINE AND COVENANTS 39:6, 23

I receive the gift of the Holy Ghost when I am confirmed.

- Consider showing a picture of someone being confirmed. Ask your children to describe what's happening in the picture. You could also invite them to point to the picture whenever they hear the words *Holy Ghost* in Doctrine and Covenants 39:6, 23 (or in a song like "The Holy Ghost," *Children's Songbook*, 105). Share with each other how the gift of the Holy Ghost has blessed you.

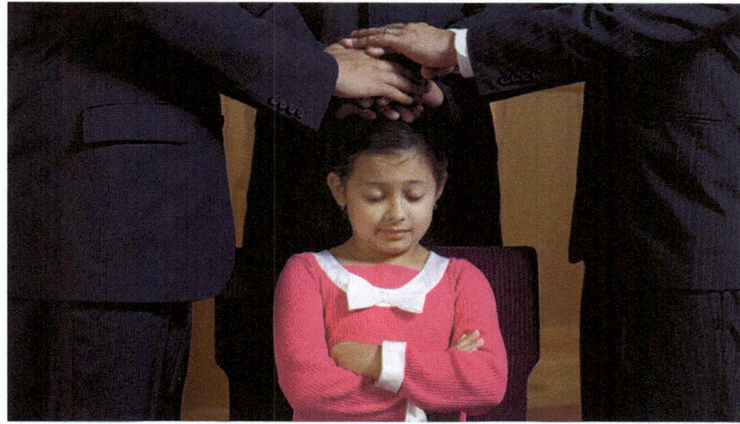

For more ideas, see this month's issue of the *Friend* magazine.

The New York, Pennsylvania, and Ohio area of the United States, 1831

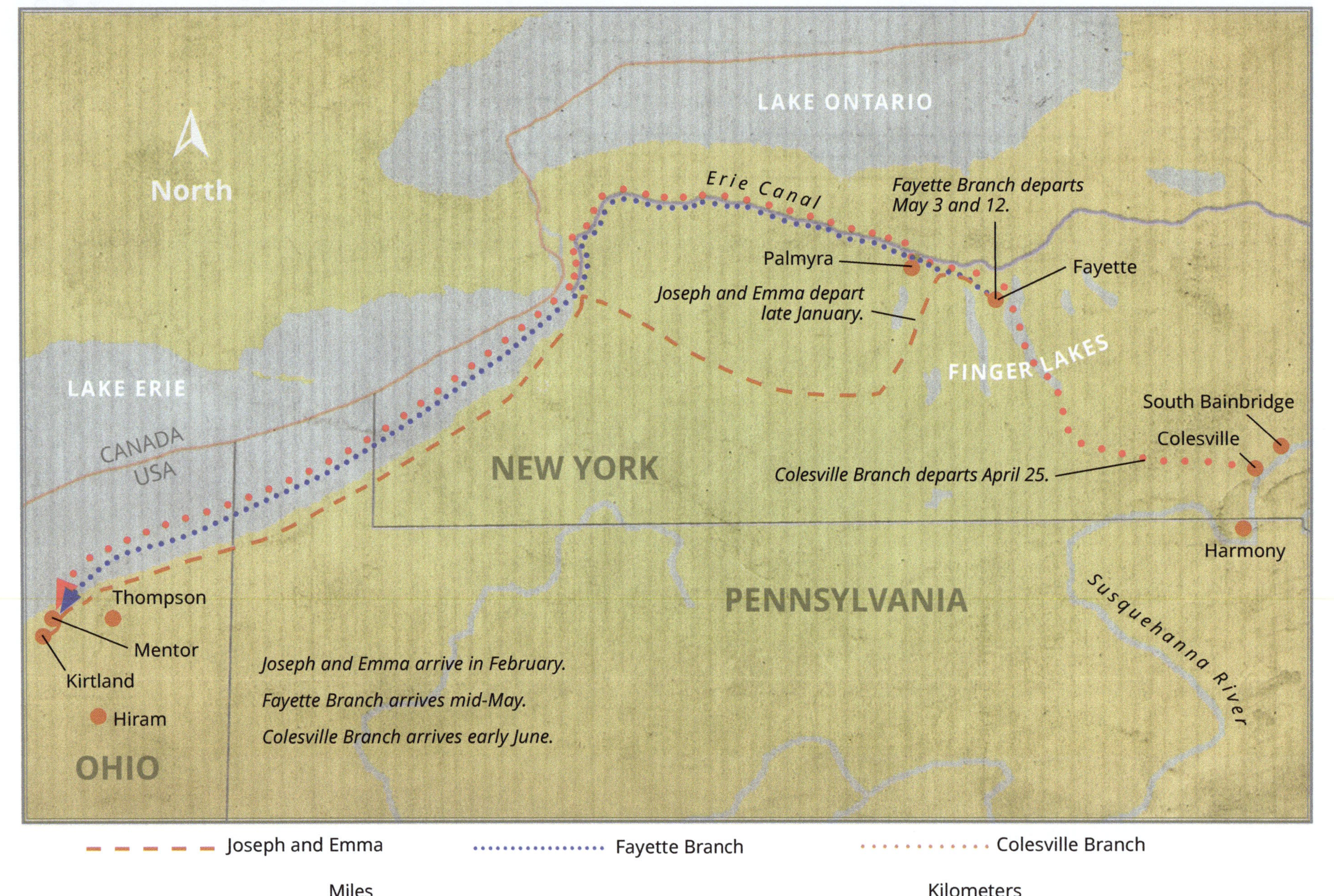

God gathers us to bless us (see Doctrine and Covenants 37; 38:31–33).

Cut out the pictures of the families, and put one of them next to the town of Fayette, New York, and the other next to the town of Colesville, New York. Move the families from their homes along the dotted paths to their new homes in Kirtland, Ohio. Draw new homes for them to live in there.

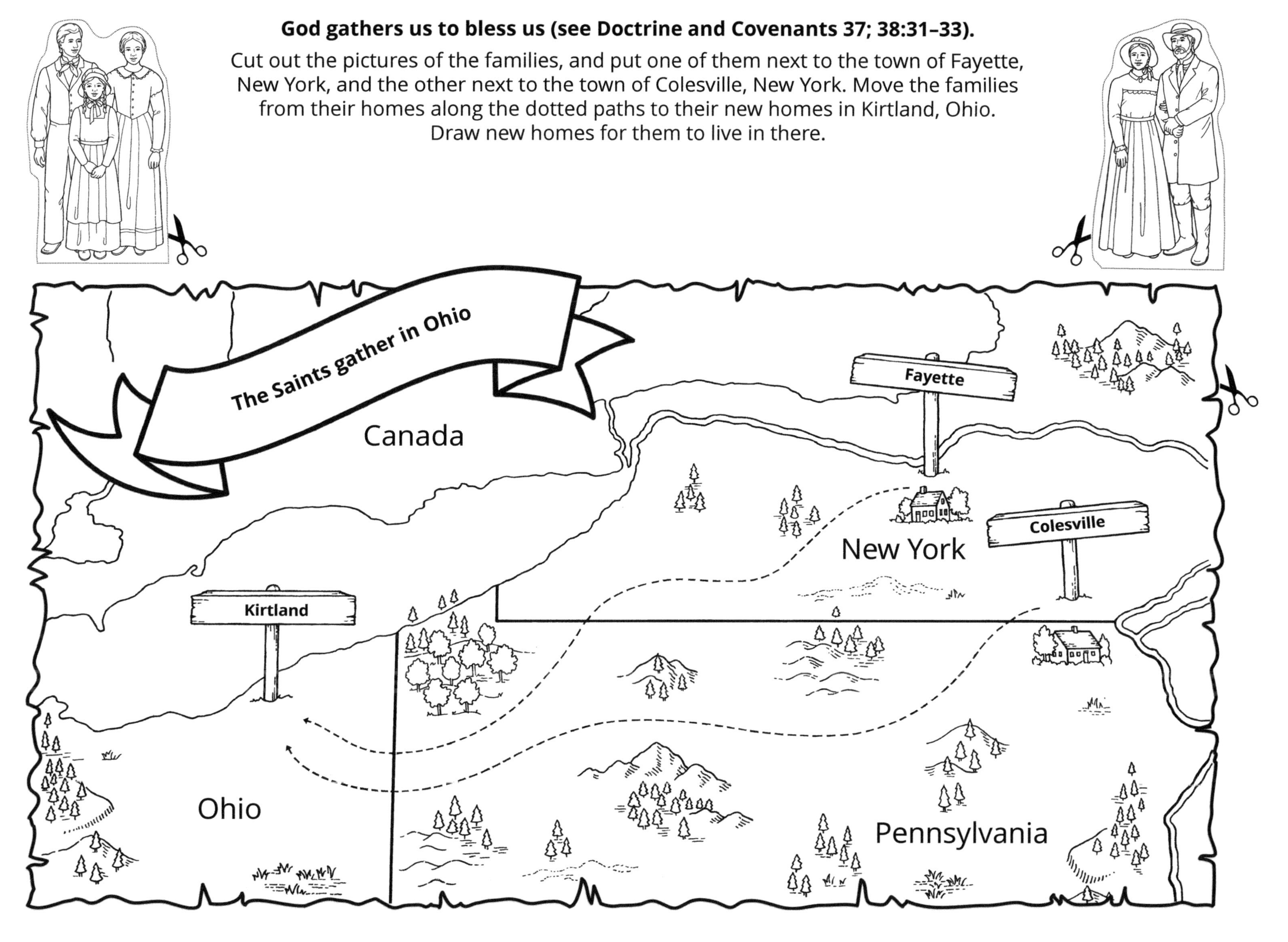

Doctrine and Covenants 41–44

The Church grew rapidly in 1830 and 1831, particularly with a rush of new members in Kirtland, Ohio. This growth was exciting and encouraging to the Saints, but it also presented some challenges. How do you unify a quickly expanding group of believers? Specifically, what do you do when they bring doctrine and practices from their previous faiths? For example, when Joseph Smith arrived in Kirtland in early February 1831, he found new members sharing common property in a genuine attempt to imitate the New Testament Christians (see Acts 4:32–37). The Lord made some important corrections and clarifications on this and other topics. He did this largely through a revelation recorded in Doctrine and Covenants 42 that He called "my law to govern my church" (verse 59). In this revelation, we learn truths that are fundamental in establishing the Lord's Church in the latter days. And we learn that we have a lot more to learn: "If thou shalt ask," the Lord promised, "thou shalt receive revelation upon revelation, knowledge upon knowledge" (Doctrine and Covenants 42:61).

See also *Saints*, 1:114–19.

 Ideas for Learning at Home and at Church

DOCTRINE AND COVENANTS 41

"He that receiveth my law and doeth it, the same is my disciple."

By early 1831, the Saints were starting to gather in Ohio. They were eager to receive the law that God had promised to reveal there (see Doctrine and Covenants 38:32). But first, He taught how His disciples should prepare to receive His law. What principles do you find in Doctrine and Covenants 41:1–6 that would have helped the Saints receive God's law? How might these principles help you receive instruction from Him?

See also "A Bishop unto the Church," in *Revelations in Context*, 77–83.

The Lord gives me commandments because He loves me.

The Saints considered the revelation found in Doctrine and Covenants 42:1–72 to be one of the most important the Prophet had received. It was one of the first revelations to be published. For many years, the Saints called it simply "the law." While the section does not include all the Lord's commandments or laws, it is worth pondering why these principles were important for the newly restored Church. Why are they important for us today?

Because section 42 is relatively long, you might consider studying it in smaller portions, like the following. Identify the principles taught in each, and consider how these laws are a sign of the Lord's love for His people.

- Verses 4–9, 11–17, 56–58

- Verses 18–29

- Verses 30–31

- Verses 40–42

- Verses 43–52

Why does God give us laws and commandments? In what ways have you been blessed by knowing and following the commandments?

"Remember the poor."

As part of the law revealed in section 42, the Lord taught His Saints how they could, like the followers of Christ anciently, have "all things common" (Acts 2:44; 4 Nephi 1:3), with "no poor among them" (Moses 7:18). What do you learn from Doctrine and Covenants 42:30–42 about how the Saints lived the law of consecration? (To consecrate means to set something aside for a sacred purpose.)

Although we don't have "all things common" today, in temples Latter-day Saints covenant to live the law of consecration. How can you consecrate what God has given you to bless people in need? Perhaps singing a song like "Because I Have Been Given Much" (*Hymns*, no. 219) can give you ideas.

See also Sharon Eubank, "I Pray He'll Use Us," *Liahona*, Nov. 2021, 53–56; "The Law," in *Revelations in Context*, 93–95.

Christ and the Rich Young Ruler, by Heinrich Hofmann

God gives revelation to guide His Church—and to guide me.

Imagine that you are having a conversation with a new member of the Church who is excited to know that the Church is guided by revelation. How could you use Doctrine and Covenants 43:1–16 to help him or her learn about the Lord's pattern for guiding His Church through His prophet? How could you use Doctrine and Covenants 42:61, 65–68 to teach about receiving personal revelation?

What are some of the "peaceable things" and joyful things you have received from the Lord through His Spirit?

To learn about how leaders of the Church have heard the Lord's voice, you could watch one of the videos in the "Hear Him" collection in the Gospel Library. Consider creating your own video, explaining how the Lord communicates with you.

See also Russell M. Nelson, "Revelation for the Church, Revelation for Our Lives," *Ensign* or *Liahona*, May 2018, 93–96; "All Things Must Be Done in Order," in *Revelations in Context*, 50–53.

Use object lessons. Object lessons or visual aids can help the people you teach understand gospel truths better and remember them longer. For example, you might use a puzzle, assembled piece by piece, to teach about receiving "revelation upon revelation, knowledge upon knowledge" (Doctrine and Covenants 42:61).

 Ideas for Teaching Children

A disciple is someone who receives God's law and obeys it.

- To help your children know what it means to be a disciple of Jesus Christ, you can write Doctrine and Covenants 41:5 on a piece of paper, leaving blanks where the word *disciple* should be. They could then look in verse 5 for the missing word. According to this verse, what does it mean to be a disciple of Jesus Christ? How are we trying to be better disciples of Christ?

I am happy when I obey the Lord.

- Your children might enjoy playing a game that requires them to listen carefully and follow instructions. You could use this game to talk about what it means to "hearken and hear and obey" the Lord (Doctrine and Covenants 42:2). What instructions has He given us? How are we blessed by obeying His laws and commandments?

- You might complete this week's activity page with your children. You could also sing a song about obeying God's laws, such as "I Want to Live the Gospel" (*Children's Songbook*, 148). Consider sharing with each other how obeying God's laws has brought you happiness.

DOCTRINE AND COVENANTS 42:38

I am serving Jesus Christ when I serve others.

- After reading together Doctrine and Covenants 42:38, help your children think of ways they can serve Jesus by serving others. They can find some ideas from the video "Pass It On" (ChurchofJesusChrist.org). They could also look at pictures of the Savior helping others, healing the sick, or being kind to children (see *Gospel Art Book*, nos. 42, 47).

- You might show your children a Tithing and Other Offerings slip and talk about how to use it to give what we have to bless others (see also "Tithing and Donations Online").

DOCTRINE AND COVENANTS 43:1–7

Only the prophet can receive revelation for the whole Church.

- Invite your children to imagine that someone stands up in testimony meeting and tells the ward that he has received a revelation for the whole Church (for example, a revelation that we should no longer eat carrots or that we should wash our hands with milk instead of water.) He says that we should listen to what he says instead of the prophet. What would be wrong with that? You could then study Doctrine and Covenants 43:1–7 together to find out how the Lord gives commandments to His Church.

- You could also show a picture of the living prophet and invite your children to share something he taught recently. If they need help, share a video clip or passage from a recent general conference message. Why is it a blessing to have a living prophet today?

For more ideas, see this month's issue of the *Friend* magazine.

Joseph Smith Preaching, by Sam Lawlor

I am happy when I obey the Lord (Doctrine and Covenants 41:5; 42:2).

Color the pictures and cut out the rectangle. Fold the picture back and forth like an accordion on the dotted lines.
Stand the paper up and look at it from each side to see how we are happy
when we are obedient or unhappy when we are disobedient.

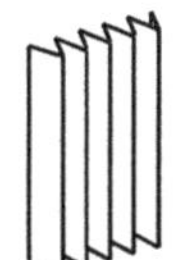

Doctrine and Covenants 45

The revelation in section 45 was received, according to the section heading, "to the joy of the Saints." And there's a lot to be joyful about in this revelation. In it the Savior gives His tender promise to plead for us before the Father (see verses 3–5). He tells of His everlasting covenant spreading throughout the world, like "a messenger . . . to prepare the way before [Him]" (verse 9). And He prophesies of His glorious Second Coming. The Savior does all of this while also acknowledging that these are troubling times (see verse 34), in part because of the perils that are to take place before His coming. But that peril, that darkness is not strong enough to extinguish the light of hope. "For verily I say unto you," the Lord declared, "that I am . . . a light that shineth in darkness" (verse 7). That alone is reason to receive this revelation—with whatever counsel and warnings and truth He wants to give—with joy.

 Ideas for Learning at Home and at Church

DOCTRINE AND COVENANTS 45:1–5

Jesus Christ is my Advocate with the Father.

When we feel inadequate or unworthy before God, we can find reassurance from the Savior's words in Doctrine and Covenants 45:1–5. As you search these verses, consider questions like these:

- What words or phrases in these verses feel especially meaningful to you?

- An advocate is someone who publicly supports or recommends a person or cause. According to these verses, how does Jesus Christ do this for you? What qualifies Him to do it?

- What impresses you about the Savior's words to the Father? (verses 4–5).

You could also study what Elder Dale G. Renlund taught about Jesus Christ, our Advocate, in "Choose You This Day" (*Ensign* or *Liahona*, Nov. 2018, 104–5). According to Elder Renlund, how does the Savior's purpose compare with Lucifer's?

The following passages may add to your understanding of the Savior's role as Advocate. As you study them, consider writing down phrases or truths you could share with others:

2 Nephi 2:8–9; Mosiah 15:7–9; Moroni 7:27–28; Doctrine and Covenants 29:5; 62:1. Why are these phrases meaningful to you?

See also "I Stand All Amazed," *Hymns*, no. 193; Topics and Questions, "Atonement of Jesus Christ," Gospel Library; "The Mediator" (video), Gospel Library.

DOCTRINE AND COVENANTS 45:9–10

The gospel is a standard to the nations.

Anciently, a standard was a banner carried into battle used to rally and unify troops. A standard is also an example or rule that other things can be measured against. As you read Doctrine and Covenants 45:9–10, ponder how your covenants with the Lord have been a standard for you.

DOCTRINE AND COVENANTS 45:11–75

Jesus Christ will return in glory.

The Second Coming of the Lord has been described as both "great" and "dreadful" (Malachi 4:5). In Doctrine and Covenants 45, both descriptions seem to fit. This revelation includes both sober warnings and hopeful promises about the Lord's coming. As you study verses 11–75, ponder how you can prepare for the Second Coming with faith in Christ rather than fear. Record what you find in a table like this one:

Prophecy or promise	What I can do
A light (the gospel) shall come to those who sit in darkness (verse 28)	Receive the light—and share it (verse 29)

In the video "Men's Hearts Shall Fail Them" (Gospel Library), what counsel did President Russell M. Nelson give to help us face fearful situations with peace?

DOCTRINE AND COVENANTS 45:31–32, 56–57

I can "stand in holy places" and not be moved.

What do you learn in Doctrine and Covenants 45:31–32, 56–57 about preparing for the Lord's coming? What are your "holy places"? What does it mean to "not be moved"? How can you make where you are more holy?

Note that the Lord referred to the parable of the ten virgins, comparing the oil in the parable to truth and the Holy Spirit. Consider reading the parable in Matthew 25:1–13 with that in mind. What insights do you gain?

See also David A. Bednar, "If Ye Had Known Me," *Ensign* or *Liahona*, Nov. 2016, 102–5.

Parable of the Ten Virgins, by Dan Burr

Zion is a place of safety for the Saints of God.

The Saints in Joseph Smith's time were eager to build Zion, the New Jerusalem (see Ether 13:2–9; Moses 7:18, 62–64). What do you learn about Zion—both the ancient city of Enoch's day and the latter-day city—from Doctrine and Covenants 45:11–15, 66–71? Today the command to establish Zion refers to establishing God's kingdom wherever we live. What can you do to help build Zion wherever you live?

 Ideas for Teaching Children

DOCTRINE AND COVENANTS 45:3–5

Jesus Christ is my Advocate with the Father.

- You might want to help your children understand that an advocate is someone who supports another person. Then you could talk about examples of being an advocate that they may be familiar with (like standing up for a friend). As you read Doctrine and Covenants 45:3–5 together, help your children discover who our Advocate is and how He helps us.

DOCTRINE AND COVENANTS 45:32

I can "stand in holy places."

- It might be fun to place pictures of a home, a Church building, and a temple around the room. Then you could give your children clues describing these places and invite them to stand near the picture you are describing. Ask them to stand still while you read the first line from Doctrine and Covenants 45:32. What are some holy places God gives us? Help your children understand that to "stand in holy places, and . . . not be moved" means to choose the right at all times, no matter what is happening. How can we make our home a more holy place?

DOCTRINE AND COVENANTS 45:9

The gospel of Jesus Christ is a standard to the world.

- You might explain to your children that anciently, a standard was a banner or flag carried into battle. It helped soldiers know where to gather and what to do. Read together Doctrine and Covenants 45:9, and discuss ways the gospel is like a standard. Your children may enjoy making their own standard or flag, including images or words that express their feelings about the Savior.

The gospel is like a standard, or a banner or flag.

DOCTRINE AND COVENANTS 45:44–45

Jesus Christ will come again.

- The destruction that will happen before the Second Coming may make children afraid. Pointing them to Jesus Christ can help them look forward with faith! Consider inviting them to think about how they feel when someone special is coming to visit, like a grandparent or friend. How do they prepare for the visit? Then you could show a picture of the Savior and read Doctrine and Covenants 45:44–45. Share with each other how you feel about the Savior's coming.

- To help your children feel excited about the Savior's Second Coming, you could write on slips of paper some of the hopeful promises from section 45 (see, for example, verses 44–45, 51–52, 55, 58–59, 66–71). Give your children the papers and ask them to raise their hand when the promise they are holding is mentioned as you read the verses. Discuss what these promises mean. You could also sing with your children a song about the Savior's Second Coming, such as "When He Comes Again" (*Children's Songbook*, 82–83).

Help children recognize the Spirit. As you teach your children, tell them when you feel the Holy Ghost. Talk about how you recognize His influence. For example, you might feel peaceful or joyful while singing a song about the Savior.

For more ideas, see this month's issue of the *Friend* magazine.

The Second Coming, by Harry Anderson

I can "stand in holy places" (Doctrine and Covenants 45:32).

Color the pictures, and draw yourself standing in the home, the church building, and the temple.
Cut out the rectangles. Make a viewer by cutting the dotted lines next to the girl and boy.
Slide the pictures of yourself standing in holy places through the viewer.

Doctrine and Covenants 46–48

As Parley P. Pratt, Oliver Cowdery, Ziba Peterson, and Peter Whitmer Jr. left Kirtland and moved on to continue preaching the gospel, they left more than 100 new members of the Church who had plenty of zeal but little experience or direction. They had no instructional handbooks, no leadership training meetings, no broadcasts of general conference—in fact, they didn't even have enough copies of the Book of Mormon to go around. Many of these new believers had been drawn to the restored gospel by the promise of marvelous manifestations of the Spirit, especially those described in the New Testament (see, for example, 1 Corinthians 12:1–11). But many found it hard to identify true manifestations of the Spirit. Seeing the confusion, Joseph Smith prayed for help. The Lord's answer is valuable today, when people often deny or ignore the things of the Spirit. He reaffirmed that spiritual manifestations are real. He also clarified what they are: gifts from a loving Heavenly Father, "given for the benefit of those who love [Him] and keep all [His] commandments, and him that seeketh so to do" (Doctrine and Covenants 46:9).

 Ideas for Learning at Home and at Church

DOCTRINE AND COVENANTS 46:1–7

The Savior welcomes all who want to worship in His Church.

Do you feel that your friends and people in your neighborhood feel welcome at your ward's worship services? What are you doing to make your Church meetings places that people want to return to? Ponder how you can apply the Lord's counsel in Doctrine and Covenants 46:1–7 (see also 2 Nephi 26:24–28; 3 Nephi 18:22–23).

You might also think about a time when you attended Church services—or a meeting of another group—for the first time. What did people do to help you feel welcome?

See also Moroni 6:5–9; "'Tis Sweet to Sing the Matchless Love," *Hymns*, no. 177; "Welcome" (video), Gospel Library.

Heavenly Father gives me spiritual gifts to bless others.

The early Saints believed in spiritual gifts but needed some help recognizing them and understanding their purpose. As you study about gifts of the Spirit in Doctrine and Covenants 46:7–33, ponder the purpose "for [which] they are given" (verse 8). What do you learn about God—the giver of these gifts?

Can you think of examples you've seen of people using these or other spiritual gifts? How did they "benefit . . . the children of God"? (verse 26). You might also see if you can identify examples of different spiritual gifts in scriptures like these: 1 Kings 3:5–15; Daniel 2:26–30; Acts 3:1–8; Helaman 5:17–19; Mormon 1:1–5; Ether 3:1–15; Doctrine and Covenants 6:10–12; Moses 7:13.

Your study of spiritual gifts might lead you to ponder what gifts God has given you. How can you use these gifts to bless His children? If you have a patriarchal blessing, it likely identifies gifts you have been given. Reading Elder John C. Pingree Jr.'s message "I Have a Work for Thee" could also open your mind to gifts you haven't thought of (*Ensign* or *Liahona*, Nov. 2017, 32–35).

If you'd like to learn about how to develop spiritual gifts, the analogy at the beginning of Elder Juan Pablo Villar's message "Exercising Our Spiritual Muscles" could help (*Ensign* or *Liahona*, May 2019, 95). What "exercises" could help you develop your spiritual gifts?

See also Topics and Questions, "Holy Ghost," Gospel Library.

The Lord wants His Church to keep a history.

John Whitmer's calling to keep a history of the Church continued a long tradition of record keepers among God's people. Why do you think keeping a history is so important to the Lord? Ponder this as you read section 47 as well as similar instructions in 2 Nephi 29:11–12; Moses 6:5; Abraham 1:28, 31. What do you feel the Lord wants you to record about your life?

John Whitmer

On FamilySearch, you can record memories and experiences from your life—and your ancestors' lives (see FamilySearch.org).

See Henry B. Eyring, "O Remember, Remember," *Ensign* or *Liahona*, Nov. 2007, 66–69.

The Holy Ghost can direct me as I fulfill my calling.

Maybe you can relate to what John Whitmer felt when he wanted reassurance that his calling came from God. What did the Lord say in Doctrine and Covenants 47 to John Whitmer—and to you—to inspire confidence in fulfilling callings He gives?

The role of a teacher. Teaching is much more than presenting information. It includes creating an environment where class members can learn and discover truths for themselves and share what they have learned with each other (see *Teaching in the Savior's Way*, 26).

Ideas for Teaching Children

DOCTRINE AND COVENANTS 46:2–6

I can help others feel welcome at church.

- After reading Doctrine and Covenants 46:5 with your children, talk about how the Savior wants people to feel when they come to His Church. Invite your children to imagine that they saw someone at church for the first time. Help them practice ways to help this person feel welcome.

DOCTRINE AND COVENANTS 46:7–26

Heavenly Father gives me spiritual gifts to bless others.

- To help your children learn about the spiritual gifts described in Doctrine and Covenants 46:13–26, consider this idea. You could write the gifts on pieces of paper and hide them around the room. As your children find each paper, help them find where that gift is mentioned in section 46. For each gift, talk with them about how it is used to bless others (the descriptions in "Chapter 20: Gifts of the Spirit," in *Doctrine and Covenants Stories*, 77–80, can help).

- Tell your children about the gifts you feel Heavenly Father has given them, and let them talk about the gifts they notice in each other. According to Doctrine and Covenants 46:8–9, 26, why does Heavenly Father give us spiritual gifts? How can we use our gifts to help others?

DOCTRINE AND COVENANTS 47:1, 3

I can record my history.

- Let your children discover what the Lord wanted John Whitmer to do in Doctrine and Covenants 47:1, 3. You might also share with each other favorite stories from the scriptures. Point out that we know about these stories because someone recorded them.

- Consider how you might inspire your children to record their personal histories. You could share some entries from your personal journal or a story about an ancestor (see FamilySearch.org or the Memories app). You might provide some journal prompts, like "What happened this week that you would like your grandchildren to know about?" or "How did you see the Lord's hand in your life this week?" Young children could draw pictures of their experiences, or you could record them telling their stories. What blessings come from keeping a "regular history"? (Doctrine and Covenants 47:1).

DOCTRINE AND COVENANTS 48:2–3

I can help others by sharing what I have been given.

- As you read Doctrine and Covenants 48:2–3 with your children, you might need to explain that people were coming to Ohio from the East, and they didn't have a place to live. What did the Lord ask the Saints to do to help? Help your children think of things God has given them that they can share with others. You could also sing with them a song like "'Give,' Said the Little Stream" (*Children's Songbook*, 236).

For more ideas, see this month's issue of the *Friend* magazine.

All who want to worship the Savior are welcome in meetings of His Saints.

Heavenly Father blesses me with His gifts (Doctrine and Covenants 46:13–25).

Match the spiritual gifts listed below with the related pictures by writing the number from the list inside the box next to the matching image. Add other spiritual gifts you find in Doctrine and Covenants 46:13–25 to the list below.

1. Know that **Jesus** is the Son of God

2. Word of **knowledge**

3. Faith to be **healed**

4. Speak with **tongues**

5. Faith to **heal**

Doctrine and Covenants 49–50

The Savior is our "good shepherd" (Doctrine and Covenants 50:44). He knows that sometimes sheep wander and the wilderness has many perils. So He lovingly leads us to the safety of His doctrine. He leads us away from dangers such as "false spirits, which have gone forth in the earth, deceiving the world" (Doctrine and Covenants 50:2). Following Him often means letting go of incorrect ideas or traditions. This was true for Leman Copley and others in Ohio. They had accepted the restored gospel but still held on to some beliefs that just weren't correct. In Doctrine and Covenants 49, the Lord declared truths that corrected Leman's previous beliefs about topics such as marriage and the Savior's Second Coming. And when the Ohio converts "received . . . spirits which [they] could not understand," the Lord taught them how to discern true manifestations of the Spirit (Doctrine and Covenants 50:15). The Good Shepherd is patient with us, His "little children," who "must grow in grace and in the knowledge of the truth" (Doctrine and Covenants 50:40).

 Ideas for Learning at Home and at Church

Jesus Christ wants me to embrace the truths of His gospel.

Before joining the Church, Leman Copley had been part of a religious group known as the United Society of Believers in Christ's Second Appearing, also known as the Shakers. After a conversation with Leman, Joseph Smith sought clarification from the Lord about some of the Shakers' teachings. The Lord responded with the revelation in section 49. Some of the Shakers' beliefs are mentioned in the section heading.

What did the Lord teach in section 49 to correct the beliefs of the Shakers? What evidence do you see in this revelation of His love and concern for people who do not have the fulness of His truth? How can you reach out to them with love and concern?

What impresses you about the Lord's observation in verse 2? You might compare this to what happens if you watch only part of a movie, see one piece of a puzzle, or hear one side of an argument. How does the Lord's warning relate to Doctrine and Covenants 50:24? Consider what you're doing to receive more light from the Lord.

See also "Leman Copley and the Shakers," in *Revelations in Context*, 117–21.

DOCTRINE AND COVENANTS 49:15–17

📖 Marriage between man and woman is essential to God's plan.

In an effort to undermine Heavenly Father's plan, Satan seeks to create confusion about marriage. The Lord, on the other hand, continues to reveal truth about marriage through His prophets. You can find some of this truth in Doctrine and Covenants 49:15–17; Genesis 2:20–24; 1 Corinthians 11:11; and "The Family: A Proclamation to the World." Make a list of the truths you find. Why is marriage so important to God's plan?

Elder Ulisses Soares taught that "the restored gospel of Jesus Christ proclaims the principle of full partnership between woman and man, both in mortal life and in the eternities" ("In Partnership with the Lord," *Liahona*, Nov. 2022, 42). You might study his message, looking for principles "that strengthen the partnership between man and woman." How can you apply these principles in your life? If someone of another faith asked you why marriage is important, how would you respond? Why are you grateful for this understanding?

See also Topics and Questions, "Marriage," "Family," Gospel Library; David A. Bednar, "Marriage Is Essential to His Eternal Plan," *Ensign*, June 2006, 83–84; "Renaissance of Marriage" (video), Gospel Library.

Be sensitive to individual circumstances. While happy marriage and family life are the ideal in the gospel of Jesus Christ, we don't all get to enjoy these blessings while in mortality. In discussing this topic, be sensitive to various individual and family circumstances, especially for people who are "waiting patiently on the Lord" for eternal promises to be fulfilled (see Doctrine and Covenants 98:1–3).

DOCTRINE AND COVENANTS 50

The Lord's teachings can protect me from Satan's deceptions.

The new members of the Church in Ohio were eager to receive the spiritual manifestations promised in the scriptures. Satan, however, was eager to deceive them. If you were asked to help these members understand how to recognize true manifestations of the Holy Ghost, what principles in Doctrine and Covenants 50 would you share? (see especially verses 22–25, 29–34, 40–46). How has the Savior helped you know the difference between truth and error?

See also 1 Corinthians 14:1–28; 2 Timothy 3:13–17.

DOCTRINE AND COVENANTS 50:23–25

"That which is of God is light."

As you ponder the Savior's words in Doctrine and Covenants 50:23–25, think about how you receive God's light in your life and how you "chase darkness" away. For example, how do these verses guide your choices about how to spend your time? what entertainment or media to seek? which conversations to engage in? What other decisions can these verses help you with? A hymn like "The Lord Is My Light" (*Hymns*, no. 89) might inspire additional thoughts.

See also "Walk in God's light," *For the Strength of Youth: A Guide for Making Choices*, 16–21.

 # Ideas for Teaching Children

DOCTRINE AND COVENANTS 49:12–14

I can follow Jesus Christ.

- To teach your children the principles in these verses, you could prepare four paper footprints and four pictures that represent faith in Jesus Christ, repentance, baptism, and receiving the Holy Ghost (see the pictures in this week's activity page). Your children could place the footprints on the floor with the pictures beside them. Then they could take turns walking on the footprints while you read Doctrine and Covenants 49:12–14. Help them understand that when we do the things in these pictures, we are following Jesus Christ.

- You could also invite your children to compare Doctrine and Covenants 49:12–14 with Acts 2:38 and with the fourth article of faith. What similarities do they find? Why are these truths important?

DOCTRINE AND COVENANTS 49:15–17

Marriage between man and woman is essential to God's plan.

- To introduce these verses, you could explain that the Shakers were a religious group that believed people should not get married (see the section heading to Doctrine and Covenants 49). Invite your children to find things the Lord taught about marriage in Doctrine and Covenants 49:15–17. What does it mean that "marriage is ordained of God"? Maybe you could read together the first three paragraphs of "The Family: A Proclamation to the World." Then talk about why marriage and family are important to Heavenly Father.

DOCTRINE AND COVENANTS 50:23–25

"That which is of God is light."

- To introduce Doctrine and Covenants 50:23–25, talk with your children about the difference between light and dark. Why do we need light? You could read together the first paragraph of "Walk in God's light" in *For the Strength of Youth: A Guide for Making Choices* (page 17) as well as Doctrine and Covenants 50:23–25. Talk about ways we receive God's light and ways we can chase darkness away. You could then sing together a song about their spiritual light, such as "Shine On" (*Children's Songbook*, 144).

DOCTRINE AND COVENANTS 50:40–46

Jesus Christ is my Good Shepherd.

- After reading Doctrine and Covenants 50:40–46 together, you could show the picture of the Savior at the end of this outline and ask questions like these: How does a shepherd feel about His sheep? How is the Savior like a shepherd to us?

For more ideas, see this month's issue of the *Friend* magazine.

Gentle Shepherd, by Yongsung Kim

I can follow Jesus Christ (Doctrine and Covenants 49:12–14).

Color the pictures, and cut out the rectangles. Fold each one on the dotted line, and tape the sides together. Put them on your fingers to remind you of ways you can follow Jesus Christ.

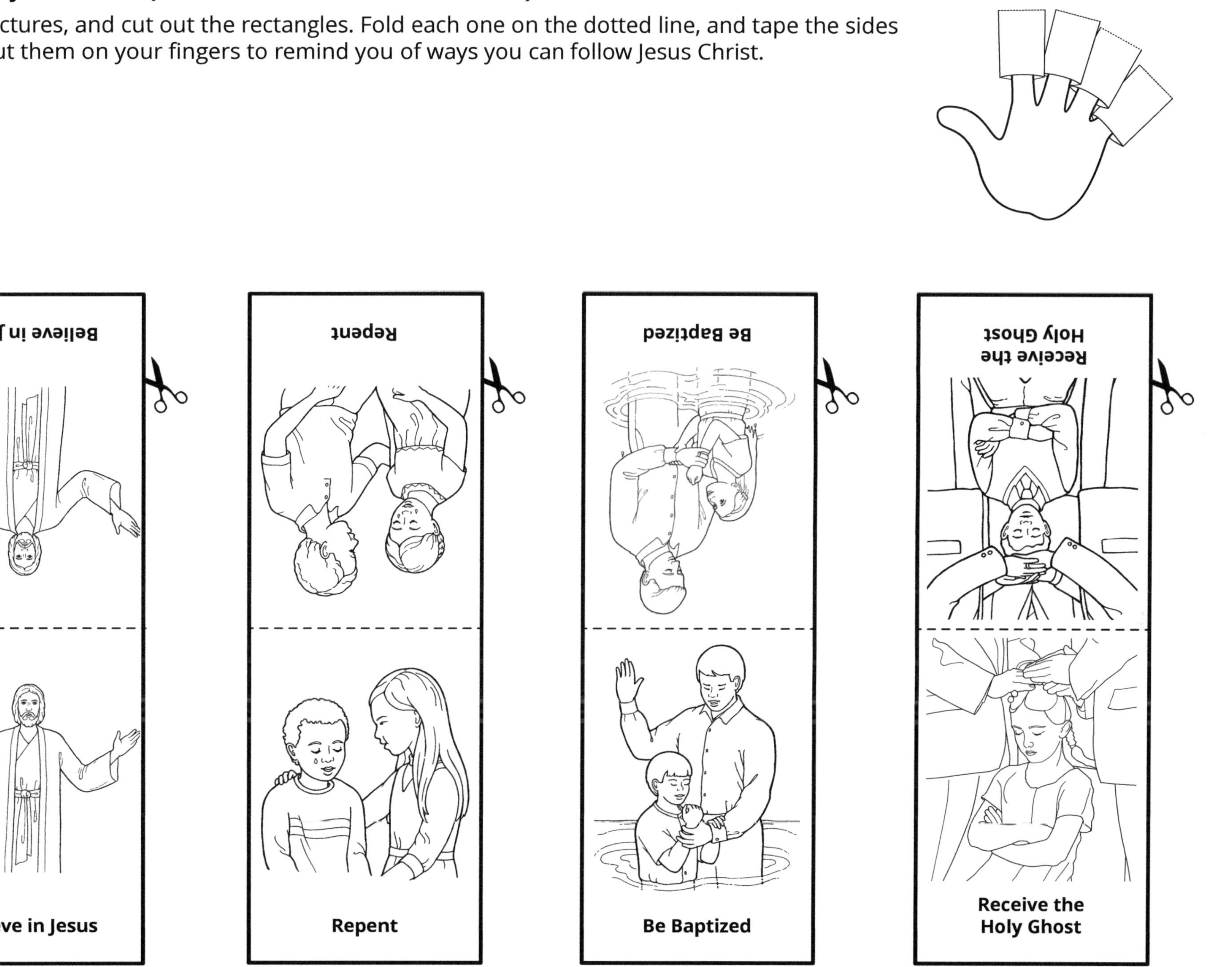

First Furrow, by James Taylor Harwood

Doctrine and Covenants 51–57

For Church members in the 1830s, gathering the Saints and building the city of Zion were spiritual as well as temporal labors, with many practical matters to address: Someone needed to buy land where the Saints could settle. Someone needed to print books and other publications. And someone needed to run a store to provide goods for people in Zion. In the revelations recorded in Doctrine and Covenants 51–57, the Lord appointed and instructed people to handle these tasks.

But while skills in such things are needed in Zion, these revelations also teach that the Lord desires His Saints to become spiritually worthy to be called a Zion people—His people. He calls each of us to be "a faithful, a just, and a wise steward," having a contrite spirit, "stand[ing] fast" in our appointed responsibilities (see Doctrine and Covenants 51:19; 52:15; 54:2). If we can do that—regardless of our temporal skills—the Lord can use us to build Zion.

 Ideas for Learning at Home and at Church

DOCTRINE AND COVENANTS 51

The Lord wants me to be a faithful, just, and wise steward.

If you were a Church member in 1831, you might have been invited to live the law of consecration by signing over your property to the Church through the bishop. He would then return to you, in most cases, what you donated, sometimes with a surplus. But it was no longer just your possession—it was your stewardship.

Today the procedures are different, but the principles are still vital to the Lord's work. As you read section 51, think about what God has entrusted to you. What do the words "steward" (verse 19) and "consecrated" (verse 5) imply about God's expectations of you?

See also "The Law of Consecration" (video), Gospel Library.

I can invite others to come unto Christ wherever I go.

When the Lord sent several Church leaders to Missouri, he told them to make use of the time spent traveling and "preach by the way" (verses 25–27). How can you share the gospel "by the way," or during the normal events of your life?

The Lord helps me avoid deception.

With many people claiming spiritual manifestations, the early Saints were concerned about being deceived. What warning did the Lord give them in Doctrine and Covenants 52:14? What was His solution? (see verses 14–19).

A pattern is something that repeats in a regular, predictable way. Examples include counting by even numbers or the sun rising and setting each day. What other examples can you think of? As you search Doctrine and Covenants 52:14–19, identify the Lord's pattern for avoiding deception. It might help to note that "contrite" implies a feeling of humility and repentance; "meek" suggests gentleness and self-control; and to "edify" means to instruct, improve, or build up. Why do you feel the Lord's pattern includes these qualities, as well as obedience? How can you apply this pattern to avoid deception?

Define difficult words. In the Gospel Library app, you can tap and hold a word and then select "Define." You will then be taken to a definition of that word. Try this when you come across unfamiliar words—or words that seem familiar that you'd like to understand better.

What are some examples of deceptions in our day? How can we know when we are being deceived?

For instance, you might consider evaluating your choices regarding movies, music, and social media based on the standards in "Walk in God's light" in *For the Strength of Youth: A Guide for Making Choices*, 16–21.

See also Gary E. Stevenson, "Deceive Me Not," *Ensign* or *Liahona*, Nov. 2019, 93–96; "Guide Me to Thee," *Hymns*, no. 101; Topics and Questions, "Seeking Truth and Avoiding Deception," Gospel Library.

Leman Copley's farm

I can turn to the Lord when I am hurt by others' choices.

Have you ever suffered disappointment when someone you depended on didn't keep their commitments? This happened to the Saints from Colesville, New York, who expected to settle on Leman Copley's land in Ohio. To learn from this experience, consider reviewing the heading to section 54 (see also *Saints*, 1:125–28; "A Bishop unto the Church," in *Revelations in Context*, 78–79). If you had a friend among the Colesville Saints, what counsel could you find in section 54 to share with them?

DOCTRINE AND COVENANTS 56:14–20

Blessed are the pure in heart.

In these verses, the Lord spoke both to the rich and to the poor; it might be interesting to compare His counsel to these two groups. What in these verses feels relevant to you personally?

For more ideas, see this month's issues of the *Liahona* and *For the Strength of Youth* magazines.

 # Ideas for Teaching Children

DOCTRINE AND COVENANTS 51:9

I can be honest.

- To help your children learn what it means to be honest, you could read together Doctrine and Covenants 51:9 and share stories of children who face decisions about being honest. You could use pictures, sock puppets, or paper dolls to make the stories more interesting. How does the Lord bless us as we strive to be honest?

- Consider playing a game with your children. Afterward, discuss how the game would have been different if someone had cheated. Why is it important to "deal honestly" with each other?

DOCTRINE AND COVENANTS 52:10; 53:3; 55:1

I receive the gift of the Holy Ghost by the laying on of hands.

- Receiving the Holy Ghost by the laying on of hands is mentioned several times in Doctrine and Covenants 51–57. This might be a good opportunity to teach your children about this ordinance. For example, they could look at a picture of a child being confirmed and describe what is happening in the picture. Ask them to clap their hands when they hear "laying on of the hands" or "laying on of hands" while you read Doctrine and Covenants 52:10; 53:3; 55:1.

- You could also sing "The Holy Ghost" (*Children's Songbook*, 105) or a similar song. Help your children find words and phrases in the song that teach about the gift of the Holy Ghost.

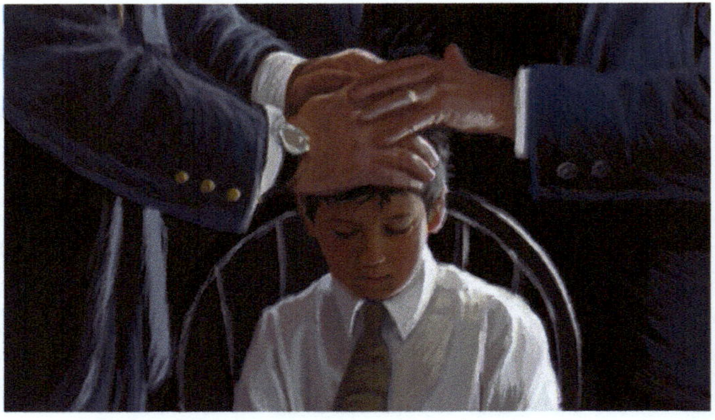

DOCTRINE AND COVENANTS 52:14–19

God has a pattern to help me not be deceived.

- To teach about the Lord's pattern for avoiding deception, you might start by helping children find examples of patterns—in nature, in colorful blankets or clothing, or in daily life. Help them find the pattern the Lord gave in Doctrine and Covenants 52:14–15. Make sure they understand any unfamiliar words in these verses. How can we use this pattern to recognize truth?

DOCTRINE AND COVENANTS 54:4–6

I should always keep my covenants.

- In your own words, share with your children what happened to the Saints who came to live on Leman Copley's land (see the heading to section 54). Your children could pretend to be a member of the Church who has arrived in Ohio. How would they have felt after Leman broke his covenant? What does this teach us about keeping our covenants or promises? Read together Doctrine and Covenants 54:6 to discover blessings for people who keep their covenants.

DOCTRINE AND COVENANTS 55:1–4

I can use the blessings God has given me to bless others.

- To introduce section 55, you may want to explain that William W. Phelps was a newspaper publisher who learned about the gospel and joined the Church. Read with your children Doctrine and Covenants 55:1–4, and help them discover what God wanted William to do. How did He plan to use William's talents? This could lead to a discussion about how God might invite us to use our talents to bless His children.

For more ideas, see this month's issue of the *Friend* magazine.

Bishop Partridge Receives Consecration, by Albin Veselka

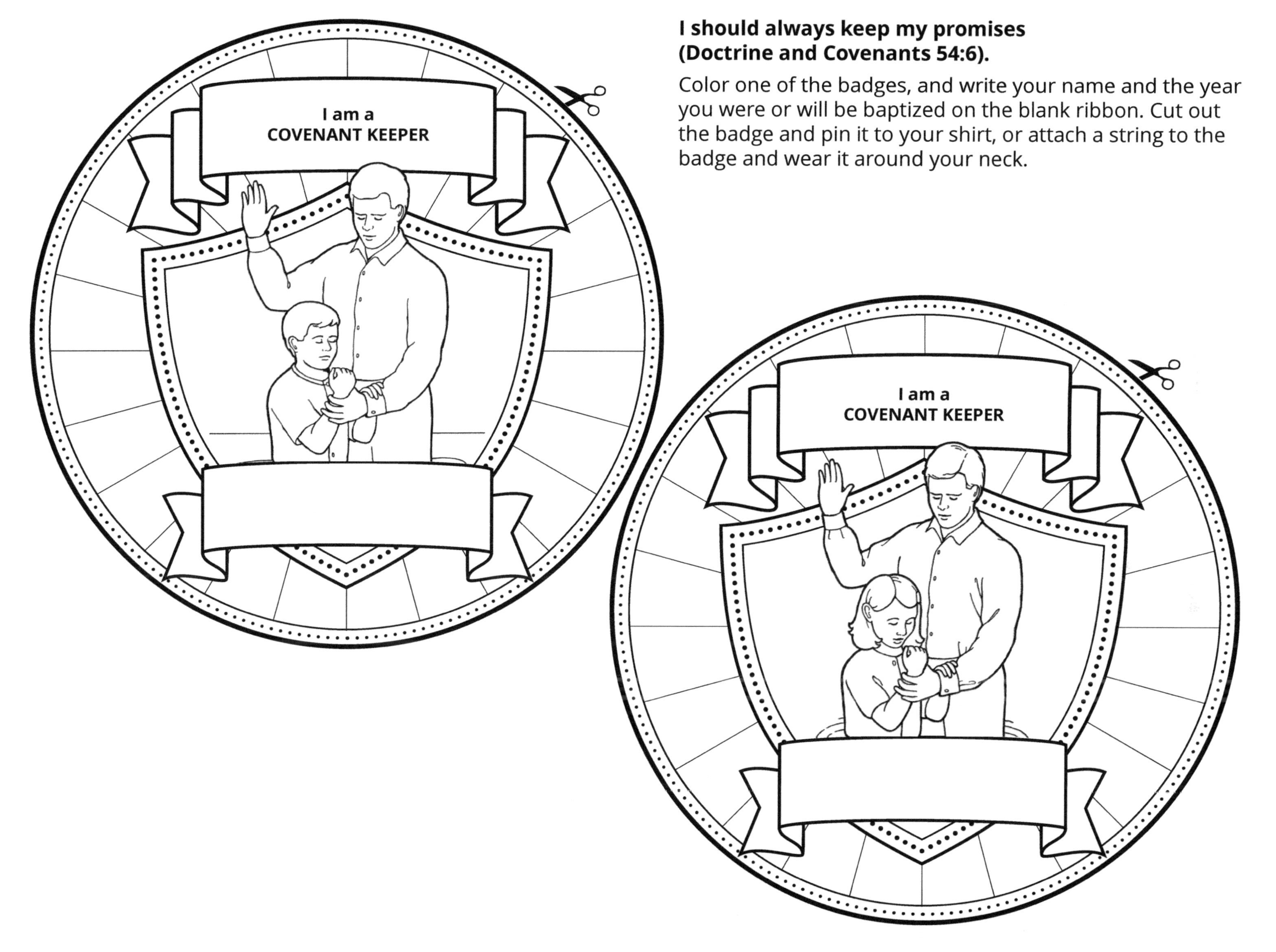

I should always keep my promises (Doctrine and Covenants 54:6).

Color one of the badges, and write your name and the year you were or will be baptized on the blank ribbon. Cut out the badge and pin it to your shirt, or attach a string to the badge and wear it around your neck.

Independence, Missouri, 1831, by Al Rounds

Doctrine and Covenants 58–59

When the elders of the Church first saw the site of the city of Zion—Independence, Missouri—it was not what they expected. Some thought they would find a thriving, industrious community with a strong group of Saints. Instead, they found a sparsely populated outpost, lacking the civilization they were used to and inhabited by rough frontier settlers rather than Saints. It turned out that the Lord wasn't asking them just to come to Zion—He wanted them to *build* Zion.

When our expectations do not match reality, we can remember what the Lord told the Saints in 1831: "Ye cannot behold with your natural eyes, for the present time, the design of your God . . . and the glory which shall follow after much tribulation" (Doctrine and Covenants 58:3). Yes, life is full of tribulation, even wickedness, but we can still "bring to pass much righteousness; for the power is in [us]" (verses 27–28).

See also *Saints,* 1:127–33.

 Ideas for Learning at Home and at Church

DOCTRINE AND COVENANTS 58:1–5; 59:23

"After much tribulation come the blessings."

The Saints hoped that during their lifetimes, Jackson County would blossom into Zion, a place where all the Saints could gather. However, their time in Jackson County was full of tribulation. Within a few years, they were forced to leave and "wait for a little season for the redemption of Zion" (Doctrine and Covenants 105:9).

What do you learn about tribulation or challenges from the Lord's words in Doctrine and Covenants 58:1–5? Why do you think some blessings come only after tribulation? What blessings have you received after tribulation?

What do you learn from Doctrine and Covenants 59:23 that brings you hope?

I can "bring to pass much righteousness" of my "own free will."

As part of your study of these verses, you might make a list of some of the things you are "anxiously engaged" in. Are all of them "good cause[s]"? Ponder what you can do to "bring to pass much righteousness"—and consider setting goals to do it.

Why do you think the Lord wants you to do "many things of [your] own free will"? What would be the result if you were "compelled in all things"? What does 2 Nephi 2:27 add to your understanding of this principle?

See also Dale G. Renlund, "Choose You This Day," *Ensign* or *Liahona*, Nov. 2018, 104–6.

The Lord forgives me as I repent.

The Lord's promise in Doctrine and Covenants 58:42 to completely forgive those who repent is inspiring, though it also raises some questions: What does it mean to repent? How do I know if I have repented? Fortunately, the Lord continued, "By this ye may know . . ." (verse 43).

Here are some additional questions people sometimes have about repentance. What does the Spirit teach you as you study the suggested resources provided below?

How does confessing my sins help me repent? See Psalm 32:1–5; Proverbs 28:13; Mosiah 27:34–37; Alma 39:12–13.

I'm trying to forsake my sins, but I keep making mistakes. Is my repentance still valid? See Bradley R. Wilcox, "Worthiness Is Not Flawlessness," *Liahona*, Nov. 2021, 61–67; "Daily Restoration" (video), Gospel Library.

How can I be sure that the Savior has forgiven me? See Tad R. Callister, "The Atonement of Jesus Christ," *Ensign* or *Liahona*, May 2019, 85–87, especially the section titled "2. Sin."

You can find more insights in the "Questions and Answers" about repentance in *For the Strength of Youth: A Guide for Making Choices* (pages 8–9).

See also Topics and Questions, "Repentance," Gospel Library.

Commandments are a blessing.

What do you think it means to be "crowned . . . with commandments"? (verse 4). Consider how the Lord blesses you as you strive to obey each of the commandments in verses 5–19.

Share what you're learning. In many cases, the spiritual insights you receive as you study the scriptures could strengthen the faith of your family, friends, and ward members. Share with them your experiences, feelings, and testimony of Jesus Christ.

The Sabbath is the Lord's day.

After promising to bless the Saints in Zion "with commandments not a few," the Lord gave special emphasis to one commandment in particular: the command to honor His "holy day"

(Doctrine and Covenants 59:4, 9). As you study Doctrine and Covenants 59:9–19, ponder why honoring the Sabbath would have been so important to these Saints as they sought to build Zion. Why is it important to you?

You could also ponder whether you are using the Sabbath day the way the Lord intended. How does keeping the Sabbath day holy help you remain "unspotted from the world"? (verse 9). What can you do to pay your "devotions unto the Most High"? (verse 10).

You might notice that the Lord used words like "rejoicing," "cheerful," and "glad" to teach about the Sabbath day. What makes the Sabbath joyful for you? How would you explain to someone why you choose to honor the Lord's day?

What do you learn from the hymn "Gently Raise the Sacred Strain" (*Hymns*, no. 146) about the purposes and blessings of the Sabbath?

See also Genesis 2:2–3; Isaiah 58:13–14; Russell M. Nelson, "The Sabbath Is a Delight," *Ensign* or *Liahona*, May 2015, 129–32.

For more ideas, see this month's issues of the *Liahona* and *For the Strength of Youth* magazines.

Ideas for Teaching Children

DOCTRINE AND COVENANTS 58:26–28

Heavenly Father has given me power to choose.

- Reading together Doctrine and Covenants 58:26–28 can give you and your children an opportunity to talk about the power Heavenly Father has given us to choose to do good. You might tell each other about various choices you've made and what happened as a result. Maybe your children would like to draw a picture of their experience.

- You could write *choice* on one side of a piece of paper and *consequence* on the other and use this paper to illustrate that our choices and their consequences are inseparable. Perhaps your children could list a few choices and talk about the consequences that come from them. Then you could read together Doctrine and Covenants 58:27–28 and talk about choices that "bring to pass much righteousness" or good consequences. How does Heavenly Father "reward" or bless us as we strive to do good? (verse 28).

"Thank the Lord thy God in all things."

- Consider reading these verses while you and your children go for a walk or look at pictures of nature, noticing things that "please the eye and . . . gladden the heart" (verse 18). You could also notice similar things in a song like "My Heavenly Father Loves Me" (*Children's Songbook*, 228–29). Or you might invite your children to draw pictures of things they are thankful for and let them tell you about their pictures. How can we show our gratitude for these things?

The Lord created many beautiful things to bring us joy.

The Sabbath is the Lord's day.

- What can we do on Sunday to worship the Lord and find joy? Help your children find ideas in Doctrine and Covenants 59:9–12 and this week's activity page. Maybe they could also find pictures or objects to represent things we do on the Sabbath (such as the pictures of the sacrament in this outline). How do these things help us feel closer to Heavenly Father and Jesus Christ?

For more ideas, see this month's issue of the *Friend* magazine.

Illustration by Marti Major

The Sabbath is a delight (Doctrine and Covenants 59:9–12).

Color the pictures of good things to do on the Sabbath day. Then draw your own ideas in the spaces provided. Attach the arrow to the center, and use the spinner when you need ideas of things to do on the Sabbath.

Doctrine and Covenants 60–63

In early August 1831, Joseph Smith and other elders of the Church were preparing to return to Kirtland after a short visit to the "land of Zion" (Doctrine and Covenants 59:3). The Lord had wanted them to preach the gospel during their trip (see Doctrine and Covenants 52:10), and some of them did so diligently. But others were hesitant. "They hide the talent which I have given unto them," the Lord said, "because of the fear of man" (Doctrine and Covenants 60:2). Many of us know how these elders felt. Even though we love the gospel, fear and doubt might keep us from sharing it. But the Lord is merciful. He "knoweth the weakness of man and how to succor [us]" (Doctrine and Covenants 62:1). Scattered throughout these revelations to early missionaries are reassurances that can help us overcome our fears and shortcomings: "I am able to make you holy." "All flesh is in mine hand." "I am with the faithful always." And "He that is faithful and endureth shall overcome the world." (Doctrine and Covenants 60:7; 61:6; 62:9; 63:47.)

 Ideas for Learning at Home and at Church

DOCTRINE AND COVENANTS 60; 62

I can share my love and testimony of Jesus Christ.

I can be open about sharing my faith in Christ.

How is your testimony of the gospel like a "talent," or a treasure from God? In what ways do we sometimes "hide [our] talent"? (Doctrine and Covenants 60:2; see also Matthew 25:14–30).

What encouraging messages from the Lord do you find in sections 60 and 62? How do these messages build your confidence in sharing the gospel? As you ponder these questions, consider singing or reading the words to "I Want to Be a Missionary Now" (*Children's Songbook*, 149). What do you learn from this children's song about sharing the gospel?

See also the "Sharing the Gospel" collection in Gospel Library.

The scriptures teach of Jesus Christ.

As He instructed His missionaries, the Lord revealed important truths about Himself. Look for these truths in Doctrine and Covenants 60:2–4; 61:1–2, 20, 36–38; 62:1, 6. What accounts from the scriptures illustrate the roles and attributes of the Savior that you found? (see, for example, John 8:1–11; Ether 2:14–15).

Signs come by faith and the will of God.

At the end of this outline, there's an illustration of a miracle that deeply impressed Ezra Booth: Elsa Johnson's arm was miraculously healed. After seeing that, Ezra was eagerly baptized. And yet, within just a few months, Ezra lost his faith and became critical of the Prophet. How could this be, considering the miracle he'd witnessed?

Ponder this as you read Doctrine and Covenants 63:7–12. What truths do you learn about signs and faith?

See also Matthew 16:1–4; John 12:37; Mormon 9:10–21; Ether 12:12, 18.

📖 I can be chaste in my thoughts and actions.

In Doctrine and Covenants 63:16, the Savior reaffirmed what He taught in the New Testament—that the law of chastity should govern not just our actions but also our thoughts (see Matthew 5:27–28). As you read Doctrine and Covenants 63:16, write down the warnings the Savior gives about lustful thoughts. You might also ponder the opposite of each warning. For example, what are some words or phrases that are the opposite of fear? What other blessings come from having chaste thoughts and actions?

Many people think the Lord's standards of chastity of thought and action are old-fashioned or even oppressive. What difference would it make if all of God's children were striving to live this law? You might look for answers to this question in Elder David A. Bednar's message "We Believe in Being Chaste" (*Ensign* or *Liahona*, May 2013, 41–44) or "Your body is sacred" (*For the Strength of Youth: A Guide for Making Choices*, 23–26). What messages of hope do you find?

Even when we know the blessings of being chaste in our thoughts and actions, that doesn't mean it's easy. You might take some time to ponder what makes it difficult for you to keep the Savior's standard of chastity—and what makes it easier. What tips might you share with others about what to do when you are tempted with unworthy thoughts?

Support one another. One of the great blessings of meeting together in Church meetings and classes is the opportunity to get support from fellow Saints in our efforts to follow the Savior. Many of us face similar challenges, and our common experiences can be a great strength. Don't be afraid to admit that you have challenges. Share with each other what helps you live God's laws and overcome temptation.

See also Doctrine and Covenants 121:45; Topics and Questions, "Virtue," Gospel Library; "Standards: Sexual Purity and Modesty—True Confidence" (video), Gospel Library; AddressingPornography.ChurchofJesusChrist.org.

DOCTRINE AND COVENANTS 63:58–64

Sacred things should be treated with reverence.

The principles in Doctrine and Covenants 63:58–64 go beyond taking the Lord's name in vain. What other sacred things come "from above," or from God? What does it mean for you to speak of these things "with care"?

For more ideas, see this month's issues of the *Liahona* and *For the Strength of Youth* magazines.

Ideas for Teaching Children

DOCTRINE AND COVENANTS 60:4; 61:1–2, 36; 62:1

The scriptures teach of Jesus Christ.

- Perhaps you could write some of the statements about the Savior found in Doctrine and Covenants 60–62 on small pieces of paper. Your children could then match these statements to pictures of Jesus from His earthly ministry (see *Gospel Art Book*, nos. 34–61) that demonstrate these attributes. How does He make Himself known to us today?

Detail from *For This Purpose*, by Yongsung Kim

DOCTRINE AND COVENANTS 60:7; 61:1–2; 62:1

The Lord will forgive me if I repent.

- As you read Doctrine and Covenants 60:7; 61:2 with your children, help them find words that these verses have in common. Remind them that these revelations were given to Joseph Smith and other Church leaders. What did the Lord want them to know? You could also talk about how the Savior feels about us when we make mistakes and what it means to repent. According to Doctrine and Covenants 62:1, how can Jesus help when we are tempted?

DOCTRINE AND COVENANTS 62:3, 9

Jesus Christ wants me to share His gospel.

- You might ask your children what they would say if someone asked them what they love about Jesus Christ and His Church. Singing together a song about sharing the gospel, such as "I Want to Be a Missionary Now" (*Children's Songbook,* 168), could give them ideas. You could then read Doctrine and Covenants 62:3 and ask your children to listen for what happens when we share our testimonies. How can the promise in verse 9 help if we feel nervous?

I can be reverent.

- To introduce Doctrine and Covenants 63:64, you could sing a song about reverence with your children, such as "Reverence Is Love" (*Children's Songbook*, no. 31). Then you could talk about different ways to show reverence for Heavenly Father and Jesus Christ.

- You can help your children understand what reverence is by talking with them about an item that is special to them, such as a favorite toy, book, or blanket. Ask them how they take care of and protect things that are special to them. You could then read together Doctrine and Covenants 63:64. What things are special—or sacred—to Heavenly Father? (see, for example, verse 61 and this week's activity page). How should we treat these things—with our words and our actions?

For more ideas, see this month's issue of the *Friend* magazine.

Healing of Elsa Johnson's Shoulder, by Sam Lawlor

I should treat sacred things with reverence (Doctrine and Covenants 63:64).

Roll two dice, and add the numbers on top together (or you could draw strips of paper numbered from 2 to 12 from a container).

Match the number you rolled to the sacred thing below that Heavenly Father has given us. Share one way you can treat that thing with reverence.

Doctrine and Covenants 64–66

In the miserable heat of August 1831, several elders were traveling back to Kirtland from the land of Zion in Missouri. The travelers were hot and weary, and tensions soon turned into quarrels. It may have seemed like building Zion, a city of love, unity, and peace, was going to take a long time.

Fortunately, building Zion—in Missouri in 1831 or in our hearts, families, and wards today—doesn't require us to be perfect. Instead, "of you it is required to forgive," the Lord said (Doctrine and Covenants 64:10). He requires "the heart and a willing mind" (verse 34). And He requires patience and diligence, for Zion is built on the foundation of "small things," accomplished by those who do not become "weary in well-doing" (verse 33).

See also *Saints*, 1:133–34, 136–37.

 Ideas for Learning at Home and at Church

DOCTRINE AND COVENANTS 64:1–11

"Forgive one another."

Consider the following as you study Doctrine and Covenants 64:1–11:

- Think about a time when the Lord forgave you. How did you feel?

- Is there someone you need to forgive? Why can forgiving others be so difficult? What helps you overcome these difficulties?

- What truths about forgiveness in Doctrine and Covenants 64:1–11 seem important to you? Why do you think the Lord commands us "to forgive all"? (verse 10).

If you struggle to forgive, consider studying Elder Jeffrey R. Holland's message "The Ministry of Reconciliation" (*Ensign* or *Liahona*, Nov. 2018, 77–79) or Kristin M. Yee's message "Beauty for Ashes: The Healing Path of Forgiveness" (*Liahona*, Nov. 2022, 36–38). What do you learn about how Christ can help you forgive?

Family relationships can provide many opportunities to forgive. Think about your family members. Whom do you need to forgive? How are we "afflicted" (verse 8) when we don't forgive each other? How would forgiveness affect your family relationships?

See also Topics and Questions, "Forgiveness," Gospel Library; "Forgiveness: My Burden Was Made Light" (video), Gospel Library.

"Ye ought to forgive one another" (Doctrine and Covenants 64:9).

DOCTRINE AND COVENANTS 64:31–34

"The heart and a willing mind"

Elder Donald L. Hallstrom suggested this possible meaning for the phrase "heart and a willing mind":

"The heart is symbolic of love and commitment. We make sacrifices and bear burdens for those we love that we would not endure for any other reason. If love does not exist, our commitment wanes. . . .

"Having 'a willing mind' connotes giving our best effort and finest thinking and seeking God's wisdom. It suggests that our most devoted lifetime study should be of things that are eternal in nature. It means that there must be an inextricable relationship between hearing the word of God and obeying it" ("The Heart and a Willing Mind," *Ensign*, June 2011, 31–32).

DOCTRINE AND COVENANTS 64:41–43

Zion shall be "an ensign unto the people."

An ensign is "a flag or standard around which people gather in a unity of purpose or identity" (Guide to the Scriptures, "Ensign," Gospel Library). How has Zion—or the Lord's Church—been like an ensign to you? Consider these other examples of things that are held up, like an ensign, to bless the people: Numbers 21:6–9; Matthew 5:14–16; Alma 46:11–20. Look for other ways the Lord describes Zion in Doctrine and Covenants 64:41–43.

See also "Let Zion in Her Beauty Rise," *Hymns*, no. 41.

DOCTRINE AND COVENANTS 65

The kingdom of God on earth prepares the world for the Savior's return.

Doctrine and Covenants 65 gives an inspiring description of the mission of the Lord's Church in the latter days. Consider searching this section, looking for answers to questions like these: What does the Lord want His kingdom to accomplish on the earth? What does He want me to do to help?

See also "Prepare Today for the Second Coming" (video), ChurchofJesusChrist.org.

DOCTRINE AND COVENANTS 66

The Lord knows the thoughts of my heart.

Shortly after joining the Church, William E. McLellin asked Joseph Smith to reveal God's will for him. Joseph didn't know it, but William had five personal questions he was hoping the Lord would answer through His Prophet. We don't know what William's questions were, but the revelation addressed to him, now Doctrine and Covenants 66, answered each question to William's "full and entire satisfaction" ("William McLellin's Five Questions," in *Revelations in Context*, 138).

As you read section 66, think about what the Lord knew about William McLellin and the concerns and intents of his heart. How has the Lord shown you that He knows you? If you have a patriarchal blessing, consider studying it. As you do, what does the Holy Ghost help you understand about God's will for you?

For more ideas, see this month's issues of the *Liahona* and *For the Strength of Youth* magazines.

Ideas for Teaching Children

DOCTRINE AND COVENANTS 64:7–10

Jesus Christ wants me to forgive everyone.

Note: As you teach your children about the Lord's command "to forgive all," you may want to clarify that forgiving does not mean allowing people to hurt us. Encourage them to tell a trusted adult if someone hurts them or touches them inappropriately.

- After reading Doctrine and Covenants 64:10 with your children, talk with them about what it means to forgive someone. You might share a few simple examples. Perhaps they could role-play these examples to practice forgiving.

- You might ask your children to plan how they would teach someone—such as a younger sibling—about forgiving others. Help them find phrases in Doctrine and Covenants 64:7–10 that they could use as they teach.

- Sing a song about forgiveness, such as "Help Me, Dear Father" (*Children's Songbook*, 99). What does this song teach us about forgiving others?

DOCTRINE AND COVENANTS 64:33

God's "great work" is built on "small things."

- You could show your children some things that are made up of small parts, like a puzzle or a rug. Then you could read together Doctrine and Covenants 64:33. What is God's "great work"? What are the "small things" we can do that will help?

DOCTRINE AND COVENANTS 64:34

I can follow Jesus with my heart and mind.

- As you read to your children from Doctrine and Covenants 64:34, you could point to your heart and head as you read "heart" and "mind," and invite the children to do it with you. How can we give our hearts (desires) and minds (thoughts) to the Savior?

DOCTRINE AND COVENANTS 66

The Lord knows who I am and loves me.

- Help your children understand that William E. McLellin had five questions for the Lord. Joseph Smith received answers to these questions even though he did not know what William's questions were. Tell your children about a time when the Lord showed you what He wanted you to do, and talk about the blessings that came from following His direction. You could then read Doctrine and Covenants 66:4 together and invite your children to seek opportunities to understand what the Lord wants them to do.

Detail from *The Second Coming*, by Kevin Keele

DOCTRINE AND COVENANTS 65

I can help prepare the world to receive Jesus Christ.

- As your children look at a picture of the Savior's Second Coming, ask them to describe what they see or what they know about this event. You could also give your children words and phrases about the Second Coming to find in Doctrine and Covenants 65. What do these words and phrases teach us? How can we prepare for the Savior's return?

For more ideas, see this month's issue of the *Friend* magazine.

Forgiven, by Greg Olsen

I can follow Jesus with my heart and mind (Doctrine and Covenants 64:34).

Draw or write inside the heart and the mind of the girl or the boy ways you can follow Jesus.

Doctrine and Covenants 67–70

From 1828 to 1831, the Prophet Joseph Smith received many revelations from the Lord, including divine counsel for individuals, instructions on governing the Church, visions of the latter days, and many inspiring truths of eternity. But many of the Saints hadn't read them. The revelations weren't yet published, and the few available copies were handwritten on loose sheets that were circulated among members and carried around by missionaries.

Then, in November 1831, Joseph called a council of Church leaders to discuss publishing the revelations. After seeking the Lord's will, these leaders made plans to publish the Book of Commandments—the precursor to today's Doctrine and Covenants. Soon everyone would be able to read for themselves the word of God revealed through a living prophet, vivid evidence that "the keys of the mysteries of the kingdom of our Savior are again entrusted to man." For these and many other reasons, Saints then and now consider these revelations to be "worth . . . the riches of the whole Earth" (Doctrine and Covenants 70, section heading).

See *Saints*, 1:140–43.

 Ideas for Learning at Home and at Church

DOCTRINE AND COVENANTS 67:1–9; 68:3–6

The Lord's servants speak His will when moved upon by the Holy Ghost.

The decision to publish the revelations received by Joseph Smith seems like an easy one, but some early Church leaders weren't sure it was a good idea. One concern had to do with imperfections in the way Joseph Smith wrote the revelations. The revelation in section 67 came in response to that concern. What do you learn about the Lord's prophets and revelation from verses 1–9? What additional insights do you gain from 68:3–6?

How have you come to know for yourself that the revelations God gives His servants are true? You might also ponder experiences when you felt the Lord was speaking to you through one of His servants (see Doctrine and Covenants 68:4). When have you felt "moved upon by the Holy Ghost" (verse 3) to say something? How did the Lord "stand by you"? (verse 6).

DOCTRINE AND COVENANTS 67:10–14

"Continue in patience."

How do jealousy, fear, and pride keep us from growing closer to the Lord? How do we overcome the "natural man" or "carnal mind" so that we can "see [Him] and know that [He is]"? (verse 12; see also Mosiah 3:19). What do you find in these verses that inspires you to "continue in patience until ye are perfected"? (verse 13).

DOCTRINE AND COVENANTS 68:25–31

📖 I can help center my home on Jesus Christ.

The Lord's words in Doctrine and Covenants 68:25–31 refer specifically to parents, but whether or not you're a parent, you can use His counsel to do your part to center your home on the doctrine of Jesus Christ. Listed below are some of the principles the Lord says should be taught in the home. Consider how you can make each one of these part of the foundation of a Christ-centered home—the home you live in now or your future home. The resources and questions provided can help.

- *Repentance*: Study Alma 36:17–20, and notice how Alma was blessed at a critical time because his father had taught him about the Savior's atoning mission. How can you help inspire your family to turn to Jesus Christ and repent? (see also 2 Nephi 25:26).

- *Faith in Christ*: Read President Russell M. Nelson's five suggestions for developing faith in "Christ Is Risen; Faith in Him Will Move Mountains" (*Liahona*, May 2021, 103). Ponder how these suggestions could create a culture of faith in your family.

- *Baptism*: Review the baptismal covenant as described in Mosiah 18:8–10, 13. How can your efforts to keep this covenant strengthen your family?

- *Gift of the Holy Ghost*: Study the invitations on pages 17–19 of *For the Strength of Youth: A Guide for Making Choices*. What do you feel inspired to do to invite the influence of the Holy Ghost in your home?

- *Prayer*: What do you learn about the power of prayer in the home in "Love Is Spoken Here"? (*Children's Songbook*, 190–91). What blessings does the Savior promise in 3 Nephi 18:15–21?

- Other principles you find in Doctrine and Covenants 68:25–31:

What counsel would you give to someone whose family members don't support their efforts to build faith in Christ?

See also "The Family: A Proclamation to the World," Gospel Library; Topics and Questions, "Parenting," Gospel Library; Dieter F. Uchtdorf, "Jesus Christ Is the Strength of Parents," *Liahona*, May 2023, 55–59.

DOCTRINE AND COVENANTS 69:1

"True and faithful" friends help me follow Jesus Christ.

Why do you think it was "wisdom in [the Lord]" for someone "true and faithful" to accompany Oliver Cowdery on the assignment described in this verse? How does this principle apply to you?

Help learners lift each other. Each individual in your class or family is a rich source of testimony, insights, and experiences living the gospel. Invite them to share with and lift each other.

DOCTRINE AND COVENANTS 70:1–4

I am accountable for the revelations the Lord has given.

The Lord gave certain elders the responsibility to oversee the publishing of the revelations. Even though you do not have that specific responsibility, what is your stewardship or responsibility "over the revelations and commandments"? (verse 3).

For more ideas, see this month's issues of the *Liahona* and *For the Strength of Youth* magazines.

 Ideas for Teaching Children

DOCTRINE AND COVENANTS 67

The Doctrine and Covenants teaches me about Jesus Christ.

- Tell your children about how Joseph Smith's revelations came to be printed in a book (see "Chapter 23: The Doctrine and Covenants," in *Doctrine and Covenants Stories*, 90–92, or the corresponding video in Gospel Library). Help them remember some of the things you've learned about Jesus Christ from Doctrine and Covenants so far this year. You might also share with each other some of your favorite verses from Doctrine and Covenants.

- You could also show your children the Bible, Book of Mormon, Doctrine and Covenants, and Pearl of Great Price and talk with them about how they are different and how they are similar (see the descriptions of these books in Guide to the Scriptures). How can we know that the scriptures are true? What do we learn from Doctrine and Covenants 67:4, 9 about the revelations the Lord gave to Joseph Smith?

I can be baptized when I am eight years old.

- In Doctrine and Covenants 68:27, the Lord specified how old a person must be to be baptized. Help your children discover what He said. Why does Jesus want us to be baptized? A song like "Baptism" (*Children's Songbook*, 100–101) can help. Using pictures or verses 25–31 (or both), help your children discover things the Lord wants children to learn.

- Read with your children about the assignment the Lord gave Oliver Cowdery in the section heading for Doctrine and Covenants 69. What counsel did the Lord give in verse 1? Why is it important to be with people "who will be true and faithful"? Maybe your children could tell about someone they know who is "true and faithful." Sing together a song that encourages the children to be true and faithful like the Savior, such as "I'm Trying to Be like Jesus" (*Children's Songbook*, 78–79). How can we make sure we are true and faithful to the Lord? How can He use us to bless others when we are true and faithful?

For more ideas, see this month's issue of the *Friend* magazine.

The Book of Commandments, precursor to the Doctrine and Covenants, was printed on a press like this one.

I can be baptized when I am eight years old (Doctrine and Covenants 68:25–28).

Color the pictures. Cut a slit along the dotted line in the font. Cut out either the girl figure or the boy figure, and glue a craft stick or piece of cardboard to the back. Put the figure through the slit in the font, and move the figure down and back up to show how we are baptized.

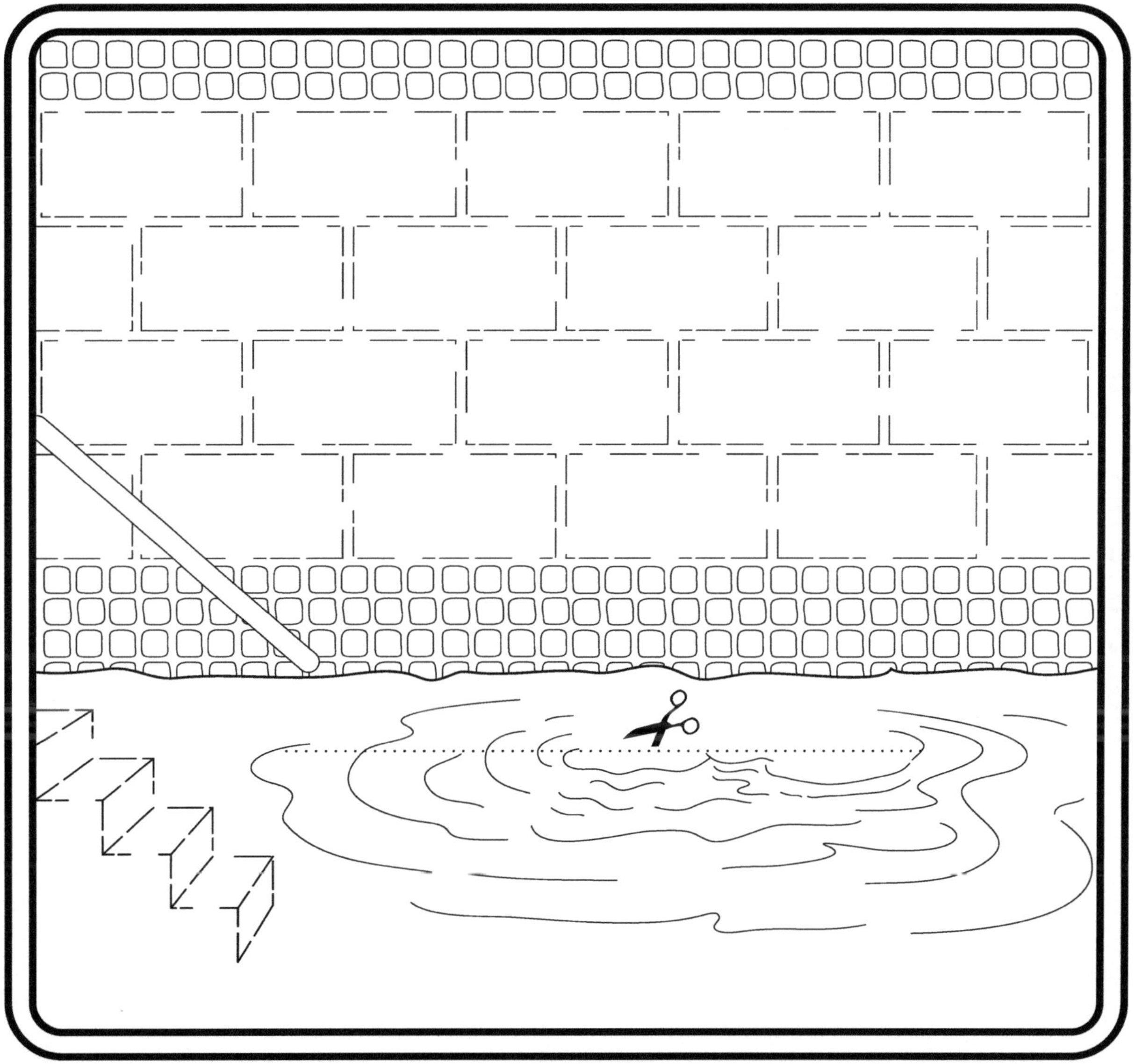

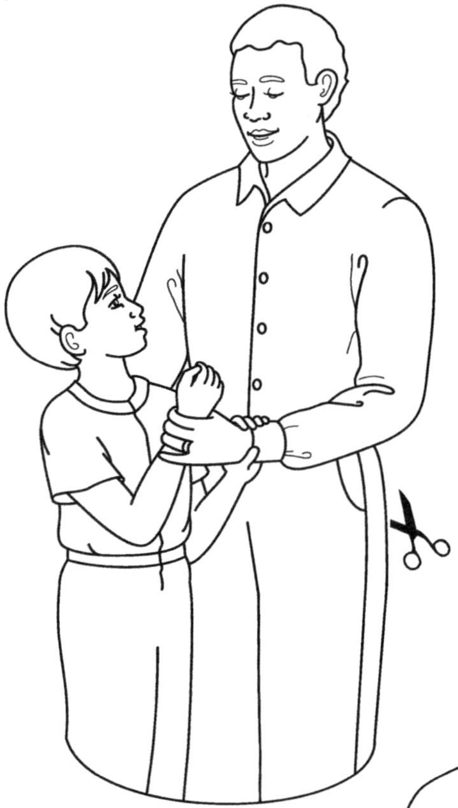

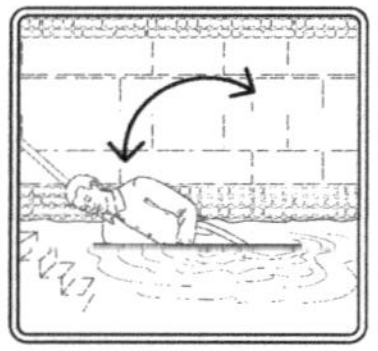

I Will Remember the Covenant, by Enrique Manuel Garcia

Doctrine and Covenants 71–75

Ever since he was a boy, Joseph Smith faced critics—even enemies—as he tried to do God's work. But it must have been particularly difficult in late 1831 when Ezra Booth began publicly berating the Church, because in this case the critic was a former believer. Ezra had seen Joseph use God's power to heal a woman. He had been invited to accompany Joseph on the first survey of the land of Zion in Missouri. But he had since lost his faith and, in an attempt to discredit the Prophet, published a series of letters in an Ohio newspaper. And his efforts seemed to be working, because "unfriendly feelings . . . had developed against the Church" in the area (Doctrine and Covenants 71, section heading). What should believers do in a case like that? While there is not one right answer for every situation, it seems that often—including in this case in 1831—part of the Lord's answer is to declare the truth and correct falsehoods by "proclaiming [the] gospel" (verse 1). Yes, the Lord's work will always have critics, but in the end, "no weapon that is formed against [it] shall prosper" (verse 9).

See "Ezra Booth and Isaac Morley," in *Revelations in Context*, 134.

 Ideas for Learning at Home and at Church

DOCTRINE AND COVENANTS 71

The Spirit will guide me as I proclaim the Savior's gospel.

It can be troubling when people criticize or ridicule your faith in the Savior, His gospel, or His Church. When that happens, what do you do? Something similar happened in Ohio in 1831 (see the section heading to Doctrine and Covenants 71). What did the Lord tell Joseph Smith and Sidney Rigdon to do about it in Doctrine and Covenants 71? Maybe you could list instructions the Lord gave them and blessings He promised.

In addition to studying section 71, you might also explore how the Savior responded to His critics during His mortal ministry. Here are some examples: Matthew 22:15–22; 26:59–64; John 10:37–38. What do you learn from Him? What additional insights do you gain from Matthew 18:15; Ephesians 4:31–32; 2 Timothy 3:12; James 1:19?

How might His counsel apply to situations you face today? You might consider ways to peacefully correct falsehoods in your own words. For example, you might start by expressing respect for the other person's views, and then you could share in a humble and kind way what you believe about Jesus Christ and His teachings. To prepare for these occasions, perhaps you could practice this approach with friends or family members.

See also Topics and Questions, "Helping Others with Questions," Gospel Library; Dallin H. Oaks, "Loving Others and Living with Differences," *Ensign* or *Liahona*, Nov. 2014, 25–28; Jörg Klebingat, "Valiant Discipleship in the Latter Days," *Liahona*, May 2022, 107–10.

DOCTRINE AND COVENANTS 72

The Lord blesses me through the ministry of leaders like bishops.

When Newel K. Whitney was called to serve as a bishop, his duties were a little different from those of today's bishops. For example, Bishop Whitney oversaw the consecration of property and permission to settle in the land of Zion in Missouri. But as you read about his calling in Doctrine and Covenants 72, you might notice some connections to what bishops do today—at least in the spirit, if not the specifics, of their duties.

For example, in what ways do you "render an account" to your bishop? (verse 5). In our day, "the Lord's storehouse" can include the donations, service, and talents of ward members (see verses 10, 12). How can you contribute to that storehouse?

How has the Lord blessed you and your family through the service of a bishop?

See also Quentin L. Cook, "Bishops—Shepherds over the Lord's Flock," *Liahona*, May 2021, 56–60.

DOCTRINE AND COVENANTS 73

I have many opportunities to share the Savior's gospel.

When Joseph Smith and Sidney Rigdon returned from their missionary assignment (see Doctrine and Covenants 71), the Lord told them to continue their translation of the Bible (see Guide to the Scriptures, "Joseph Smith Translation (JST)," Gospel Library). But that didn't mean He wanted them to stop sharing the gospel. After all, it's part of the life of a disciple.

As you read Doctrine and Covenants 73, consider how you can make sharing the gospel an ongoing, "practicable" (verse 4)—or realistic—part of your life among your other responsibilities.

Sharing the gospel of Jesus Christ can be normal and natural.

DOCTRINE AND COVENANTS 75:1–16

"Labor with your might . . . proclaiming the truth."

The revelation in section 75 was addressed to people who had "given [their] names to go forth to proclaim [the Savior's] gospel" (verse 2). One way to study this revelation is to make two lists: (1) how to share the gospel effectively and (2) how the Lord blesses and supports us as we do.

What do you think it means to "tarry" or "be idle" in sharing the gospel? What does it look like to "labor with your might"? (verse 3).

See also "I'll Go Where You Want Me to Go," *Hymns*, no. 270.

For more ideas, see this month's issues of the *Liahona* and *For the Strength of Youth* magazines.

 # Ideas for Teaching Children

DOCTRINE AND COVENANTS 71

I can defend the truth by sharing my testimony.

- You can use the section heading for Doctrine and Covenants 71 or "Chapter 25: Joseph Smith and Sidney Rigdon Go on a Mission" (in *Doctrine and Covenants Stories*, 96, or the corresponding video in Gospel Library) to teach your children about the circumstances that inspired section 71. Then help them discover in verse 1 what the Lord wanted Joseph and Sidney to do about "unfriendly feelings" toward the Church. How did He say He would help them? How can we be like Joseph and Sidney?

- You could also sing a song that inspires your children to be true to the Savior, such as "Stand for the Right" (*Children's Songbook*, 159). Help your children practice how to share what they know about Jesus Christ.

DOCTRINE AND COVENANTS 72:2

The Lord has called a bishop to help me.

- Reading Doctrine and Covenants 72:2 together could create an opportunity to discuss why the Lord gives us bishops (see also "Chapter 17: The First Bishops of the Church," in *Doctrine and Covenants Stories*, 64–66, or the corresponding video in Gospel Library). You and your children could find pictures or objects that represent the responsibilities of a bishop. The picture and activity page at the end of this outline provide some ideas. Then you could talk together about bishops you've known and how the Lord has blessed your family through their service.

Always teach about Jesus Christ. "No matter what you are teaching, remember that you are really teaching about Jesus Christ and how to become like Him" (*Teaching in the Savior's Way*, 6). For example, when you teach your children about bishops, emphasize that they are representatives of Jesus Christ, called by Him to do His work (see 1 Peter 2:25).

The Lord asks bishops to care for people in need.

DOCTRINE AND COVENANTS 75:3

I can give my best effort to the Lord.

- To talk about the difference between being "idle" and "labor[ing] with [our] might," perhaps you could select some acts of service or household chores and invite your children to demonstrate doing them idly and then with all their might. As you read "neither be idle" in Doctrine and Covenants 75:3, your children could show how they would do the chores lazily. When you read "but labor with your might," they could show how they work hard. Why is it important that we do our best when serving the Lord?

- In his message "Two Principles for Any Economy" (*Ensign* or *Liahona*, Nov. 2009, 55–58), President Dieter F. Uchtdorf told two stories about work. Maybe you could share them with your children and talk about how it feels to know we have worked hard and done our best.

For more ideas, see this month's issue of the *Friend* magazine.

Recognizing the Tender Mercies in Your Life, by Keith Larson

The Lord has called a bishop to help me (Doctrine and Covenants 72:2, 10, 14).

Draw a line between each picture and the matching description of what a bishop does to help us.

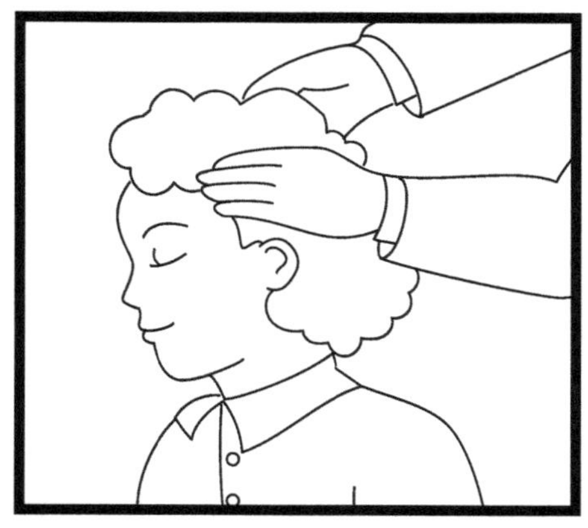

Presides at meetings

Interviews and counsels

Gives blessings

Oversees ward finances

Gives food to the needy

Teaches the scriptures

Visits those in need

Serves children and youth

Oversees the meetinghouse

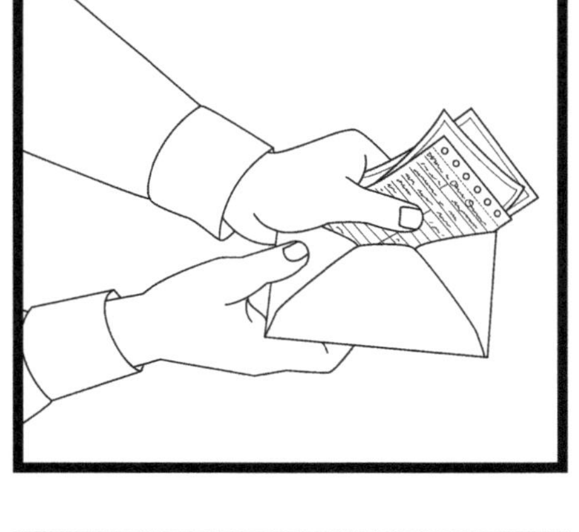

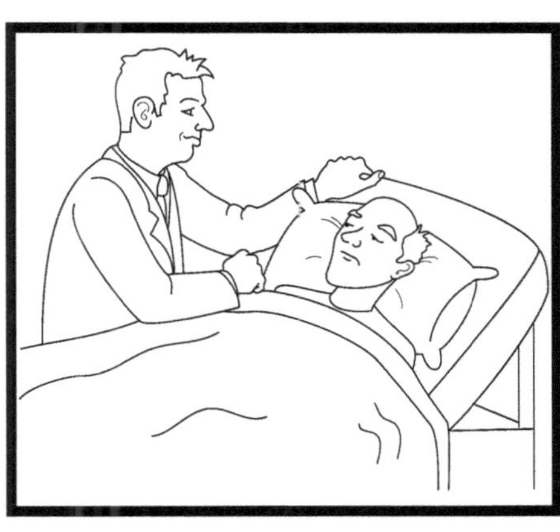

Refuge, by Shaelynn Abel

Doctrine and Covenants 76

"What will happen to me after I die?" Nearly everyone asks this question in some form or another. For centuries, many Christian traditions, relying on biblical teachings, have taught of heaven and hell, of paradise for the righteous and torment for the wicked. But can the entire human family really be divided so strictly? In February 1832, Joseph Smith and Sidney Rigdon wondered if there was more to know about the subject (see Doctrine and Covenants 76, section heading).

There certainly was. While Joseph and Sidney were pondering these things, the Lord "touched the eyes of [their] understandings and they were opened" (verse 19). They received a revelation so stunning, so expansive, so illuminating that the Saints simply called it "the Vision." It threw open heaven's windows and gave God's children a mind-stretching view of eternity. The vision revealed that heaven is grander and broader and more inclusive than most people had previously supposed. God is more merciful and just than we can comprehend. And God's children have an eternal destiny more glorious than we can imagine.

See *Saints*, 1:147–50; "The Vision," in *Revelations in Context*, 148–54.

 Ideas for Learning at Home and at Church

DOCTRINE AND COVENANTS 76

Salvation comes through Jesus Christ, the Son of God.

Section 76 reveals important truths about our eternal destiny, but it would be incomplete to say that this revelation is about the three kingdoms of glory or even just about the plan of salvation. More accurately, section 76 is about Jesus Christ, who makes God's plan for our salvation and eternal glory possible. As you read, you might look for words or phrases that describe the relationship between Jesus Christ and the people who inherit the different kingdoms of glory. Perhaps a table like the following could help you record what you find.

Kingdom of glory	Relationship with Jesus Christ	Eternal blessings
Celestial (verses 50–70, 92–96)	• Received testimony of Jesus • Made and kept covenants with Him	• Cleansed from sin • Overcome by faith
Terrestrial (verses 71–79, 97)		
Telestial (verses 81–90, 98–106, 109–12)		

What do you feel inspired to do to strengthen your relationship with the Savior?

When Wilford Woodruff read this vision, he said, "I felt to love the Lord more than ever before in my life" (see "Voices of the Restoration: Testimonies of 'the Vision,'" Gospel Library.) What do you learn about Jesus Christ from verses 1–5, 20–24, 39–43, 107–8 that causes you to love Him more?

See also 1 Peter 3:18–19; 4:6; Dallin H. Oaks, "What Has Our Savior Done for Us?," *Liahona*, May 2021, 75–77; "I Stand All Amazed," *Hymns*, no. 193.

Focus on Heavenly Father, Jesus Christ, and Their doctrine. Of everything we can learn in the scriptures, the most important truths help us build faith in Heavenly Father and Jesus Christ, repent, make and keep covenants with Them, and receive the Holy Ghost. Although it may be interesting to compare or analyze the attitudes or behavior of people who will receive the different kingdoms of glory, it's more important to focus on Heavenly Father and the Savior. Everything They do to prepare us for that glory will turn us toward Them.

In this room, Joseph Smith saw the vision recorded in Doctrine and Covenants 76.

DOCTRINE AND COVENANTS 76:5–10, 114–18

I can understand God's will "by the power of the Holy Spirit."

Not all members of the Church easily accepted the revelation in section 76, because it taught that almost everyone would be saved and receive some degree of glory. For example, Brigham Young said: "My traditions were such, that when the Vision came first to me, it was directly contrary and opposed to my former education. I said, Wait a little. I did not reject it; but I could not understand it." He explained that he had to "think and pray, to read and think, until I knew and fully understood it for myself" (in "The Vision," in *Revelations in Context*, 150). What do you learn from his experience that can help you when God reveals things that are different from your current understanding? What do you learn about God in Doctrine and Covenants 76:5–10, 114–18? What do these verses teach about how you can understand "the good pleasure of [God's] will"? (verse 7).

DOCTRINE AND COVENANTS 76:39–44, 50–70

Exaltation is the highest form of salvation.

Doctrine and Covenants 76:39–44 describe salvation generally. Verses 50–70 describe exaltation, a specific kind of salvation. How would you explain the difference between salvation and exaltation? What is the Savior's role in both? What do you find in these verses that inspires you to seek exaltation?

See also John 3:16–17; Doctrine and Covenants 132:20–25.

DOCTRINE AND COVENANTS 76:50–70, 92–95

My Heavenly Father wants me to receive eternal life in the celestial kingdom.

Have you ever wondered—or worried—about whether you can become the kind of person who will receive celestial glory, as described in Doctrine and Covenants 76:50–70, 92–95? While it's important to know what God expects of us, consider also looking in these verses for what God has done for us—and is doing—to help us become like Him. Why do you feel your efforts matter to Him?

How does this vision of celestial glory affect the way you want to live your daily life?

See also Moses 1:39; J. Devn Cornish, "Am I Good Enough? Will I Make It?," *Ensign* or *Liahona*, Nov. 2016, 32–34.

> For more ideas, see this month's issues of the *Liahona* and *For the Strength of Youth* magazines.

 Ideas for Teaching Children

DOCTRINE AND COVENANTS 76:24

We are all children of God.

- To help your children understand their divine potential, you could show them pictures of children and their parents. You could then read Doctrine and Covenants 76:24 and share with each other why you're happy to know that we are all "sons and daughters unto God."

- You could also sing together "I Am a Child of God" (*Children's Songbook*, 2–3) and invite your children to point to themselves when they sing "I." Then sing the song again, replacing "I am" with "you are" while pointing to someone else.

Jesus Christ is my Savior.

- Consider role-playing with your children a scenario in which someone asks, "What has Jesus Christ done for me?" You and your children can look for possible answers in verses 5, 41–42, or 69 in section 76. You could also sing "He Sent His Son," *Children's Songbook*, 34–35. How can we show our gratitude for what the Savior has done for us?

Detail from *Suffer the Children*, by J. Kirk Richards

Heavenly Father wants me to return to live with Him forever.

- You and your children could read or watch part or all of "Chapter 26: The Three Kingdoms of Heaven" (in *Doctrine and Covenants Stories*, 97–103, or the corresponding video in Gospel Library) and share with each other what you like about the vision Joseph Smith had. Let your children share their thoughts and feelings about what it would be like to live with Heavenly Father in the celestial kingdom.

- You could also read Doctrine and Covenants 76:62 and invite your children to draw pictures of themselves with Heavenly Father and Jesus Christ in the celestial kingdom (see this week's activity page).

Studying the scriptures can help me "understand the things of God."

- You could invite your children to read verses 15–19 to find out what Joseph Smith and Sidney Rigdon were doing when they saw the vision in Doctrine and Covenants 76. Tell your children about a time when you received inspiration while reading the scriptures, and ask your children if they have had similar experiences.

For more ideas, see this month's issue of the *Friend* magazine.

Glory in Degrees, by Annie Henrie Nader

**Heavenly Father wants me to return to live with Him forever
(Doctrine and Covenants 76:62).**

Joseph Smith and Sidney Rigdon saw a vision of the celestial kingdom (see Doctrine and Covenants 76:50–70, 92–94). Draw something Joseph and Sidney saw in their vision (see verses 20–21, 62, 92–94, for example). Or draw a picture of you and your family in the celestial kingdom.

Doctrine and Covenants 77–80

Less than two years after the Church of Jesus Christ was restored, it had more than 2,000 members and was growing quickly. In March 1832, Joseph Smith met with other Church leaders "to discuss Church business": the need to publish revelations, purchase land to gather on, and care for the poor (see Doctrine and Covenants 78, section heading). To meet these needs, the Lord called on a small number of Church leaders to form the United Firm, a group that would join their efforts to "advance the cause" of the Lord (verse 4) in these areas. But even in such administrative matters, the Lord focused on the things of eternity. Ultimately, the purpose of a printing press or a storehouse—like everything else in God's kingdom—is to prepare His children to receive "a place in the celestial world" and "the riches of eternity" (verses 7, 18). And if those blessings are hard to comprehend right now, in the midst of the busyness of daily life, He reassures us, "Be of good cheer, for I will lead you along" (verse 18).

 Ideas for Learning at Home and at Church

DOCTRINE AND COVENANTS 77

God gives knowledge to people who seek it.

Translation of the Bible, by Liz Lemon Swindle

As Joseph Smith and Sidney Rigdon worked on the inspired translation of the Bible, they had questions about the book of Revelation, as many people do. And as Joseph knew well, when he lacked wisdom, he could ask of God. The insights he gained are in Doctrine and Covenants 77. As you read this section, consider recording your insights in the relevant chapters in the book of Revelation. What do you learn from your study about receiving revelation?

I can help "advance the cause" of Christ and His Church.

The Lord told Joseph Smith and other Church leaders that managing a storehouse and a printing press would help "advance the cause, which ye have espoused" (Doctrine and Covenants 78:4). What would you say is the "cause" of the Savior's Church? Ponder this as you read Doctrine and Covenants 78:1–7. What are some of the various ways you can help advance that cause—including in your family?

See also *General Handbook*, 1.2.

The Lord will lead me along.

Why do you think the Lord sometimes calls His followers "little children"? (Doctrine and Covenants 78:17). When have you felt like a little child, perhaps because of something you "have not as yet understood" or "cannot bear"? (verses 17–18). What do you find in these verses that can help you "be of good cheer" (verse 18) in such times? Consider finding a picture of yourself when you were a child, and ponder how you have grown spiritually since then. Or think of something that was hard for you when you were young but is easier now. In what ways does Heavenly Father still want you to be like a child? (see Mosiah 3:19). How is He "[leading] you along"?

I can receive all things with thankfulness.

To prepare to study Doctrine and Covenants 78:19, you could make a list of good things that have happened to you today. Then make a list of things that don't really seem like blessings to you. Ponder these lists as you read Doctrine and Covenants 78:19. What difference does it make in your life if you receive "all things" with thankfulness—even things that might not seem like blessings?

To learn more about how gratitude to God can influence your life, explore these scriptures and make a list of the truths you find: Psalm 107:8–9; Luke 17:11–19; Philippians 4:6–7; Mosiah 2:19–24; Alma 34:38; 37:37; Doctrine and Covenants 46:32; 59:7, 15–21.

Consider searching President Dieter F. Uchtdorf's message "Grateful in Any Circumstances" (*Ensign* or *Liahona*, May 2014, 70–77) for counsel about how to be grateful. You could look for similar counsel in the video "President Russell M. Nelson on the Healing Power of Gratitude" (Gospel Library). How does gratitude affect your relationship with Jesus Christ?

Search and share. If you are assigned to teach, look for ways to help people search the scriptures or words of prophets—on their own or in small groups—and share what they learn. For example, in this activity you could give each individual or group a section of President Uchtdorf's message and ask them to share a phrase or sentence that they feel summarizes what he taught.

See also "Count Your Blessings," *Hymns*, no. 241; Topics and Questions, "Gratitude," Gospel Library.

DOCTRINE AND COVENANTS 79–80

The call to serve God matters more than where I serve.

Regarding Doctrine and Covenants 80, Elder David A. Bednar taught, "Perhaps one of the lessons the Savior is teaching us in this revelation is that an assignment to labor in a specific place is essential and important but secondary to a call to the work" ("Called to the Work," *Ensign* or *Liahona*, May 2017, 68). What experiences have helped you learn that Elder Bednar's words are true? What additional lessons can you find in Doctrine and Covenants 79–80 that could help someone who has just received a calling?

For more ideas, see this month's issues of the *Liahona* and *For the Strength of Youth* magazines.

 Ideas for Teaching Children

DOCTRINE AND COVENANTS 77:2

God created every creature on earth.

- As you and your children read Doctrine and Covenants 77:2 together, you might look at pictures of animals, including insects and birds. Your children could point to the pictures when you read the words "beasts," "creeping things," and "fowls of the air." Share with each other how God's creations help you feel His love.

God created all creatures on earth.

DOCTRINE AND COVENANTS 78:4

I can help "advance the cause" of Jesus Christ.

- To help your children think about their roles in the Lord's work, consider reading with them Doctrine and Covenants 78:4 to identify the "cause" we "espoused" (accepted or chose to support) when we were baptized. Help them look in scripture passages like these for possible answers: Mosiah 18:8–10; Doctrine and Covenants 20:37; Moses 1:39. Your children might enjoy role-playing how they can help with the Lord's work. For example, what does it look like to "bear one another's burdens" or "take upon [ourselves] the name of Jesus Christ"? How does this "advance the cause" of Christ?

I can share what I have with others.

- To teach what it means to be "equal in earthly things" (verse 6), you could give your children pictures of people in need (hungry, injured, or cold) and objects that would help (such as food, a bandage, or a blanket). Then your children could match the pictures with the objects. What can we share to help people in need?

- To get some context for section 78, read with your children the sentences under the first two pictures of "Chapter 28: The Prophet Joseph Goes to Missouri Again" (in *Doctrine and Covenants Stories*, 108, or the corresponding video in Gospel Library). Then your children could pretend they are helping someone build a house, sharing food, or serving in another way.

Jesus Christ will lead me along.

- It may be fun for your children to talk about what it means to be a leader and then lead an activity. After reading together Doctrine and Covenants 78:18, you could discuss times when we need Jesus to lead us. Consider singing a song such as "I Will Walk with Jesus" (Gospel Library).

I can receive "all things with thankfulness."

- Read with your children Doctrine and Covenants 78:19 to discover what the Lord promises to people who are thankful. Help your children understand what "an hundred fold" means, perhaps by showing them a small object and then 100 of that same object. Perhaps they could draw pictures of things they have received from God "with thankfulness."

For more ideas, see this month's issue of the *Friend* magazine.

God's Garden, by Sam Lawlor

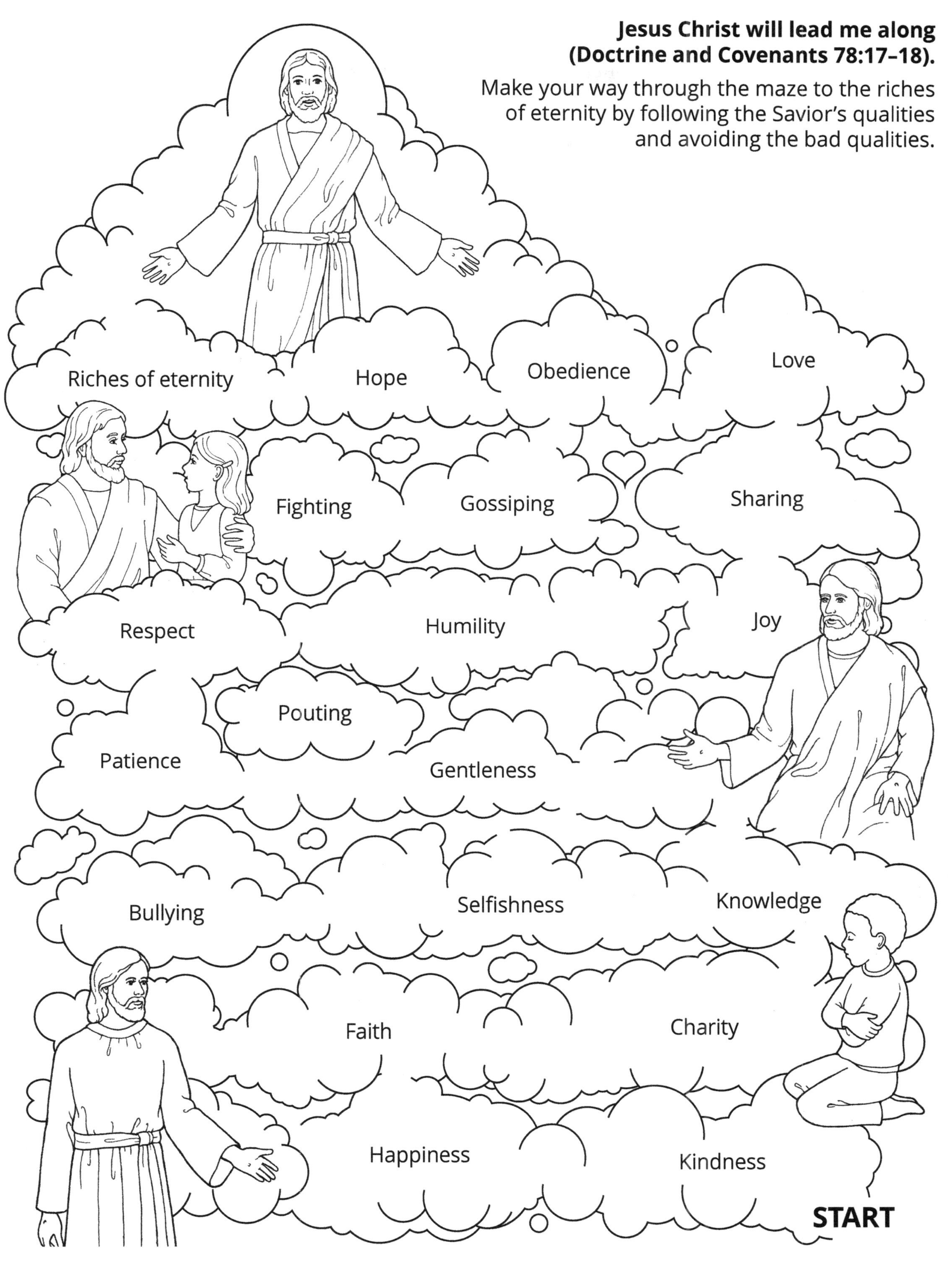

Jesus Christ will lead me along (Doctrine and Covenants 78:17–18).
Make your way through the maze to the riches of eternity by following the Savior's qualities and avoiding the bad qualities.
Riches of eternity
Hope
Obedience
Love
Fighting
Gossiping
Sharing
Respect
Humility
Joy
Pouting
Patience
Gentleness
Bullying
Selfishness
Knowledge
Faith
Charity
Happiness
Kindness
START

Doctrine and Covenants 81–83

In March 1832, the Lord called Jesse Gause to be a counselor to Joseph Smith in the Presidency of the High Priesthood (now called the First Presidency). Doctrine and Covenants 81 is a revelation to Brother Gause about his new calling. But Jesse Gause did not serve faithfully, so Frederick G. Williams was called to replace him. Brother Williams's name replaced Brother Gause's name in the revelation.

That may seem like a minor detail, but it implies a significant truth: most revelations in the Doctrine and Covenants are addressed to specific people, but we can always seek ways to apply them to ourselves (see 1 Nephi 19:23). When we read the Lord's counsel to Frederick G. Williams to "strengthen the feeble knees," we can think of people we might strengthen (Doctrine and Covenants 81:5). When we read the Lord's invitation to members of the United Firm to "bind yourselves by this covenant," we can think of our own covenants. And we can read His promise, "I . . . am bound when ye do what I say," as if He's speaking to us (Doctrine and Covenants 82:10, 15). We can do this because, as the Lord declared, "What I say unto one I say unto all" (verse 5).

See "Newel K. Whitney and the United Firm," "Jesse Gause: Counselor to the Prophet," in *Revelations in Context*, 142–47, 155–57.

 Ideas for Learning at Home and at Church

DOCTRINE AND COVENANTS 81:4–5; 82:18–19

"Thou wilt do the greatest good unto thy fellow beings."

In several passages in Doctrine and Covenants 81–83, the Lord invites us to help people in need around us. Consider marking the passages as you find them. One of the most descriptive examples is in Doctrine and Covenants 81:4–5. Here are some questions to help you ponder these verses:

- What are some ways a person can be "weak"? What does it mean to "succor" them? When has the Christlike service of others helped me when I felt weak?

- What might cause a person's hands to figuratively "hang down"? How can I "lift up" those hands?

- What might "feeble knees" mean? How are they strengthened?

How does the Savior do these things for you?

Perhaps studying this verse has brought to mind someone you could "succor," "lift up," or "strengthen." What will you do to minister to that person?

What else do you learn about service to others in Doctrine and Covenants 82:18–19? You might also watch the video "Teachings of Thomas S. Monson: Rescuing Those in Need" (Gospel Library). How did Bishop Monson's ward members exemplify what these verses teach?

See also Jacob 2:17–19; Mosiah 18:8–9; "Works of God" (video), ChurchofJesusChrist.org.

Carl Heinrich Bloch (1834–1890), *Christ Healing the Sick at Bethesda*, 1883, oil on canvas, 100 ¾ x 125 ½ inches. Brigham Young University Museum of Art, purchased with funds provided by Jack R. and Mary Lois Wheatley, 2001.

DOCTRINE AND COVENANTS 82:3

The Savior has given me much and requires much of me.

Reading this verse might prompt you to review what God has given you—both physical and spiritual blessings. Keep this in mind as you read the rest of section 82. What do you feel God requires of you?

See also "Because I Have Been Given Much," *Hymns*, no. 219.

DOCTRINE AND COVENANTS 82:8–10

Commandments are evidence of God's love for us.

If you or someone you know has ever wondered why the Lord gives so many commandments, Doctrine and Covenants 82:8–10 could help. Which insights from these verses could help you explain to someone why you choose to follow the Lord's commandments? What could you compare the commandments to that might help? You could find additional insights in Doctrine and Covenants 1:37–38; 130:20–21 and the video "Blessed and Happy Are Those Who Keep the Commandments of God" (Gospel Library). What experiences have taught you to see commandments as blessings?

Think about some of the commandments God has given you. What have these commandments taught you about Him and His will? (see verse 8). How has your life been affected by keeping these commandments?

What do you learn about the Lord from verse 10? What do you think it means for the Lord to be "bound"? (see also verse 15).

How has the Lord kept His promises in your life? What might you say to someone who doesn't feel motivated to keep the commandments because they haven't received the blessings they hoped for? Do you find any helpful insights in Elder D. Todd Christofferson's message "Our Relationship with God"? (*Liahona*, May 2022, 78–80).

See also Topics and Questions, "Commandments," Gospel Library.

For more ideas, see this month's issues of the *Liahona* and *For the Strength of Youth* magazines.

 ## Ideas for Teaching Children

DOCTRINE AND COVENANTS 81:3

I can pray to God "vocally and in [my] heart."

- As you read Doctrine and Covenants 81:3 with your children, help them think of different "public" and "private" places where they can pray. You might also listen to or sing with them a hymn about prayer, such as "Secret Prayer" (*Hymns*, no. 144). Share with each other something from the hymn that teaches an important truth about prayer. You could also talk about speaking reverently to Heavenly Father.

- To encourage your children to pray in their hearts, you could give them paper hearts and invite them to draw or write something they want to pray about to Heavenly Father. Testify that Heavenly Father knows what we are thinking and feeling and He can hear our prayers even if we don't say them out loud. You might share with them an experience when you prayed in your heart and Heavenly Father heard you.

DOCTRINE AND COVENANTS 81:5

The Lord wants me to help people in need.

- With your children, draw pictures of hands and knees, and ask your children to find these body parts in Doctrine and Covenants 81:5. What is the Lord asking us to do in this verse? You might share with each other some ways that people have strengthened you when you felt "weak" or "feeble." The video "Pass It On" (ChurchofJesusChrist.org) could give your children ideas about how they serve others. You could also sing a song about service, such as "Have I Done Any Good?" (*Hymns*, no. 223). Consider helping your children make a plan to help at least one person in need this week.

- You could also use pictures or videos to tell simple stories of Jesus Christ serving others (see the pictures in this outline; *Gospel Art Book*, nos. 41, 42, 46, 47, 55; or one of the Bible Videos in Gospel Library). How can we follow the Savior's example of helping others?

We can reach out to people in need as the Savior did.

Help your children receive their own inspiration. Teaching means more than just sharing truth—it means helping other people become independent learners. Instead of simply telling your children how they can serve others, for example, encourage them to seek the Lord's guidance to know who they can help.

Heavenly Father promises blessings as I strive to obey Him.

- You and your children could look in Doctrine and Covenants 82:8–10 for answers to the question "Why does Heavenly Father give us commandments?" You might want to help your children think of examples of His commandments (see, for example, Exodus 20:4–17; Matthew 22:37–39; Doctrine and Covenants 89:5–17). It might help if you and your children find or draw pictures to represent some of them. How do Heavenly Father's commandments show His love for us?

- Perhaps a simple game would help your children see God's commandments as blessings, not burdens. One person could give instructions to help another person, who is blindfolded, to do something like make a sandwich or draw a picture. Think of something fun and creative! Then talk about how God's commandments are like the instructions in this game.

For more ideas, see this month's issue of the *Friend* magazine.

Illustration of Jesus healing a man, by Dan Burr

The Lord wants me to help people in need (Doctrine and Covenants 81:5).

Cut out several paper hearts. Then write on them ways you can serve others and share the Savior's love for them. As you serve each person, glue the hearts to the hand.

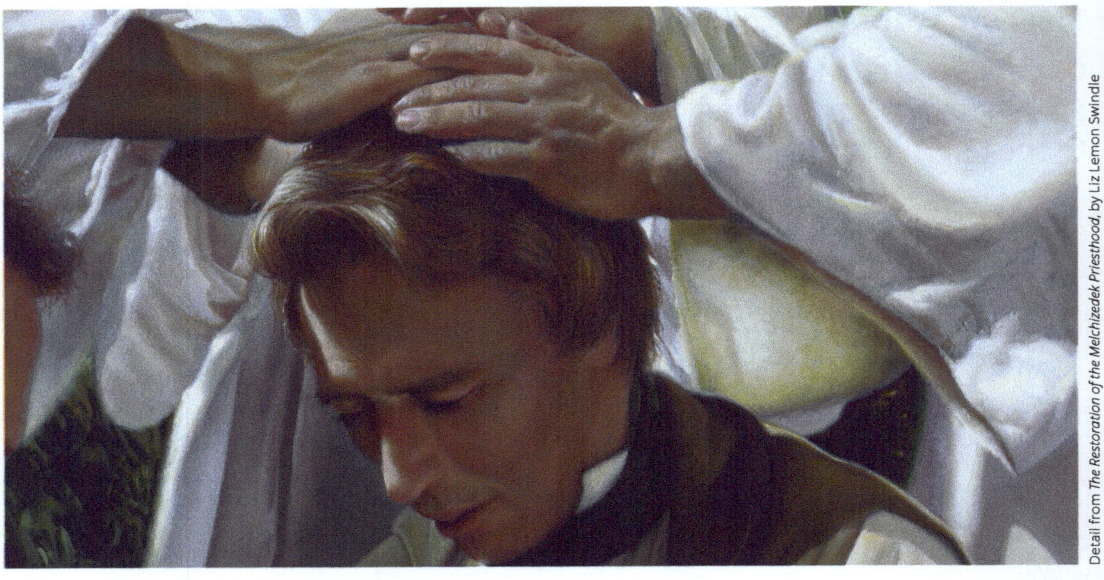

Doctrine and Covenants 84

Ever since the priesthood was restored in 1829, the early Saints had been blessed by the Lord's sacred power. They were baptized, confirmed, and called to serve by priesthood authority, much like we are today. But having access to priesthood power is not the same thing as completely understanding it, and God had more He wanted His Saints to understand—particularly with the coming restoration of temple ordinances. The 1832 revelation on the priesthood, now Doctrine and Covenants 84, expanded the Saints' vision of what the priesthood really is. And it can do the same for us today. After all, there is a lot to learn about the divine power that holds "the key of the knowledge of God," that makes manifest "the power of godliness," and that prepares us to "see the face of God, even the Father, and live" (verses 19–22).

 Ideas for Learning at Home and at Church

DOCTRINE AND COVENANTS 84:17–32

I have access to God's priesthood power and blessings.

When you think of the word *priesthood*, what comes to mind? How does God's priesthood power influence your life?

After pondering these questions, you might study Doctrine and Covenants 84:17–32, looking for what God wants you to know about His priesthood power. Consider how you could use these verses to describe the priesthood and its purposes to someone.

One thing you'll find is that through priesthood ordinances "the power of godliness is manifest" (see verses 19–21). Perhaps you could list the priesthood ordinances you have participated in (the lists in *General Handbook*, 18.1, 18.2, can help). How have these ordinances—and the associated covenants—brought God's power into your life? What would your life be like without them?

President Russell M. Nelson taught: "Every woman and every man who makes covenants with God and keeps those covenants, and who participates worthily in priesthood ordinances, has direct access to the power of God" ("Spiritual Treasures," *Ensign* or *Liahona*, Nov. 2019, 77). Consider studying President Nelson's message, looking for ways you can "draw the Savior's power into [your] life."

See also Doctrine and Covenants 25:10, 13, 15; 121:34–37, 41–46; Topics and Questions, "Priesthood," "Joseph Smith's Teachings about Priesthood, Temples, and Women," Gospel Library; *General Handbook*, 3.6, Gospel Library.

DOCTRINE AND COVENANTS 84:31–44

The priesthood is obtained with an oath and covenant.

The oath and covenant of the priesthood (see Doctrine and Covenants 84:31–44) has special application for Heavenly Father's sons who are ordained to a priesthood office, but many of the promised blessings in these verses are available to all of God's children. What are these promises, and what does God ask us to do to receive them?

Elder Paul B. Pieper taught: "It is interesting that in the oath and covenant of the priesthood [see Doctrine and Covenants 84:31–44], the Lord uses the verbs *obtain* and *receive*. He does not use the verb *ordain*. It is in the temple that men and women—together—obtain and receive the blessings and power of both the Aaronic and Melchizedek Priesthoods" ("Revealed Realities of Mortality," *Ensign*, Jan. 2016, 21).

As you study Doctrine and Covenants 84:31–44, ponder what it might mean to "obtain" and "receive" the priesthood. How is this different from being ordained to a priesthood office? What else does the Lord invite you to receive in these verses? How are you doing that?

What do you find that inspires you to be more faithful in receiving the Savior, His Father, His servants, and His priesthood power?

See also Doctrine and Covenants 121:36–46.

DOCTRINE AND COVENANTS 84:43–61

Living by the word of God brings light and truth into my life.

What truths do you find in Doctrine and Covenants 84:43–61 that help you understand why you need to consistently study the word of God? Note the contrast between light and darkness in these verses; how has your "diligent heed to the words of eternal life" brought light, truth, and "the Spirit of Jesus Christ" into your life? (verses 43, 45).

See also 2 Nephi 32:3.

Compare gospel principles to familiar things. Can you think of an analogy that would illustrate the truths in verses 43–44? For example, how is following all the steps in a recipe like living "by every word . . . of God"?

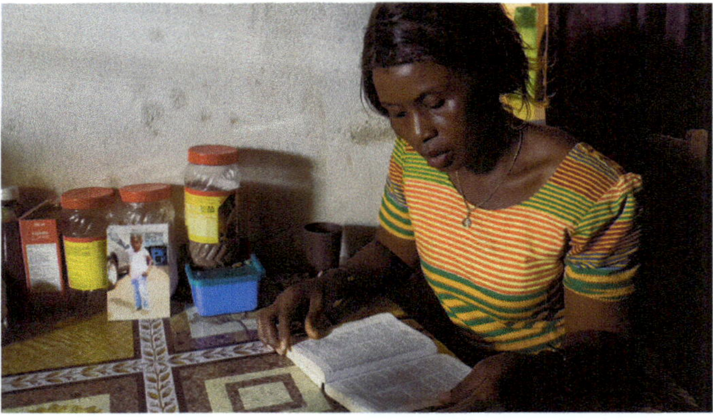

"Give diligent heed to the words of eternal life."

The Lord will be with me when I am in His service.

As you read these verses, you could identify ways the Lord said He would support His servants. How might these promises apply to the work He has asked you to do? For example, how have the promises in verse 88 been fulfilled in your life?

DOCTRINE AND COVENANTS 84:106–110

Everyone can contribute to the work of God.

What do you learn from these verses about how the Lord accomplishes His work? What counsel and blessings do you find? You might also think about how you have been "edified in all meekness" because you served with someone who was "strong in the Spirit," including people in your family.

For more ideas, see this month's issues of the *Liahona* and *For the Strength of Youth* magazines.

 # Ideas for Teaching Children

DOCTRINE AND COVENANTS 84:4–5

Temple ordinances help me prepare to live with Heavenly Father again.

- To help your children look forward to going to the temple, you could create a puzzle out of a picture of a temple. On the back of each piece, you could write something we do in the temple, such as being baptized for ancestors, being sealed to our families, and making covenants with God. Read Doctrine and Covenants 84:4–5 with your children, and ask them to listen for what the Lord commanded the Saints to build. As you and your children put the puzzle together, share with each other things we can do to prepare to enter the temple.

DOCTRINE AND COVENANTS 84:19–22

I can receive Heavenly Father's power through priesthood ordinances.

- To help your children understand what an ordinance is, consider looking at pictures of several priesthood ordinances with them, such as *Gospel Art Book*, nos. 103–8, or this week's activity page. Ask them to describe what is happening in each picture. You could then read together Doctrine and Covenants 84:19–22. Why does Heavenly Father want us  to receive these ordinances? Tell your children how you have felt God's power because of ordinances you received and covenants you made. (See also "Priesthood Power, Authority, and Keys" in appendix A or appendix B.)

I am Jesus's friend as I follow Him.

- After reading Doctrine and Covenants 84:77 together, ask your children about what it means to be a friend. You might talk about good friends you've had. How does Jesus show us that He wants us to be His friends? How can we show that we want that too? A song like "I'm Trying to Be like Jesus" (*Children's Songbook*, 78–79) could help with this conversation.

Heavenly Father helps His servants.

- Your children might enjoy hearing about how missionaries helped you, your family, or your ancestors receive the gospel. Then you could read about a special promise the Lord made to missionaries in Doctrine and Covenants 84:88. Maybe your children could think of actions that go with this verse. Consider sharing about a time when you were serving the Lord and felt that He was with you, as described in verse 88. You might also help your children think of ways they can be missionaries now. Testify that Heavenly Father helps us know what to say when we talk with others about Jesus Christ.

For more ideas, see this month's issue of the *Friend* magazine.

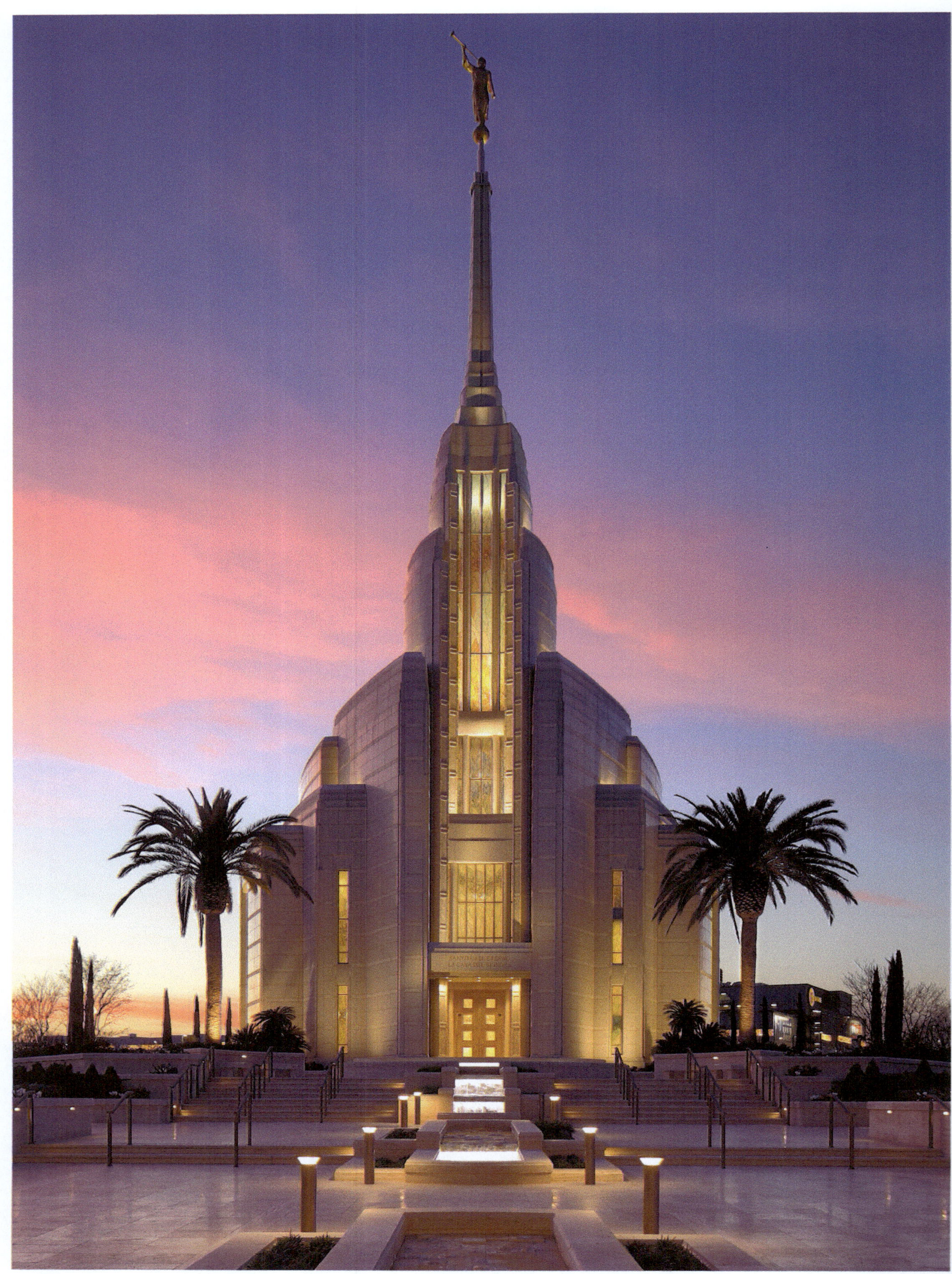

Rome Italy Temple

I can receive Heavenly Father's power through priesthood ordinances (Doctrine and Covenants 84:19–22).

Color the pictures, and cut out the shape on the solid black lines. Fold all of the dotted lines, and glue or tape the tabs together to make a cube.

Toss the cube and share why you are thankful for the priesthood ordinance that lands on top. If the word *priesthood* lands on top, share something you can do because the priesthood was restored.

. . . partake of the sacrament

. . . be sealed to my family

. . . be confirmed

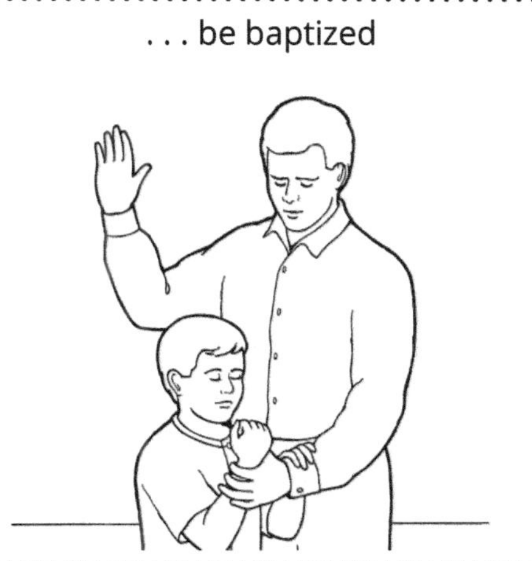

. . . be baptized

. . . receive priesthood blessings

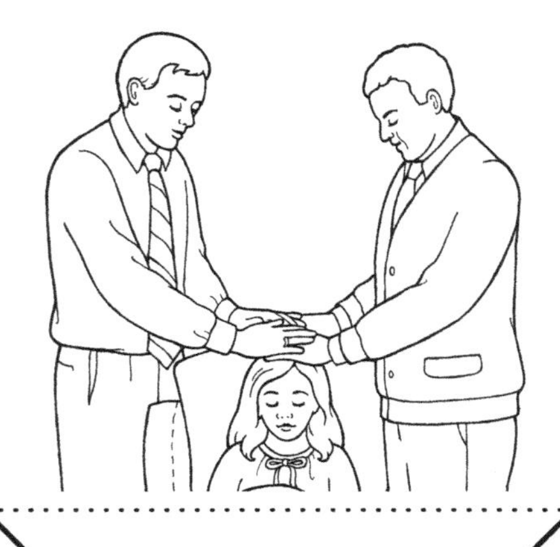

Doctrine and Covenants 85–87

Christmas Day is usually a time to ponder messages like "peace on earth" (see Luke 2:14). But on December 25, 1832, Joseph Smith's mind was occupied with the threat of war. The state of South Carolina in the United States had just defied the government and was preparing for battle. And the Lord revealed that this was only the beginning: "War," He declared, "will be poured out upon all nations" (Doctrine and Covenants 87:2). It seemed like this prophecy would be fulfilled very soon.

But then it wasn't. Within a few weeks, South Carolina and the United States government reached a compromise, and war was averted. Prophecy, however, is not always fulfilled at the time or in the way we expect. Nearly 30 years later, long after Joseph Smith was martyred, South Carolina rebelled and civil war followed. Today, war throughout the world continues to cause "the earth [to] mourn" (Doctrine and Covenants 87:6). The value of this revelation is less in predicting when calamity will come and more in teaching what to do when it comes. The counsel is the same in 1831, 1861, and 2025: "Stand ye in holy places, and be not moved" (verse 8).

 Ideas for Learning at Home and at Church

The Lord wants me "to keep a history."

Notice what the Lord wanted to be included in the "history" described in Doctrine and Covenants 85:1–2. Why do you think He wants His Saints to keep a history? What could you record about your "manner of life, [your] faith, and works" that might be a blessing to you and future generations? How might keeping a personal history help you come unto Christ?

See also "Journals: 'Of Far More Worth than Gold,'" *Teachings of Presidents of the Church: Wilford Woodruff* (2011), 125–33; "Turning Hearts" (video), ChurchofJesusChrist.org.

The scriptures describe the voice of the Spirit as a still, small voice.

The Spirit speaks with a "still small voice."

Ponder the words Joseph Smith used to describe the Spirit in Doctrine and Covenants 85:6. In what sense is the Spirit's voice "still" and "small"? Consider these additional descriptions given through Joseph Smith: Doctrine and Covenants 6:22–24; 8:2–3; 9:7–9; 11:12–13; 128:1. How does the Spirit speak to you?

See also Luke 24:32; Mosiah 5:2; Alma 32:28; Helaman 5:30; Doctrine and Covenants 6:22–23; 11:12–13.

Use object lessons. People remember a gospel lesson better when they see or participate in an object lesson related to what they are learning. For example, when teaching about the still, small voice of the Spirit, maybe you could play a recording of soft, sacred music, and learners could talk about how the music makes them feel and how much harder it would be to hear if there were distracting noises. This could lead to a discussion about distractions in our lives that keep us from hearing the still, small voice.

The righteous are gathered to Christ in the last days.

Doctrine and Covenants 86 contains an interpretation of the parable of the wheat and the tares, found in Matthew 13:24–30, 37–43. As you learn about the meaning of this parable, consider filling out a table like this one:

Symbols	Possible meanings	Questions to ponder
Sowers of the seed	Prophets and apostles	What kinds of "seeds" do prophets and apostles plant?
The enemy	Satan	How does the adversary try to stop the Lord's work?

Here are a few additional questions to consider:

- After interpreting the parable, the Lord spoke of priesthood, restoration, and the salvation of His people (see verses 8–11). What connections do you see between these themes and the parable of the wheat and the tares?

- What is your role in being a "light unto the Gentiles" and "a savior unto [the Lord's] people"? (verse 11).

DOCTRINE AND COVENANTS 87

📖 Peace is found in "holy places."

The prophecy in section 87 warns about physical dangers related to war in the last days. But the counsel in this revelation also applies to spiritual dangers. Ponder questions such as the following:

- A prophecy is a revelation from God to a prophet, often about the future. What are some examples of prophecies that ancient and modern prophets have given? (see John 3:14; Mosiah 3:5; Helaman 14:2–6). How were they fulfilled? (see Luke 23:33; Matthew 15:30–31; 3 Nephi 1:15–21).

- What are the blessings of accepting the prophecies of God's prophets?

With those thoughts in mind, read section 87. (For some historical context, you might also want to read the introduction to this outline.) What do you learn about prophecy from this revelation and the way it was fulfilled? What would you say to someone who doubts a prophecy because it is not fulfilled right away?

What counsel does the Lord give in verse 8? What are your "holy places" where you find peace and safety? What makes a place holy? In addition to physical locations, perhaps there are holy times, holy practices, or holy thoughts that can provide peace. For example, how can the words of God's prophets be a holy place for you? What does it mean to "stand" and "be not moved" from these places?

See also "Where Love Is," *Children's Songbook*, 138–39; *Saints*, 1:163–64; "Peace and War," in *Revelations in Context*, 158–64.

For more ideas, see this month's issues of the *Liahona* and *For the Strength of Youth* magazines.

 ## Ideas for Teaching Children

DOCTRINE AND COVENANTS 85:6

The Spirit speaks with a "still small voice."

- What would your children say if someone asked them how they know when the Holy Ghost speaks to them? Invite them to read about one way Joseph Smith described the Spirit's voice in Doctrine and Covenants 85:6. They could then practice listening to and speaking in a small voice. You might also share experiences when the Spirit spoke to you in a still, small voice.

- To help your children understand the phrase "still small voice," you could play a children's song quietly, such as "The Holy Ghost" (*Children's Songbook*, 105). Ask one of the children to guess what song it is while other children make distracting noises. Then you could repeat the song with no distractions. What distractions can we remove from our lives to feel the Spirit more often?

DOCTRINE AND COVENANTS 86

I can help gather God's people.

- To help your children understand the parable described in section 86, you could prepare several small pictures or drawings of wheat and hide them around the room. Explain to your children the parable of the wheat and the tares (see Matthew 13:24–30), and read together the Lord's commentary in Doctrine and Covenants 86:1–7. Your children could then gather the hidden pictures of wheat and write on them the name of someone they can "gather" to Jesus Christ. What does it mean to gather people to Jesus Christ? What are some ways we can do this?

DOCTRINE AND COVENANTS 86:11

I can be like a light to others.

- Here are some questions you can ask your children as you discuss Doctrine and Covenants 86:11: How does light bless us? What is it like when we have no light? How can we be a light to other people? Help your children think of ways we can "continue in [Jesus's] goodness" and share it with others.

DOCTRINE AND COVENANTS 87:6, 8

I can "stand . . . in holy places."

- Read together Doctrine and Covenants 87:6 to learn about things the Lord said would happen in the latter days. Then you could talk about some of the challenges you and your children face. In verse 8, what did the Lord say we can do during hard times?

- Help your children make a list of holy places, holy thoughts, and holy actions that can help them face spiritual danger. For ideas, see the videos "Standing in Holy Places" and "Stand Ye in Holy Places—Bloom Where You're Planted" (Gospel Library).

The temple is a holy place.

For more ideas, see this month's issue of the *Friend* magazine.

The Lord gathers His people like wheat.

My home can be a holy place (Doctrine and Covenants 87:8).

Write or draw things in the house that you can do to make your home a holy place.

The School of the Prophets was held in this room.

Doctrine and Covenants 88

Every so often, the Lord gives us a glimpse of His boundless "majesty and power" (Doctrine and Covenants 88:47) through stunning revelations. Doctrine and Covenants 88 is that kind of revelation—one about light and glory and kingdoms that can make our earthly cares seem small by comparison. Even if we can't comprehend it all, we can at least sense that there's far more to eternity than we ever realized. Of course, the Lord doesn't share these grand truths to intimidate us or make us feel small. In fact, He promised, "The day shall come when you *shall* comprehend even God" (verse 49; emphasis added). Perhaps it was to that glorious end that the Lord commanded His Saints in Kirtland to form the School of the Prophets. "Organize yourselves," He said. "Prepare every needful thing; and establish . . . a house of God" (verse 119). More than anywhere else, it is within God's holy house—and in our homes—that He can lift our vision beyond the mortal world, "unveil his face unto [us]," and prepare us to "abide a celestial glory" (verses 68, 22).

See *Saints*, 1:164–66.

 Ideas for Learning at Home and at Church

DOCTRINE AND COVENANTS 88

Jesus Christ offers me peace.

Just days after warning that war would be "poured out upon all nations" (Doctrine and Covenants 87:2), the Lord gave a revelation that Joseph Smith called an "olive leaf," which is a traditional symbol of peace (Doctrine and Covenants 88, section heading; see also Genesis 8:11). Throughout your study of section 88 this week, look for the Lord's messages of peace to you.

DOCTRINE AND COVENANTS 88:6–67

Light and law come from Jesus Christ.

The words *light* and *law* are repeated many times in section 88. Mark or note verses where you find these words in verses 6–67, and write down what you learn about light and law— and about Jesus Christ. What do you feel inspired to do to receive light and live the "law of Christ"? (verse 21).

See also Isaiah 60:19; John 1:1–9; 3 Nephi 15:9; Timothy J. Dyches, "Light Cleaveth unto Light," *Liahona*, May 2021, 112–15; Sharon Eubank, "Christ: The Light That Shines in Darkness," *Ensign* or *Liahona*, May 2019, 73–76.

The scriptures contain the law of Christ.

DOCTRINE AND COVENANTS 88:62–64

"Draw near unto me."

What experiences have shown you that the promises in these verses are true? What is your next step to "draw near unto" Christ? Consider making the hymn "Nearer, My God, to Thee" (*Hymns*, no. 100) part of your study and worship.

DOCTRINE AND COVENANTS 88:67–76

I can become clean through the Atonement of Jesus Christ.

The Lord's command to "sanctify yourselves" appears twice in section 88 (verses 68, 74). What do you think this phrase means? You might review some of the passages under "Sanctification" in the Guide to the Scriptures (Gospel Library). How do we become sanctified? Let this question guide your study of Doctrine and Covenants 88:67–76, and record any spiritual insights you gain.

DOCTRINE AND COVENANTS 88:77–80, 118–26

"Seek learning, even by study and also by faith."

The Lord told the Saints to establish a "school of the prophets" in Kirtland (Doctrine and Covenants 88:137). Much of the instruction in section 88 taught them how to do it. This instruction could also help you "establish . . . a house of learning" (verse 119) in your own life. In fact, you could look at verses 77–80 and 118–26 as blueprints to "remodel your home [or your life] into a center of gospel learning" and "a sanctuary of faith" (Russell M. Nelson, "Becoming Exemplary Latter-day Saints," *Ensign* or *Liahona*, Nov. 2018, 113). It could be interesting to sketch what your personal "remodel" might look like, including phrases from these verses that you feel you need to apply.

It might also help to explore these questions: *Why* are learning and education important to the Lord? *What* does He want me to study? *How* does He want me to learn? Look for answers to these questions in verses 77–80 and in "Truth will make you free" (*For the Strength of Youth: A Guide for Making Choices*, 30–33).

What do you think it means to learn "by study and also by faith"? (verse 118). What insights do you gain from Elder Mathias Held's message "Seeking Knowledge by the Spirit"? (*Ensign* or *Liahona*, May 2019, 31–33).

See also Topics and Questions, "Seeking Truth and Avoiding Deception," Gospel Library; "A School and an Endowment," in *Revelations in Context*, 174–82.

For more ideas, see this month's issues of the *Liahona* and *For the Strength of Youth* magazines.

 ## Ideas for Teaching Children

DOCTRINE AND COVENANTS 88:33

Heavenly Father gives good gifts.

- You could start a discussion about Doctrine and Covenants 88:33 by asking your children to talk about gifts they have been given—both those they received joyfully and others they did not. Maybe they could act out receiving a gift with joy. Then you could talk about gifts Heavenly Father gives us (such as the gift of the Holy Ghost). How do we receive these gifts with joy?

DOCTRINE AND COVENANTS 88:63

If I seek the Savior, I will find Him.

- Doctrine and Covenants 88:63 contains action words that might inspire some fun activities to encourage your children to seek the Lord's presence in their lives. For instance, can you and your children think of a game for discussing the phrase "*seek* me diligently and ye shall *find* me" (emphasis added) or "knock, and it shall be opened"?

Children need variety. "Most children learn best when multiple senses are involved. Find ways to help children use their senses of sight, hearing, and touch as they learn. In some situations, you may even find ways to include their senses of smell and taste!" (*Teaching in the Savior's Way*, 32).

- To emphasize the Savior's invitation to "draw near unto me," you could ask one child to hold a picture of Jesus (like the picture at the end of this outline) on one side of the room while the other children stand on the other side. As your children think of things they can do to come closer to the Savior, they can take a step toward the picture, and the child holding the picture could take a step toward the other children. Talk with your children about how you draw near to the Savior and how He draws near to you. You could also sing with them a song about this topic, like "I Feel My Savior's Love" (*Children's Songbook*, 74–75).

DOCTRINE AND COVENANTS 88:77–80, 118

Heavenly Father wants me to learn.

- Ask your children to tell you about what they are learning in school or Primary. You might also share some things you are learning. Then you could show your children the words *what*, *why*, and *how*. Help them search Doctrine and Covenants 88:77–79 to find out *what* the Lord wants us to learn about. Then look together in verse 80 to find out *why* He wants us to learn and in verse 118 to find out *how* we should learn.

"Seek learning . . . by study and also by faith."

DOCTRINE AND COVENANTS 88:119

Our home can be holy like the temple.

- As you read Doctrine and Covenants 88:119 to your children, they could make a temple spire with their arms every time they hear the word "house." Explain that Heavenly Father wanted Joseph Smith and the Saints to build a temple, or a "house of God."

- You could ask your children to choose seven words that describe their home. Then help them find, in Doctrine and Covenants 88:119, the seven words the Lord uses to describe His house. How can we make our home a "house of God"?

For more ideas, see this month's issue of the *Friend* magazine.

Be Not Afraid, by Michael Malm

Our home can be holy like the temple (see Doctrine and Covenants 88:119).

Cut out the puzzle on the dotted lines. As you put the puzzle together, think of ways you can make your home more like the temple.

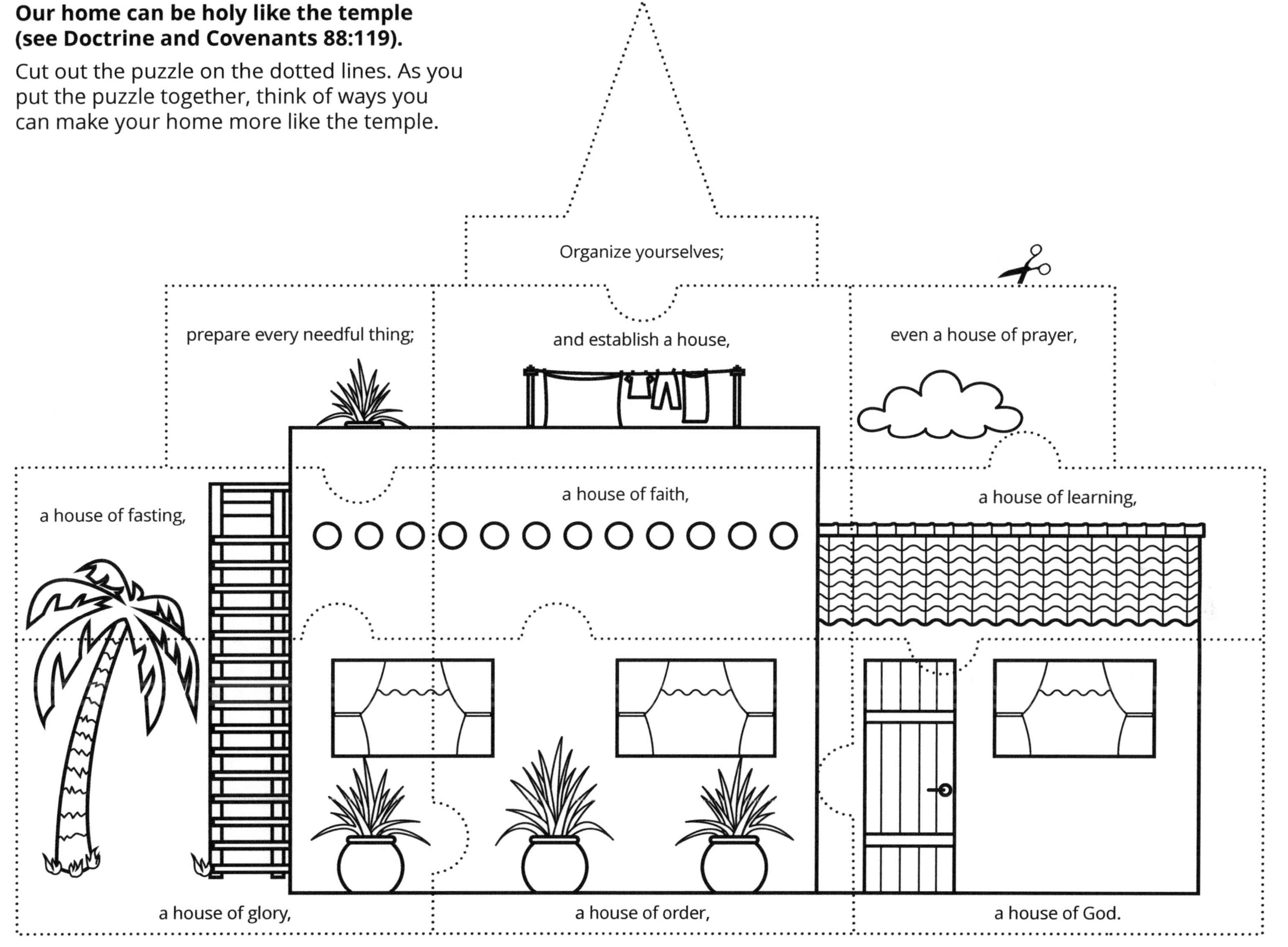

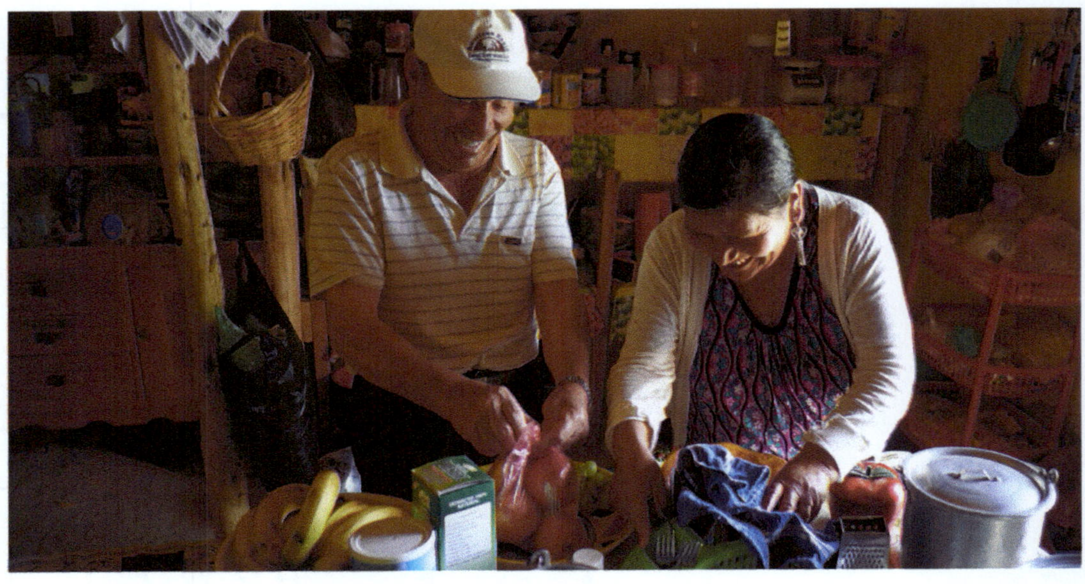

Doctrine and Covenants 89–92

In the School of the Prophets, the Prophet Joseph Smith taught the elders of Israel about building God's kingdom on earth. They discussed spiritual truths, prayed together, fasted, and prepared to preach the gospel. But there was something about the atmosphere that might seem odd to us today, and it didn't seem right to Emma Smith either. During the meetings, the men smoked and chewed tobacco, which wasn't unusual for the time, but it stained the wood floors black and left a strong odor in the air. Emma shared her concerns with Joseph, and Joseph asked the Lord. His response was a revelation that went far beyond smoke and tobacco stains. It gave the Saints, for generations to come, "a principle with promise"—promises of physical health, "wisdom," and "great treasures of knowledge" (Doctrine and Covenants 89:3, 19).

See also *Saints*, 1:166–68.

 Ideas for Learning at Home and at Church

DOCTRINE AND COVENANTS 89

 **The Lord gave me the Word of Wisdom to help me be healthy in body and spirit.**

When the elders in the School of the Prophets first heard Joseph Smith read the Word of Wisdom, they immediately "tossed their pipes and plugs of chewing tobacco into the fire" (*Saints*, 1:168). They wanted to show their willingness to obey the Lord. Perhaps you have already "tossed" from your life the substances the Word of Wisdom warns against, but what else can you learn from this revelation? Consider these ideas:

- Think of the revelation as "a principle with promise" (verse 3)—enduring truths that guide decision-making. What principles do you find that can guide your decisions? What blessings does the Lord promise? (see verses 18–21). How has He fulfilled those promises in your life?

- What examples have you seen of "evils and designs . . . in the hearts of conspiring men" related to the Word of Wisdom? (verse 4). In addition to this revelation, what has the Lord given to help you avoid or overcome these evils?

- What does this revelation teach you about the Lord? How does the Word of Wisdom relate to Doctrine and Covenants 29:34–35?

- What are you prompted to do to better care for your body?

You may have had opportunities to explain to others why you live the Word of Wisdom—and you may have more opportunities in the future. Consider how you might use these opportunities to testify of the Savior, the sacredness of our bodies, and other spiritual truths. For ideas, see "Your body is sacred," *For the Strength of Youth: A Guide for Making Choices*, 22–29.

See also 1 Corinthians 6:19–20; Thomas S. Monson, "Principles and Promises," *Ensign* or *Liahona*, Nov. 2016, 78–79; Topics and Questions, "Word of Wisdom," Gospel Library; "The Word of Wisdom," in *Revelations in Context*, 183–91; "Addiction," "Physical Health," Life Help, Gospel Library.

Learn and teach through principles. Rather than creating lists of dos and don'ts, we can live by principles to exercise our agency and faith in Christ. For example, consider principle-based questions like these regarding the Word of Wisdom: Which principles can give encouragement to someone who struggles to obey the Word of Wisdom? Which principles can comfort me when I have health problems despite living the Word of Wisdom?

Heavenly Father wants us to take care of our bodies.

DOCTRINE AND COVENANTS 90:1–17

DOCTRINE AND COVENANTS 90:1–17

The First Presidency holds the "keys of the kingdom."

In section 90, the Lord gave instructions about "the ministry and presidency" (verse 12) of Joseph Smith, Sidney Rigdon, and Frederick G. Williams—members of what we now call the First Presidency. What do you learn about the First Presidency from verses 1–17? Consider reviewing recent messages from members of the First Presidency. What do they do to "set in order all the affairs of this church and kingdom"? (verse 16). How can you show that they are not "a light thing" to you? (verse 5).

Consider singing or reading the words to "Come, Listen to a Prophet's Voice" (*Hymns*, no. 21) or another song about prophets that relates to teachings in these verses. How has the service of the First Presidency helped you know Heavenly Father and Jesus Christ?

DOCTRINE AND COVENANTS 90:24

"All things shall work together for [my] good."

Ponder any experiences you have had that testify of the Lord's promise in Doctrine and Covenants 90:24. Consider recording your experiences and sharing them with a family member or loved one—maybe someone who needs reassurance or encouragement. If you are still waiting for certain blessings, ponder what you can do to remain faithful as you wait to see how "all things shall work together for your good."

DOCTRINE AND COVENANTS 91

"The Spirit manifesteth truth."

We all encounter messages that contain "many things . . . that are true" and "many things . . . that are not true" (Doctrine and Covenants 91:1–2). What counsel do you find in section 91 that can help you discern truth in the messages you encounter? How has the Spirit helped you discern truth from error?

For more ideas, see this month's issues of the *Liahona* and *For the Strength of Youth* magazines.

 Ideas for Teaching Children

DOCTRINE AND COVENANTS 89

The Word of Wisdom helps me be healthy in body and spirit.

- To introduce section 89, perhaps you and your children could look at a picture of a temple or sing a song about physical health, such as "The Lord Gave Me a Temple" (*Children's Songbook*, 153), to teach that our bodies are like temples for our spirits. Help your children act out ways they can care for their bodies.

- To learn about the Lord's commandments in Doctrine and Covenants 89:10–17, you and your children could draw or look at pictures of good things we can eat or do to keep our bodies healthy (see the picture and activity page at the end of this outline). What has the Lord warned us not to use? Why does He want us to care for our bodies?

- Elder Gary E. Stevenson counseled young people to plan in advance what they will do when tempted with alcohol or drugs. He taught: "You will find that temptation has less control over you. You will have already made the decision of how you will react and what you will do. You won't need to decide every time" ("Your Priesthood Playbook," *Ensign* or *Liahona*, May 2019, 48). After reading together Doctrine and Covenants 89:4 and Elder Stevenson's statement, counsel with your children about how they can decide now—for the rest of their lives—to live the Word of Wisdom. You could even role-play how they might respond if someone, even a friend, offers them something that is against the Word of Wisdom. How does the Lord bless us as we obey the Word of Wisdom? (see verses 18–21).

Our bodies are gifts from God.

God gives me prophets to guide and protect me.

- You could look at pictures of ancient prophets or sing a song like "Follow the Prophet" (*Children's Songbook*, 110–11). How has God blessed His children through His prophets? Why should we listen to God's prophets? (see Doctrine and Covenants 90:5). Then you and your children could look at a picture of the living prophet and share some things the Lord has taught or warned us about through him. How can we follow the prophet?

DOCTRINE AND COVENANTS 91

The Spirit can help me know what is true.

- You could summarize the section heading for Doctrine and Covenants 91 to help your children understand why this revelation was given. They could then think of places, such as in the media, where we find "many things . . . that are true" and "many things . . . that are not true" (verses 1–2). What do verses 4–6 teach us about the Holy Ghost? How does the Holy Ghost help us know what is right?

For more ideas, see this month's issue of the *Friend* magazine.

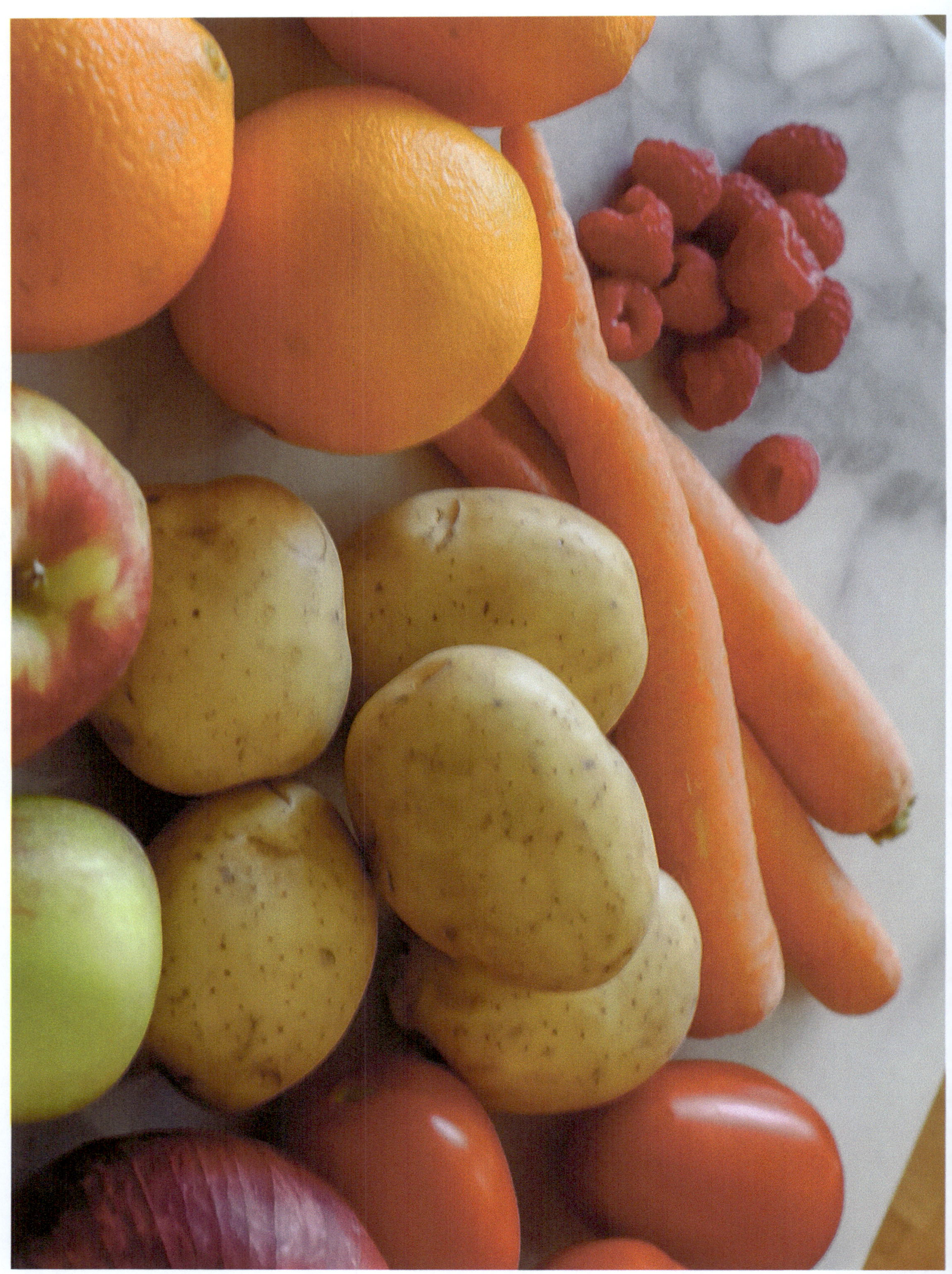

"All grain is good for the food of man; as also the fruit of the vine."

The Word of Wisdom helps me be healthy in body and spirit (Doctrine and Covenants 89).

Cut out the cards, mix them up, and place them face down. Turn over two cards at a time. If the pictures match, set the cards aside and say whether the things in the picture are good or bad for your body. If the cards don't match, turn them back over and try again. Discuss the blessings Heavenly Father will give us if we obey the Word of Wisdom (see verses 18–21).

Doctrine and Covenants 93

"When you climb up a ladder," Joseph Smith taught, "you must begin at the bottom, and ascend step by step, until you arrive at the top; and so it is with the principles of the gospel—you must begin with the first, and go on until you learn all the principles of exaltation" (*Teachings of Presidents of the Church: Joseph Smith* [2007], 268).

Sometimes that ladder of exaltation seems impossibly high, but we were born to climb to the top with the Savior's constant help. Whatever limitations we may see in ourselves, Heavenly Father and His Son see something glorious in us, something godlike. Just as Jesus Christ "was in the beginning with the Father," so "ye were also" (Doctrine and Covenants 93:21, 23). Just as He "continued from grace to grace, until he received a fulness," so also "you shall receive grace for grace" (verses 13, 20). The restored gospel teaches about the true nature of God, and so it also teaches about your true nature and destiny. You are a literal child of God with the potential to "in due time receive of his fulness" (verse 19).

 Ideas for Learning at Home and at Church

Like Jesus Christ, I can be glorified and receive God's "fulness."

The Prophet Joseph Smith taught, "If men do not comprehend the character of God, they do not comprehend themselves" (*Teachings: Joseph Smith*, 40). As you learn about the Savior by studying Doctrine and Covenants 93, look for what you also learn about yourself. For example, what do you learn about Him from verses 3, 12–13, 21, and 26? What similar truths do you find about yourself in verses 20, 23, and 28–29? (see also 1 John 3:2; 3 Nephi 27:27). The following questions may help you understand and apply the truths in this section:

- What do you feel it means to receive "grace for grace" and to continue "from grace to grace"? (verses 12–13). If it helps, you could read "Grace" in Guide to the Scriptures (Gospel Library).

- What do you discover in this revelation about how God helps you grow and learn? How does knowing this affect the way you treat others—and yourself?

- What do you learn about "how to worship, and . . . what you worship"? (verse 19; see also Guide to the Scriptures, "Worship," Gospel Library).

The glory of God is light and truth.

You might notice that words like *glory*, *light*, and *truth* appear frequently in this revelation. As you study verses 20–39 in particular, list the truths you learn about these concepts. Making a table like this one might help:

Verse	What I learn	Questions to ponder
24		There are many deceptions in the world. How can I know the truth? (see also Jacob 4:13).
28		
36	God is a being of light and truth.	
37		Who do I know that seems to be able to resist evil influences? Why are they able to do this?
See also: Doctrine and Covenants 50:24		

What do you find in these verses that inspires you to seek greater light and truth? Why are *light* and *truth* good titles for Jesus Christ? (see John 8:12; 14:6). How do these truths affect your life?

You might also make note of promises about your eternal destiny in verses 20, 22, 28, 33–35. What is the relationship between these promises and obtaining light?

Consider searching "Walk in God's light" (*For the Strength of Youth: A Guide for Making Choices*, 18–21) to find out what you can do to obtain light and how the Lord promises to bless you. The videos "Light and Truth, Part 1" and "Part 2" (Gospel Library) may provide additional ideas.

See also "Teach Me to Walk in the Light," *Hymns*, no. 304; Topics and Questions, "Holy Ghost," Gospel Library.

DOCTRINE AND COVENANTS 93:40–50

"Set in order your own house."

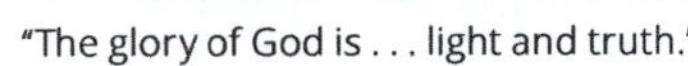

"The glory of God is . . . light and truth."

The command to "set in order your own house" (verse 43) isn't about organizing cupboards and closets but about teaching—and learning—"light and truth" (verse 42). Consider how you are trying to follow this counsel. What challenges do you face? Which truths in Doctrine and Covenants 93 can help?

See also David A. Bednar, "More Diligent and Concerned at Home," *Ensign* or *Liahona*, Nov. 2009, 17–20; Henry B. Eyring, "A Home Where the Spirit of the Lord Dwells," *Ensign* or *Liahona*, May 2019, 22–25.

For more ideas, see this month's issues of the *Liahona* and *For the Strength of Youth* magazines.

Ideas for Teaching Children

The Lord commands parents to "bring up [their] children in light and truth.

DOCTRINE AND COVENANTS 93:2–21

Jesus Christ is the Light and Life of the World.

• Consider showing a picture of the Savior and asking your children why it is important to learn about and follow Jesus Christ. Then you could read together Doctrine and Covenants 93:19 to discover one important reason.

• You may want to choose several truths about Christ in section 93 that are inspiring to you and help your children discover and understand them (see also "Chapter 33: A Revelation about Jesus Christ," in *Doctrine and Covenants Stories*, 126–27, or the corresponding video in Gospel Library). For each truth you choose, you could give your children a word or phrase to listen for as you read the verse together. For example, Jesus Christ:

- Did the works of the Father (verse 5).

- Is the Light of the World (verse 9).

- Is the Creator of the world (verse 10).

- Received all power in heaven and on earth (verse 17).

- Was with God in the beginning (verse 21).

DOCTRINE AND COVENANTS 93:23, 29, 38

I lived with Heavenly Father before I came to earth.

- The Savior emphasized three times in section 93 that we lived with God "in the beginning" (verses 23, 29, 38). To help your children discover this, you could invite them to read Doctrine and Covenants 93:23, 29, 38 and look for a truth about themselves that is repeated in these verses. Why does Heavenly Father want us to know this truth? You might also ask your children what they know about our life with Heavenly Father before we were born. To help them learn more, read with them one or more of the following scripture passages: Jeremiah 1:5; Doctrine and Covenants 138:53–56; Moses 3:5; Abraham 3:22–26.

- You could also sing together "I Am a Child of God" or "I Lived in Heaven" (*Children's Songbook*, 2–3, 4) and discuss truths we learn from these songs about our purpose for coming to earth.

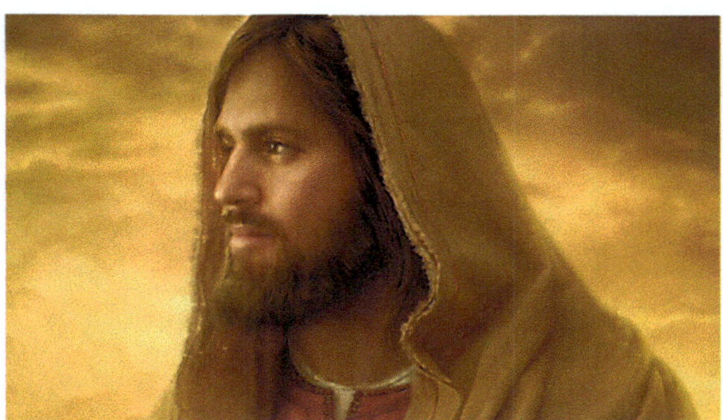

Detail from *Light of the World*, by Howard Lyon

DOCTRINE AND COVENANTS 93:24–39

I receive light and truth as I obey God.

- To help your children apply the truths about obedience in Doctrine and Covenants 93, consider writing a few scripture references from this section on pieces of paper. On different pieces of paper, write the truths that each of these verses teaches. Your children could work together to read the verses and match the truths to the scripture references. Examples could include:

  - Verse 24: Truth is knowing things that are real in the past, present, and future.

  - Verse 28: I can receive light and truth as I keep the commandments.

  - Verse 37: When I have light and truth, I am able to resist evil.

  - Verse 39: I lose light and truth when I am disobedient.

You may want to share examples of truths you have come to know as you have kept the commandments of the Lord.

Adapt to the ages of your children. You know the needs and abilities of your children; feel free to adapt the activity ideas to meet their needs. For example, in this activity, if you are teaching young children, it may be better to focus on one simple truth from section 93.

For more ideas, see this month's issue of the *Friend* magazine.

Light and Truth, by Simon Dewey

Jesus Christ is the Light and Life of the World (Doctrine and Covenants 93:2–21).

Color the pictures and cut out the rectangle on the solid line. To make a booklet, fold the rectangle in half on the horizontal dotted line, and then fold it in half again.

Doctrine and Covenants 94–97

Anciently, the Lord commanded Moses to build a tabernacle "according to the pattern shewed to [him] in the mount" (Hebrews 8:5; see also Exodus 25:8–9). The tabernacle was to be the center of Israel's wilderness camp (see Numbers 2:1–2).

In 1833, the Lord commanded Joseph Smith to build temples "not after the manner of the world" but rather "after the manner which I shall show" (Doctrine and Covenants 95:13–14; see also 97:10). Like the tabernacle in the wilderness, the temple was meant to be a central feature in Kirtland (see Doctrine and Covenants 94:1).

Today, temples are found around the world. Even if they aren't at the center of our cities, they point us to Christ, who should be the center of our lives. Though each temple differs in appearance, within them we learn the same divine pattern—a heavenly plan to bring us back into the presence of God. Sacred ordinances and covenants connect us to Christ and strengthen our families "not after the manner of the world" but after the pattern God shows us.

See *Saints*, 1:169–70; "A House for Our God," in *Revelations in Context*, 165–73.

 Ideas for Learning at Home and at Church

DOCTRINE AND COVENANTS 94; 97:10–17

I can be "wholly dedicated unto the Lord."

In Doctrine and Covenants 94, the Lord gives instructions about constructing administrative buildings in Kirtland—an office and a printing house. What impresses you about what the Lord says about these buildings in Doctrine and Covenants 94:2–12? How does it compare with what He says about the temple in 97:10–17?

What does it mean to you to be "wholly dedicated unto the Lord"?

DOCTRINE AND COVENANTS 95

The Lord chastens those He loves.

When the revelation in section 95 was received, about five months had passed since the Lord commanded the Saints to build a house of God (see Doctrine and Covenants 88:117–19)—and they hadn't started yet. Notice how the Lord corrected them in this revelation. You might even make a list of principles you find for giving inspired correction. What do you learn about the Lord from the way He corrected His Saints?

See also Doctrine and Covenants 121:43–44; D. Todd Christofferson, "As Many as I Love, I Rebuke and Chasten," *Ensign* or *Liahona*, May 2011, 97–100.

DOCTRINE AND COVENANTS 95:8, 11–17; 97:10–17

📖 The temple is the house of the Lord.

After being chastised for not building a house of the Lord in Kirtland, Church leaders chose a site in a wheat field where they would build. Hyrum Smith, the Prophet's brother, immediately ran to get a scythe to begin clearing the field. "We are preparing to build a house for the Lord," he said, "and I am determined to be the first at the work" (in *Teachings of Presidents of the Church: Joseph Smith* [2007], 271, 273). Why do you think Hyrum was so eager to build the temple? Ponder this as you read Doctrine and Covenants 95:8, 11–17; 97:10–17.

In our day, the Lord "is accelerating the pace at which we are building temples" (Russell M. Nelson, "Focus on the Temple," *Liahona*, Nov. 2022, 121). If someone asked you why the Church of Jesus Christ builds so many temples, what would you say? Look for possible answers in:

- President Russell M. Nelson's messages announcing new temples (such as "Now Is the Time," *Liahona*, May 2022, 126).

- "Why Latter-day Saints Build Temples" (temples.ChurchofJesusChrist.org).

- The video "Temples" (Gospel Library).

You might compare the Saints' efforts to build the Kirtland Temple to your efforts to prepare for meaningful experiences with the Lord in the temple. How can you show the same sense of urgency that Hyrum Smith felt toward the Lord's holy house? For example, what could you do that would be like clearing the field, as Hyrum did? What sacrifices do you feel the Lord wants you to make? (see Doctrine and Covenants 97:12).

See also "Holy Temples on Mount Zion," *Hymns*, no. 289; Topics and Questions, "Temples," Gospel Library.

Hyrum Smith clearing land for the Kirtland Temple.

DOCTRINE AND COVENANTS 97:8–9

"They are accepted of me."

Think about a time when you were accepted—or not accepted—into a group or team. How is that similar to or different from what Doctrine and Covenants 97:8–9 teaches about what it means to be accepted of the Lord? What do you think the Lord is trying to teach you with the metaphor in verse 9?

See also Erich W. Kopischke, "Being Accepted of the Lord," *Ensign* or *Liahona*, May 2013, 104–6.

Create a spiritual environment for learning and teaching. "The Holy Ghost," Jesus promised, "shall teach you all things" (John 14:26). So whether you're learning on your own or with others, make it a priority to invite the Spirit. Sacred music, prayer, and loving interactions can all help create a peaceful, spiritual setting where the Holy Ghost can teach you truth.

DOCTRINE AND COVENANTS 97:18–28

Zion is "the pure in heart."

To the Saints in the 1830s, Zion was a place. In the revelation in section 97, the Lord expanded the definition to describe a people—"the pure in heart" (verse 21). As you read verses 18–28, you could substitute this definition when you read the word *Zion*. What does it mean to you to be pure in heart?

See also Moses 7:18.

For more ideas, see this month's issues of the *Liahona* and *For the Strength of Youth* magazines.

 Ideas for Teaching Children

DOCTRINE AND COVENANTS 95:8; 97:10–17

The temple is the house of the Lord.

- For some background on sections 95 and 97, you could share with your children "The Kirtland Temple" in *Doctrine and Covenants Stories for Young Readers* (Gospel Library; see also *Saints*, 1:210). Your children might enjoy pretending they are helping to build the Kirtland Temple (cutting wood, hammering nails, painting walls, and so on). You could also show them a picture of the Kirtland Temple, like those in this outline, while you read Doctrine and Covenants 95:8 to teach your children why the Lord wants us to build temples.

- After reading together Doctrine and Covenants 97:15–16, you and your children could share with each other why the temple is special to you. You could also sing together a song to help your children feel reverence for the Lord's house, such as "I Love to See the Temple" (*Children's Songbook*, 95). Why is the temple sacred?

DOCTRINE AND COVENANTS 97:1–2, 8–9, 21

Zion is "the pure in heart."

- To help your children understand what the word *pure* could mean in Doctrine and Covenants 97:21, you could look at a glass of clean water together and add something to the water that makes it impure (such as dirt or pepper). Why is it important for water to be pure? Then your children could read verse 21 and put their finger on the word *pure*. What does it mean for our hearts to be pure? Verses 1–2 and 8–9 could provide some ideas. How does the Savior help make our hearts pure?

Heavenly Father wants me to be pure in heart.

DOCTRINE AND COVENANTS 97:8–9

The Lord blesses people who keep covenants with Him.

- Do your children know what covenants we make with the Lord when we are baptized or in the temple? Consider reviewing those covenants with them by reading Mosiah 18:9–10, 13 or *General Handbook*, 27.2. Share with each other how you are striving to "observe [your] covenants by sacrifice" (Doctrine and Covenants 97:8).

- You could invite your children to draw pictures of what Doctrine and Covenants 97:9 describes. As they share their pictures, talk about how the Lord has blessed you for keeping your covenants. How are those blessings like being a "fruitful tree which is planted . . . by a pure stream"?

For more ideas, see this month's issue of the *Friend* magazine.

Building the Kirtland Temple, by Walter Rane

The temple is the house of the Lord (Doctrine and Covenants 95:8; 97:15–16).

Color the Kirtland Temple, and then cut around the edges. Fold the temple on the dotted lines and tape the sides and the roof together to make a model of the temple.

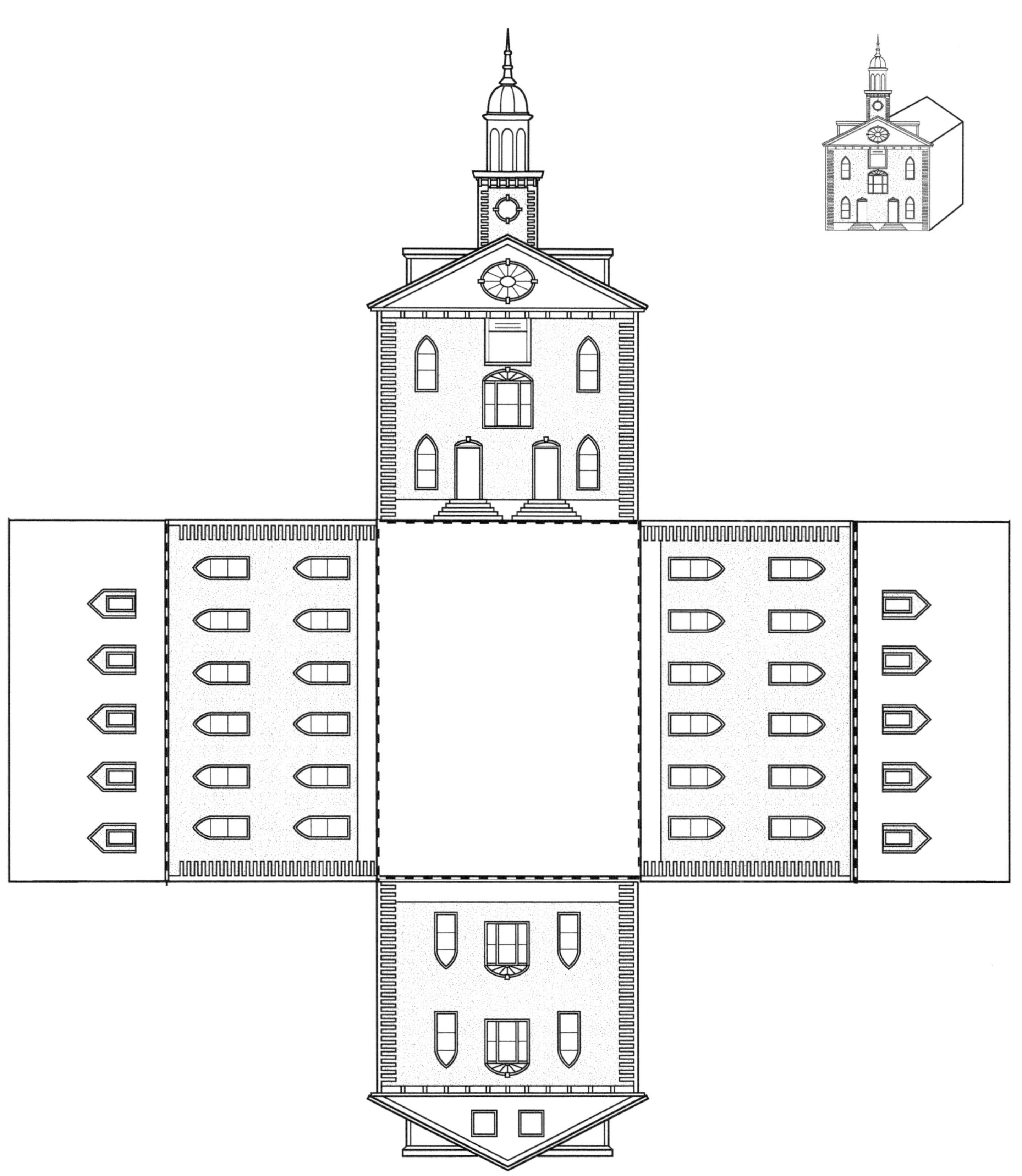

C.C.A. Christensen (1831–1912), *Saints Driven from Jackson County Missouri*, c. 1878, tempera on muslin, 77 ¼ x 113 inches. Brigham Young University Museum of Art,

Doctrine and Covenants 98–101

For the Saints in the 1830s, Independence, Missouri, was literally the promised land. It was "the center place" of Zion (Doctrine and Covenants 57:3)—the city of God on earth—and the gathering of Saints there was an exciting prelude to the Second Coming. But their neighbors in the area saw things differently. They objected to the claim that God had given the land to the Saints, and they were uncomfortable with the political, economic, and social consequences of so many unfamiliar people moving in so quickly. Discomfort soon turned into persecution and violence. In 1833, the Church's printing office was destroyed, and the Saints were forced from their homes.

Joseph Smith was more than 800 miles away in Kirtland, and this news took weeks to reach him. But the Lord knew what was happening, and He revealed to His Prophet principles of peace and encouragement that would comfort the Saints—principles that can also help us when we face persecution, when our righteous desires go unfulfilled, or when we need a reminder that our daily afflictions will eventually, somehow, "work together for [our] good" (Doctrine and Covenants 98:3).

See *Saints*, 1:171–93; "Waiting for the Word of the Lord," in *Revelations in Context*, 196–201.

 Ideas for Learning at Home and at Church

DOCTRINE AND COVENANTS 98:1–3, 11–14, 22; 101:1–16, 22–31, 36

My trials can work together for my good.

Some of our challenges in life are caused by our own choices. Others are caused by the choices of others. And sometimes things just happen that are part of mortality. Regardless of the cause, adversity can help fulfill divine purposes as we turn to God.

This was true for the Saints in Missouri in 1833, and it's true for us today. As you read what the Lord told the Saints in Doctrine and Covenants 98 and 101, ponder how His message applies to the various trials or difficulties you might have. Here are some questions and resources to help you.

If a trial is a result of:

- **Personal choices:** What counsel—and promises—do you find in Doctrine and Covenants 98:11–12; 101:1–9? What do you learn from these verses about Heavenly Father and Jesus Christ? What do you feel God would have you do?

- **The choices of others:** What comfort do you find in Doctrine and Covenants 98:1–3, 22; 101:10–16, 22? How does the Lord want us to respond to abuse, bullying, or violence? (See Life Help, "Abuse," Gospel Library; Topics and Questions, "Abuse," Gospel Library.) What do these verses teach about how to put your trust in the Lord?

- **The difficulties of mortality:** What perspective do you gain from Doctrine and Covenants 98:1–3; 101:22–31, 36? What are you learning from your trials? What are you doing to invite God's help? How is He helping you?

To learn more about how God can make "all things wherewith you have been afflicted . . . work together for your good" (Doctrine and Covenants 98:3), consider studying Elder Anthony D. Perkins's message "Remember Thy Suffering Saints, O Our God" (*Liahona*, Nov. 2021, 103–5). You might look for a passage in his message that helps you understand how the Savior invites you to view your challenges. In what ways have your trials worked together for your good or accomplished God's purposes?

See also Romans 8:28; 2 Nephi 2:2; Doctrine and Covenants 90:24; D. Todd Christofferson, "Come to Zion," *Ensign* or *Liahona*, Nov. 2008, 37–40; "Trial of Adversity," "Feeling the Lord's Love and Goodness in Trials," "The Refiner's Fire" (videos), ChurchofJesusChrist.org.

DOCTRINE AND COVENANTS 98:23–48

The Lord wants me to seek peace in His way.

While not everything in Doctrine and Covenants 98:23–48 will apply to your personal interactions with others, what principles do you find that can guide you to end personal conflicts in your life? You could find additional truths in a song about peace or forgiveness, such as "Truth Reflects upon Our Senses" (*Hymns*, no. 273).

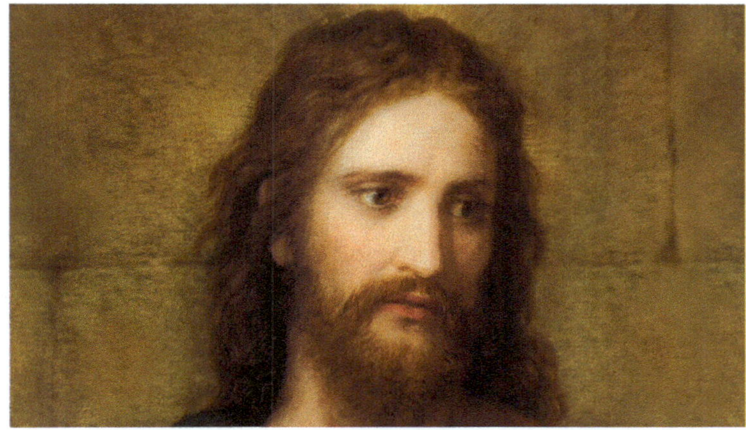

Detail from *Christ and the Rich Young Ruler*, by Heinrich Hofmann

DOCTRINE AND COVENANTS 99–100

The Lord takes care of people who serve Him.

The revelations in sections 99 and 100 were given to people who had important Church responsibilities but were also concerned about their families. What do you find in these revelations that could have helped them? What message does the Lord have for you in these revelations?

See also "John Murdock's Missions to Missouri" in "'I Quit Other Business': Early Missionaries" and "A Mission to Canada," in *Revelations in Context*, 87–89, 202–7.

DOCTRINE AND COVENANTS 101:43–65

Following God's counsel helps keep me safe.

The parable in Doctrine and Covenants 101:43–62 explains why the Lord allowed the Saints to be driven out of Zion. As you read these verses, do you see any ways you are like the servants in the parable? How do you show God that you're "willing to be guided in a right and proper way for [your] salvation"? (see verses 63–65).

Act out accounts or parables. Sometimes it's easier to learn from and relate to stories and parables in the scriptures when we put ourselves in the place of the people they describe. If you're teaching Doctrine and Covenants 101:43–62, you might invite learners to act out the parable as someone reads it aloud. What insights do you gain from putting actions to the words?

For more ideas, see this month's issues of the *Liahona* and *For the Strength of Youth* magazines.

Ideas for Teaching Children

DOCTRINE AND COVENANTS 98:1–3

Jesus Christ can turn my trials into blessings.

- You might begin a discussion by asking your children about some of the challenges that children their age face. You could then read together Doctrine and Covenants 98:1–3 and talk about how Jesus Christ can turn trials into blessings. You might share with your children examples of how He has turned your trials into blessings.

DOCTRINE AND COVENANTS 98:39–40

The Savior helps me forgive.

Note: As you teach your children the importance of forgiveness, make sure they also understand that if someone hurts them, they should always tell a trusted adult.

- Chapters 34 and 35 in *Doctrine and Covenants Stories* (128–34) could help you teach about how the Saints were treated in Missouri in 1833. You and your children could talk about how these Saints might have felt. Then you could read together Doctrine and Covenants 98:23, 39–40 to find out what the Lord wanted them to do. You and your children could talk about times you needed to forgive someone and how the Savior helped you.

- You could also show your children pictures of a happy face and a sad face. Talk about situations in which someone is unkind, and suggest ways to respond. Help your children choose if each response would make them happy or sad by pointing to the corresponding face. Why does Jesus want us to forgive people, even those who are not nice to us?

DOCTRINE AND COVENANTS 101:16, 23–32

Jesus Christ can bring me peace.

- After reading Doctrine and Covenants 101:16, help your children recognize the peaceful feelings that come when we are being still and thinking about Jesus—for example, when we are praying or taking the sacrament. You could also sing together a song about reverence, such as "Reverently, Quietly" or "To Think about Jesus" (*Children's Songbook*, 26, 71). How can we feel His peace in our home?

- Your children might be interested in learning about what life will be like when Jesus Christ comes again. Read Doctrine and Covenants 101:23–32 together, and talk about things they find in these verses that will bring us joy when He comes. Why is it helpful to know about these things when we are having a hard time?

Jesus Christ will bring peace and joy when He comes again.

For more ideas, see this month's issue of the *Friend* magazine.

Missouri Burning, by Glen S. Hopkinson

Thinking of Jesus can bring me peace (Doctrine and Covenants 101:16).

Color and cut out the picture viewer and the picture strips. Tape the two picture strips together to form one long strip. Cut two slits along the dotted lines of the picture viewer. Slide the picture strip through the viewfinder to see things about Jesus Christ that you can think about to feel peace.

C.C.A. Christensen (1831–1912), *Zion's Camp*, c. 1878, tempera on muslin, 78 x 114 inches. Brigham Young University Museum of Art, gift of the grandchildren of C.C.A. Christensen, 1970.

Doctrine and Covenants 102–105

The Saints in Kirtland were heartbroken to hear that their brothers and sisters in Jackson County, Missouri, were being driven from their homes. It must have been encouraging, then, when the Lord declared that "the redemption of Zion" would "come by power" (Doctrine and Covenants 103:15). With that promise in their hearts, over 200 men and about 25 women and children enlisted in what they called the Camp of Israel, later known as Zion's Camp. Its mission was to march to Missouri and redeem Zion.

To the members of the camp, redeeming Zion meant restoring the Saints to their land. But just before they arrived in Jackson County, the Lord told Joseph Smith to disband Zion's Camp. Some members of the camp were confused and upset; it seemed the expedition had failed and the Lord's promises were not fulfilled. Others, however, saw it differently. While the exiled Saints did not get their lands and homes back, the experience did bring a degree of "redemption" to Zion, and it did "come by power." Faithful members of Zion's Camp, many of whom later became leaders of the Church, testified that the experience deepened their faith in God's power, in Joseph Smith's divine call, and in Zion—not just Zion the place but Zion the people of God. Rather than questioning the value of this seemingly unsuccessful task, they learned that the real task is to follow the Savior, even when we don't understand everything. This is how Zion, ultimately, will be redeemed.

See *Saints*, 1:194–206; "The Acceptable Offering of Zion's Camp," in *Revelations in Context*, 213–18.

 Ideas for Learning at Home and at Church

What is the purpose of membership councils?

Section 102 contains the minutes of the meeting in Kirtland, Ohio, where the first high council of the Church was organized. In verses 12–23, the Lord describes procedures that high councils follow when holding membership councils for those who have committed serious transgressions.

President M. Russell Ballard taught: "Members sometimes ask why Church [membership] councils are held. The purpose is threefold: to save the soul of the transgressor, to protect the innocent, and to safeguard the Church's purity, integrity, and good name" ("A Chance to Start Over: Church Disciplinary Councils and the Restoration of Blessings," *Ensign*, Sept. 1990, 15).

See also Topics and Questions, "Membership Councils," Gospel Library.

DOCTRINE AND COVENANTS 103:1–12, 36; 105:1–19

Zion can be built only on principles of righteousness.

Why did the Saints lose their promised land in Missouri? There may have been many reasons—at least one, the Lord said, was "the transgressions of my people." If not for that, Zion "might have been redeemed" (Doctrine and Covenants 105:2). As you read Doctrine and Covenants 103:1–12, 36; 105:1–19, you may notice some things that hindered the establishment of Zion in Missouri and others that could have helped. What do you learn that can help you establish Zion in your heart, home, and community?

DOCTRINE AND COVENANTS 103:12–13, 36; 105:1–6, 9–19

Blessings come after trials of faith.

In many ways, participating in Zion's Camp was a trial of faith. The journey was long, the weather was hot, and food and water were sometimes scarce. And after all they endured, Zion's Camp was still unsuccessful in returning the Saints to their land. Imagine you had the opportunity to write a letter to a member of Zion's Camp whose faith in the Lord was shaken by his or her experience. What might you say to encourage this person? What truths do you find in Doctrine and Covenants 103:5–7, 12–13, 36; 105:1–6, 9–19 that could help?

The Camp of Israel camped along the banks of Little Fishing River.

Then you might think about a more modern example of a trial like Zion's Camp—such as a missionary who works hard, but no one joins the Church because of his or her efforts. Based on what you've studied, how would you help that missionary see that his or her mission was still successful?

How has the Lord blessed you "after much tribulation"? (Doctrine and Covenants 103:12).

See also 1 Nephi 11:16–17; Alma 7:11–12; Doctrine and Covenants 6:33–36; 84:88; 101:35–36; David A. Bednar, "On the Lord's Side: Lessons from Zion's Camp," *Ensign*, July 2017, 26–35, or *Liahona*, July 2017, 14–23; Topics and Questions, "Endure to the End," Gospel Library; "How Firm a Foundation," *Hymns*, no. 85.

Prepare by studying the historical context of the revelations. Understanding the setting of the revelations in the Doctrine and Covenants may help you understand and apply the principles they teach. *Come, Follow Me* provides links to many of these resources. For Doctrine and Covenants 102–5, see *Saints*, 1:194–206; "The Acceptable Offering of Zion's Camp," in *Revelations in Context*, 213–18; and "Voices of the Restoration: Zion's Camp."

The Lord has made me a "steward over earthly blessings."

In addition to trials in Missouri, in 1834 the Church faced financial difficulties, including heavy debts and expenses. In section 104 the Lord gave counsel on the Church's financial situation. How can you apply the principles in verses 11–18 and 78–83 to your own financial decisions?

See also "Treasure in Heaven: The John Tanner Story" and "The Labor of His Hands" (videos), Gospel Library.

For more ideas, see this month's issues of the *Liahona* and *For the Strength of Youth* magazines.

Ideas for Teaching Children

DOCTRINE AND COVENANTS 103:9

I can be "a light unto the world" by following Jesus.

- You could invite your children to hold pictures of a light bulb, a candle, or another source of light while you read Doctrine and Covenants 103:9. How can we be like a light to others when we follow Jesus Christ? See also "Jesus Wants Me for a Sunbeam" (*Children's Songbook*, 60–61).

I can be like a light to others when I follow Jesus Christ.

DOCTRINE AND COVENANTS 104:13–18

The Lord wants me to share what I have with people in need.

- You may want to give your children a few minutes to make a list of blessings God has given them (such as food, clothing, talents, faith, and a home). Encourage them to list as many as they can. Then you could read together Doctrine and Covenants 104:13–18, looking for answers to questions like these: Who is the true owner of all things? What does He want us to do with these things? You and your children could share experiences in which someone gave you something you needed (see also "The Coat" [video], Gospel Library).

DOCTRINE AND COVENANTS 104:42

The Lord will bless me as I keep His commandments.

- Several times in section 104 the Lord promises "a multiplicity of blessings" to people who faithfully obey His commandments. To help the children understand what "multiplicity" means, you could draw a circle and ask your children to help you multiply the number of circles—drawing two, then four, then eight, then sixteen, and so on. Each time you add circles, help your children think of a blessing Heavenly Father has given them.

DOCTRINE AND COVENANTS 105:38–40

I can be a peacemaker.

- To help your children learn the story of Zion's Camp, you could share "Chapter 36: Zion's Camp" (in *Doctrine and Covenants Stories*, 135–39, or the corresponding video in Gospel Library). Pause periodically to talk about lessons we can learn from Zion's Camp—for example, that the Lord wants us to be peaceful and work together instead of arguing and fighting (see also Russell M. Nelson, "Peacemakers Needed," *Liahona*, May 2023, 98–101).

- You could also read Doctrine and Covenants 105:38–40 and ask the children to stand up each time they hear the word "peace." Explain that the Lord wanted the Saints to make peace with the people who were being unkind. Help your children think of things that they can do to be peacemakers, and invite them to role-play some situations.

For more ideas, see this month's issue of the *Friend* magazine.

Zion's Camp (Zion's Camp at Fishing River), by Judith A. Mehr

I can be a peacemaker (Doctrine and Covenants 105:38–40).

Color the figures and cut them out. Glue a craft stick or piece of card stock to the back of one of the figures, and then glue the two figures back-to-back. Flip the figures over to tell how the Lord wanted the Saints in Missouri not to be angry but to be peacemakers.

Doctrine and Covenants 106–108

At first glance, Doctrine and Covenants 107 seems to be only about organizing priesthood offices into a leadership structure for the Lord's Church. By the time this revelation was published, Church membership was outgrowing the capacity of the few leaders it had in place. Outlining the roles and responsibilities of the First Presidency, the Quorum of the Twelve Apostles, the Seventy, bishops, and quorum presidencies was definitely needed and helpful. But there's so much more to the divine instruction in section 107 than just how Church leadership should be organized. Here, the Lord teaches us about His power and authority, "the Holy Priesthood, after the Order of the Son of God" (verse 3). The purpose of the priesthood is to unlock "all the spiritual blessings of the church" so that all of God's children can "have the heavens opened unto them" and "enjoy the communion and presence of God the Father, and Jesus the mediator of the new covenant" (verses 18–19). In teaching us about His priesthood, the Savior is teaching us about Himself and how we can come unto Him.

See "Restoring the Ancient Order," in *Revelations in Context*, 208–12.

 Ideas for Learning at Home and at Church

The Lord supports me when He calls me to serve.

In Doctrine and Covenants 106 and 108, the Lord gave counsel and promises to two members who were called to serve in His Church. As you study His counsel, you might think about your own opportunities to serve the Lord—perhaps a ministering assignment, a Church calling, responsibilities in your family, or spiritual promptings to do good.

What do you feel the Lord's message to you is in these revelations? Which phrases seem particularly meaningful to you? Here are a few to consider:

- When has the Lord given you "grace [or divine help] and assurance" to be able to serve Him? (Doctrine and Covenants 106:8).

- What do you think it means to strengthen others "in all your doings"? (Doctrine and Covenants 108:7).

When Elder Carl B. Cook received a difficult Church assignment, he drew strength from the experience of an ancestor. Read about it in his message "Serve" (*Ensign* or *Liahona*, Nov. 2016, 110–12). Consider writing a letter to encourage your descendants—or your future self—to accept opportunities to serve the Lord. Include in your letter the truths you learn from Elder Cook's message, Doctrine and Covenants 106 and 108, and your own experiences.

See also Henry B. Eyring, "Walk with Me," *Ensign* or *Liahona*, May 2017, 82–85; Topics and Questions, "Serving in Church Callings," Gospel Library; "Warren Cowdery" and "'Wrought Upon' to Seek a Revelation," in *Revelations in Context*, 219–23, 224–28.

DOCTRINE AND COVENANTS 107:1–4, 18–20

The priesthood is "after the Order of the Son of God."

The Lord begins His "revelation on the priesthood" (Doctrine and Covenants 107, section heading) by teaching us the original name of the Melchizedek Priesthood (see verses 1–4). Why do you think it's important to know that? How does this name influence the way you think about the priesthood?

Keep these thoughts in mind as you read about the priesthood, especially in verses 18–20. What does it mean to "have the heavens opened"? What does it mean to "enjoy the communion and presence of God the Father, and Jesus"? How do the Savior's priesthood power and authority make all of this available to you?

See also Alma 13:2, 16; Doctrine and Covenants 84:19–27.

Focus on Jesus Christ. "There are many things to teach about in the restored gospel of Jesus Christ—principles, commandments, prophecies, and scripture stories. But all of these are branches of the same tree, for they all have one purpose: to help all people come unto Christ and be perfected in Him (see Jarom 1:11; Moroni 10:32). So no matter what you are teaching, remember that you are really teaching about Jesus Christ and how to become like Him" (*Teaching in the Savior's Way*, 6). For example, as you teach—and learn—about the priesthood in Doctrine and Covenants 107, frequently ask, "What are we learning about the Savior?"

DOCTRINE AND COVENANTS 107:22

The Lord's servants are "upheld by the confidence, faith, and prayer of the Church."

What do you think it means to uphold the Lord's servants by your confidence? by your faith? by your prayer?

See also "God Bless Our Prophet Dear," *Hymns*, no. 24.

DOCTRINE AND COVENANTS 107:23–24, 33–35, 38, 91–92

Prophets and Apostles testify of Jesus Christ.

Joseph Smith shared section 107 in 1835 with the newly called Quorum of the Twelve Apostles (see the section heading). What did the Lord teach them about their calling in verses 23–24, 33–35, 38? How has your witness of Jesus Christ been strengthened by the teaching and ministry of His living Apostles?

In verses 91–92, the Lord teaches about His senior Apostle, the President of the Church. How is he "like unto Moses"? (see Guide to the Scriptures, "Moses," Gospel Library).

See also David A. Bednar, "Chosen to Bear Testimony of My Name," *Ensign* or *Liahona*, Nov. 2015, 128–31.

DOCTRINE AND COVENANTS 107:27–31, 85–89

The Lord accomplishes His work through councils.

Notice what the Lord taught about councils in Doctrine and Covenants 107:27–31, 85–89. What makes a council effective? How might you apply these principles in your Church calling, your home, or your other responsibilities?

See also M. Russell Ballard, "Family Councils," *Ensign* or *Liahona*, May 2016, 63–65; *General Handbook*, 4.3–4.4, Gospel Library.

The Lord invites families to counsel together.

For more ideas, see this month's issues of the *Liahona* and *For the Strength of Youth* magazines.

 Ideas for Teaching Children

DOCTRINE AND COVENANTS 107:18–20

Jesus Christ blesses me through His priesthood power.

- As you and your children read together Doctrine and Covenants 107:18–19, emphasize the phrase "all the spiritual blessings." Perhaps you and your children could list blessings that come from the priesthood. You might make a game of it—see who can make the longest list. Your children could also draw or find pictures to represent these blessings (see this week's activity page). You could then talk about how priesthood ordinances (like baptism or the sacrament) help us receive God's blessings.

DOCTRINE AND COVENANTS 107:21–26, 33–35, 91–92

The Lord's chosen servants lead His Church.

- Every conference issue of the *Liahona* includes a page of pictures of the General Authorities. Consider looking at these pictures with your children as you read about their responsibilities in Doctrine and Covenants 107:21–26, 33–35, 91–92. You and your children could talk about why you are grateful the Lord has given them these responsibilities.

- Your children can learn more about the Lord's servants at "General Church Leadership" on ChurchofJesusChrist.org. Maybe each of your children could learn about one of these leaders and teach each other about him or her. Share with each other how you know that these leaders are true servants of Jesus Christ.

- After reading Doctrine and Covenants 107:22 together, you and your children could take turns holding up a picture of the First Presidency and sharing ways you can sustain them as the Lord's servants.

I can be careful in living my covenants.

- To start a conversation about this verse, you could invite your children to do something that requires careful attention, like filling a cup without spilling. What happens when we are not careful? Then you could read Doctrine and Covenants 108:3 to find out what the Lord wants us to do carefully. What "vows" (promises or covenants) do we make with God? How can we be more careful about keeping them? You might share parts of Sister Becky Craven's message "Careful versus Casual" (*Ensign* or *Liahona*, May 2019, 9–11) that you feel could inspire your children to keep their covenants. You could also sing a song about keeping covenants, such as "I Will Be Valiant" (*Children's Songbook*, 162).

Carefully pouring water could be compared
to carefully keeping our covenants.

For more ideas, see this month's issue of the *Friend* magazine.

Melchizedek Blesses Abram, by Walter Rane

Jesus Christ blesses me through His priesthood power (Doctrine and Covenants 107:18–20).

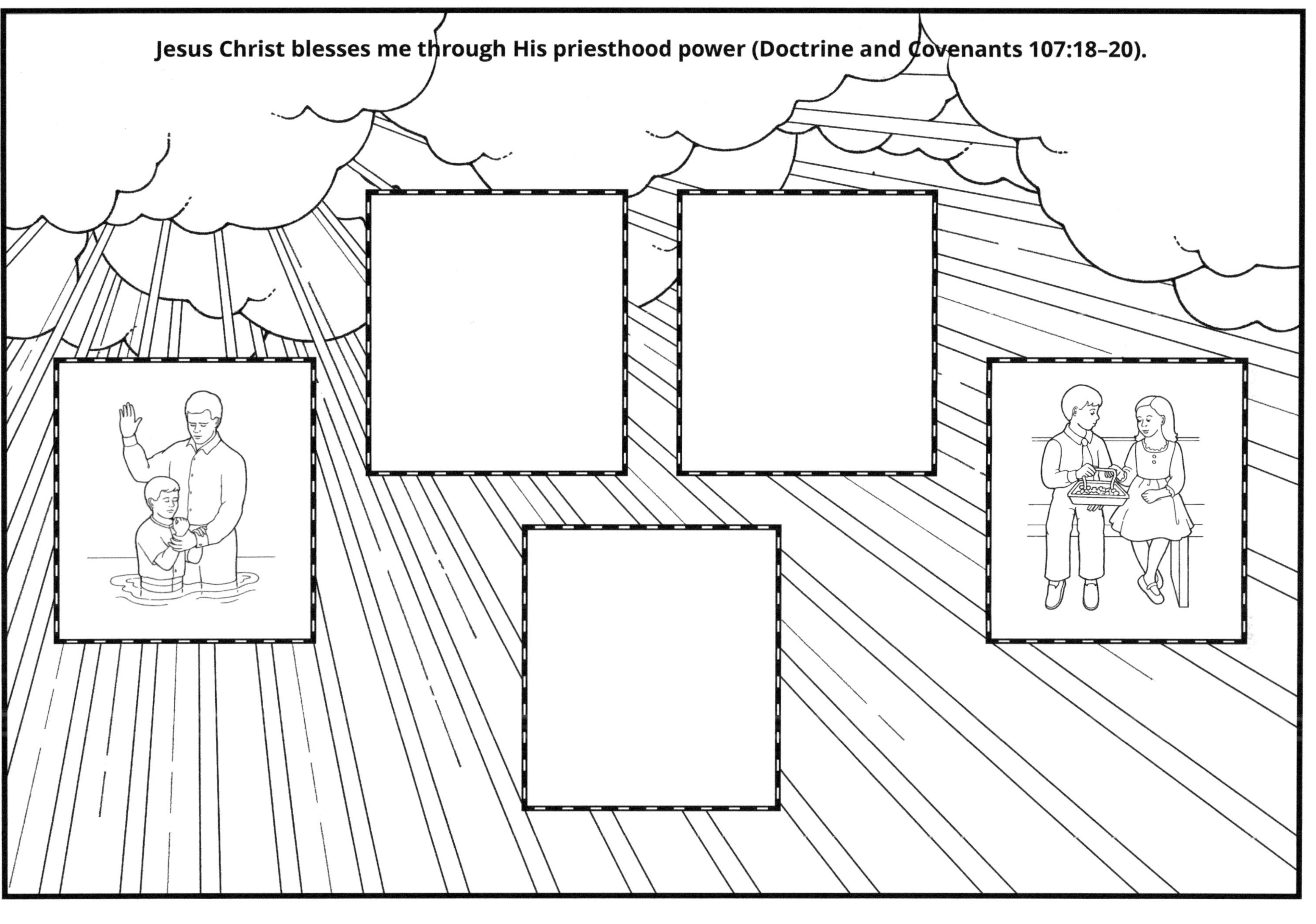

In the empty boxes, draw ways you have been blessed through the Lord's priesthood power.
For example, you could draw a picture of a temple.

A Glorious Light—Kirtland Temple, by Glen S. Hopkinson

Doctrine and Covenants 109–110

The doors to the Kirtland Temple weren't supposed to open until eight o'clock on the morning of March 27, 1836. But Saints who were hoping to attend the dedication services started lining up as early as seven. An overflow location and then a second session were needed to accommodate everyone. And it wasn't just the living who were eager to be present. Multiple witnesses saw angels inside the temple and even on the roof, during and after the dedication. It really did seem that "the armies of heaven" had come to "sing and [to] shout" with the Latter-day Saints ("The Spirit of God," *Hymns*, no. 2).

Why the great excitement—on both sides of the veil? After centuries, there was a house of the Lord again on the earth. The Lord was fulfilling His promise to endow His Saints "with power from on high" (Doctrine and Covenants 38:32). And this, He declared, was only "the beginning of the blessing" (Doctrine and Covenants 110:10). The era we now live in—with accelerated temple work and ordinances available to millions of the living and the dead—had its beginning in Kirtland, when "the veil o'er the earth [was] beginning to burst" ("The Spirit of God").

See also *Saints*, 1:232–41; "A House for Our God," in *Revelations in Context*, 169–72.

 Ideas for Learning at Home and at Church

The Lord offers me rich blessings through temple covenants.

The Kirtland Temple was different from temples we know today. There were no altars and no baptismal font, for example. But the blessings described in section 109, the dedicatory prayer for the Kirtland Temple, are also available in the Lord's house today. Review the following verses to find some of these blessings, and ponder how they can help strengthen your relationship with Heavenly Father and Jesus Christ.

Verses 5, 12–13 (see also Doctrine and Covenants 110:6–8): In the Lord's house, He can manifest Himself to me, and I can feel His power.

Verses 9, 15–19, 26, 78–79: _______________________________

Verses 21–23: ____

Verses 24–33, 42–46: ____

Verses 35–39: ____

Other blessings: ____

If you have been to the house of the Lord, think about how these promises have been fulfilled in your life.

The hymn "The Spirit of God" (*Hymns*, no. 2) was written for the Kirtland Temple dedication—and it has been sung at every temple dedication since. Consider singing or listening to it as part of your study and worship. What blessings of the temple do you find described in this hymn?

DOCTRINE AND COVENANTS 109

Prayer is communication with Heavenly Father.

Section 109 is a dedicatory prayer that was given to the Prophet Joseph Smith by revelation (see section heading). What do you learn about prayer from this section? For example, you might make note of what the Prophet gave thanks for and what blessings he asked for. What else did he say in this prayer? As you study, you might evaluate your own communication with Heavenly Father. What do you learn about Him and His Son from this prayer?

DOCTRINE AND COVENANTS 110:1–10

The Lord can manifest Himself to me in His house.

As you read the descriptions of the Savior in Doctrine and Covenants 110:1–10, including the section heading, ponder what these verses suggest about Him.

How does Jesus Christ manifest Himself—or make Himself known to you—in His house? How does He help you know that He accepts your sacrifices?

Inside the Kirtland Temple.

DOCTRINE AND COVENANTS 110:10–16

The Savior directs His work through priesthood keys.

Just before Moses, Elias, and Elijah appeared in the temple to restore priesthood keys, Jesus Christ said, "This is the beginning of the blessing which shall be poured out upon the heads of my people" (Doctrine and Covenants 110:10). As you read verses 11–16, think about the blessings that the Savior is pouring out on you through the work directed by these keys. For example:

- Verse 11: Moses and the keys of the gathering of Israel (or missionary work). How has the Lord blessed you and your family through the missionary efforts of His Church?

- Verse 12: Elias and the keys of the gospel of Abraham, including the Abrahamic covenant. How could the Lord bless you and the "generations after [you]" because of your covenants? (See Russell M. Nelson, "The Everlasting Covenant," *Liahona*, Oct. 2022, 4–11; Guide to the Scriptures, "Elias," Gospel Library.)

- Verses 13–16: Elijah and the sealing power, manifested through temple and family history work. Why do you think Heavenly Father wants you to be connected to your ancestors through temple ordinances? (See Gerrit W. Gong, "Happy and Forever," *Liahona*, Nov. 2022, 83–86.)

What connections do you see between these keys and our responsibilities in God's work of salvation and exaltation (living the gospel, caring for people in need, inviting all to receive the gospel, and uniting families for eternity)?

What experiences have you had with God's work of salvation and exaltation? What are these experiences teaching you about the Savior, His Church, and His work?

Find ways to include others. If you are teaching about Doctrine and Covenants 110:11–16, you might consider assigning each learner to study about Moses, Elias, or Elijah and the keys he restored. Then learners could share with each other what they discovered. An approach like this involves everyone in learning and teaching. (See *Teaching in the Savior's Way*, 24–27).

For more ideas, see this month's issues of the *Liahona* and *For the Strength of Youth* magazines.

 # Ideas for Teaching Children

The temple is the house of the Lord.

- You and your children could talk about something you love about your home. Then you could look at a picture of the Kirtland Temple and use Doctrine and Covenants 109:12–13; 110:1–7 to talk about how that temple was dedicated and became the Lord's house (see also "Chapter 39: The Kirtland Temple Is Dedicated," in *Doctrine and Covenants Stories*, 154, or the corresponding video in Gospel Library). Share with each other something you love about the Lord's house.

- Perhaps you and your children could imagine that a friend is trying to find your house. How would we help our friend know which house is ours? How do we know that the temple is the Lord's house? (see Doctrine and Covenants 109:12–13).

DOCTRINE AND COVENANTS 110

The Savior is blessing His people through priesthood keys.

- You could use this week's activity page or "Chapter 40: Visions in the Kirtland Temple" (in *Doctrine and Covenants Stories*, 155–57, or the corresponding video in Gospel Library) to tell the children about the heavenly beings who visited the temple. You could also use the picture at the end of this outline.

- To learn about the importance of what happened in the Kirtland Temple, you and your children could talk about what keys do. Maybe your children could take turns holding keys and pretending to open a locked door. Help them find the word *keys* in Doctrine and Covenants 110:11–16, and talk about the blessings that these keys unlock. You might explain that priesthood keys are God's permission to lead His Church. Share your gratitude that the Lord gave us priesthood keys.

DOCTRINE AND COVENANTS 110:15

The Savior wants me to turn my heart to my ancestors.

- After reading Doctrine and Covenants 110:15 together, tell your children about an experience that helped turn your heart to your ancestors. You could also sing a song together like "Family History—I Am Doing It" (*Children's Songbook*, 94).

- What might help "turn the hearts" of your children to their ancestors? You can find some fun ideas at FamilySearch.org/discovery. You could work together to identify ancestors who need temple ordinances. Why does Jesus want us to do this work?

For more ideas, see this month's issue of the *Friend* magazine.

Vision in the Kirtland Temple, by Gary E. Smith

Priesthood keys were revealed in the Kirtland Temple (Doctrine and Covenants 110).

Color the pictures of the heavenly messengers who came to the Kirtland Temple. Cut out the pictures. Put the messengers in the space above Joseph Smith and Oliver Cowdery one at a time to show how they visited the temple.

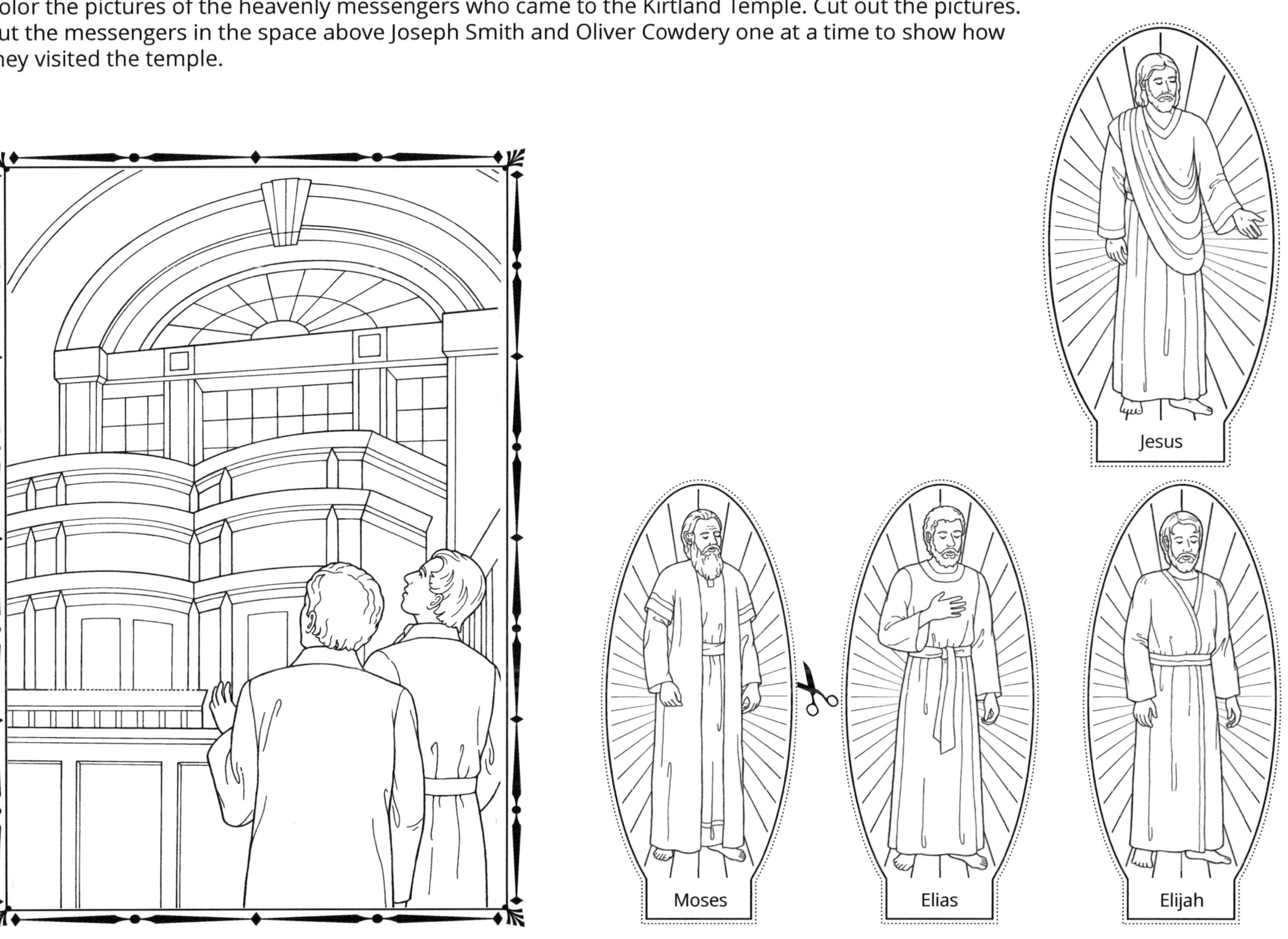

Doctrine and Covenants 111–114

Have you ever had a spiritual experience that made you feel confident and secure in your faith in Christ—but then life's afflictions tried your faith, and you found yourself struggling to recover the peace you felt before? Something similar happened to the Saints in Kirtland. Less than a year after the spiritual outpourings connected with the dedication of the Kirtland Temple, troubles arose. A financial crisis, conflict in the Quorum of the Twelve, and other trials caused some Saints to waver in their faith despite their earlier experiences.

We can't avoid trials, so how can we keep them from threatening our faith and testimony? Maybe part of the answer can be found in the Lord's counsel in Doctrine and Covenants 112, given while adversity in Kirtland was swelling. The Lord said, "Purify your hearts before me" (verse 28), "Rebel not" (verse 15), "Gird up thy loins for the work" (verse 7), and "Be thou humble" (verse 10). As we follow this counsel, the Lord will "lead [us] by the hand" through adversity and into healing and peace (see verses 10, 13).

Ideas for Learning at Home and at Church

The Lord can "order all things for [my] good."

By 1836, the Church had accumulated heavy debts in doing the Lord's work. Joseph Smith and others worried about these debts and considered ways to pay them (see the section heading to Doctrine and Covenants 111).

As you read section 111, consider how the Lord's words to Joseph may apply to you—and the things you worry about. For example, when have you felt God's love "notwithstanding your follies" (verse 1)? How has the Lord helped you find unexpected "treasures" (verse 10)? What has He done to "order all things for your good" (verse 11)? What does the phrase "as fast as ye are able to receive them" teach you about Heavenly Father?

See also Matthew 6:19–21, 33; "More Treasures Than One," in *Revelations in Context*, 229–34.

The Lord will lead me as I humbly seek His will.

Thomas B. Marsh, President of the Quorum of the Twelve Apostles, was upset that Joseph Smith had, without consulting him, called two members of his quorum to preach the gospel in England. He met with the Prophet, who received a revelation that helped Thomas put aside his hurt feelings. That revelation is recorded in Doctrine and Covenants 112.

Keep this context in mind as you study Doctrine and Covenants 112. What do you find that might have healed Thomas's hurt feelings? In verses 3–15 and 22, you could look for answers to questions like these: What is humility? What does it mean for the Lord to lead you "by the hand"? Why do you think being humble helps you receive the Lord's guidance? You could find additional answers in "Pattern of Humility" in Elder Joseph W. Sitati's message "Patterns of Discipleship" (*Liahona*, Nov. 2022, 87–88).

Think of someone you know who is humble. What does this person do to show humility? What do you learn from the Savior about being humble? Perhaps you can find pictures of times in His life when He showed humility.

When have you felt guided by the Lord as you humbled yourself?

See also Ulisses Soares, "Be Meek and Lowly of Heart," *Ensign* or *Liahona*, Nov. 2013, 9–11; "The Faith and Fall of Thomas Marsh," in *Revelations in Context*, 54–60; Topics and Questions, "Humility," Gospel Library; "Be Thou Humble," *Hymns*, no. 130.

Engage learners. Think about how you can help the people you teach to actively participate in learning the truths in the scriptures. For instance, to help them understand what the Lord said in Doctrine and Covenants 112:10, you could blindfold someone and carefully lead him or her by the hand around a small obstacle course of chairs or other objects. What can we learn about humility from this demonstration?

Those who are truly converted come to know Jesus Christ.

The fact that some Apostles in 1837 turned against the Prophet is a good reminder that regardless of our Church calling or how much we know about the gospel, we must individually make sure we nourish our conversion to Jesus Christ. Perhaps you could read Doctrine and Covenants 112:12–26, 28, 33–34 and look for truths that could help you overcome a trial of faith or become more fully converted to the Lord. You might feel inspired to share what you find to help someone else strengthen their conversion to Christ.

Joseph Smith was "a servant in the hands of Christ."

The prophet Isaiah referred to one of Jesse's descendants as a "rod" and a "root" (Isaiah 11:1, 10). In section 113, the Lord explained that this descendant, a servant of Christ, would be instrumental in gathering the Lord's people in the last days (see Doctrine and Covenants 113:4, 6). This prophecy describes the Prophet Joseph Smith quite well. How might this and

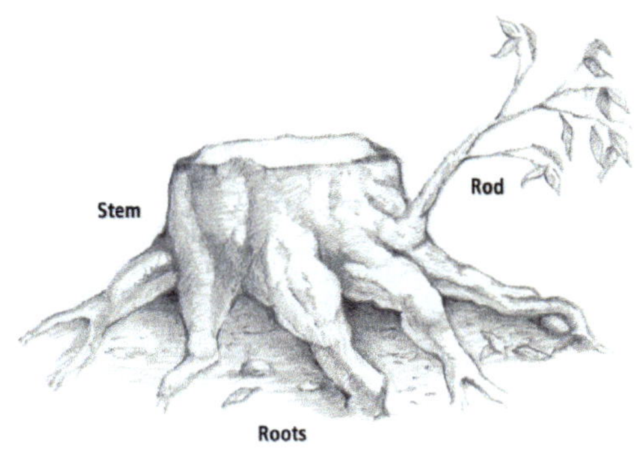

Isaiah wrote of a "rod" and "roots" coming out of the "stem of Jesse" (Isaiah 11:1).

other truths in section 113 have encouraged the Saints during the turmoil they experienced in Kirtland? What do you find in this revelation that inspires you to stay strong and continue to participate in the work of the Lord today?

See also Guide to the Scriptures, "Jesse," Gospel Library; 2 Nephi 21:10–12; Joseph Smith—History 1:40.

For more ideas, see this month's issues of the *Liahona* and *For the Strength of Youth* magazines.

 # Ideas for Teaching Children

DOCTRINE AND COVENANTS 111:2, 10–11

The things of God can be a treasure to me.

- You and your children could draw what comes to mind when you hear the word *treasure*. Then you could read together Doctrine and Covenants 111:2, 10–11 and contrast earthly treasures with the things the Lord treasures. (See this week's activity page.) How can we treasure more the things of God?

DOCTRINE AND COVENANTS 112:10

The Lord will lead me by the hand and answer my prayers.

- After reading Doctrine and Covenants 112:10 together, you and your children could sing together "Be Thou Humble" (*Hymns*, no. 130). You could also play a game that involves leading each other "by the hand" (such as an obstacle course). How does the Lord lead us "by the hand," even though He isn't physically with us? Why do we need the Lord to lead us? When have we felt the Lord leading us?

- You or your children could write the words of Doctrine and Covenants 112:10 and underline the blessings the Lord gives us when we humbly turn to Him. Encourage your children to share times when they humbly asked for the Lord's help and received answers to their prayers or were led to do something good (see Moroni 7:13, 16).

Detail from *Arise and Walk,* by Simon Dewey

DOCTRINE AND COVENANTS 112:11

Jesus wants me to love everyone.

- You and your children could take turns reading from "Chapter 41: Trouble in Kirtland" (in *Doctrine and Covenants Stories*, 158–60). Who in the story made the problems in Kirtland worse? Who was trying to make them better? Then you could read Doctrine and Covenants 112:11 and talk about why the Savior wants us to love everyone. When did He show love for people who were unkind to Him? (for example, see Luke 23:34). You could also sing a song about loving others, such as "I'll Walk with You" (*Children's Songbook*, 140–41).

DOCTRINE AND COVENANTS 112:11–14, 24–26

Those who are truly converted come to know Jesus Christ.

- After reading Doctrine and Covenants 112:24–26, you and your children could talk about the difference between knowing someone's name and knowing them. What teachings from verses 11–14 help us understand what it means to know the Lord?

For more ideas, see this month's issue of the *Friend* magazine.

Be Thou Humble, by Julie Rogers

The things of God can be a treasure to me (Doctrine and Covenants 111:2, 10–11).

Color and cut out the treasure chest and coins. Fold the chest on the dotted
lines, and tape or staple the ends together. As you place the coins inside the chest,
think about how you can better treasure the thing pictured on each coin.
On the backs of the coins, draw more things that God treasures.

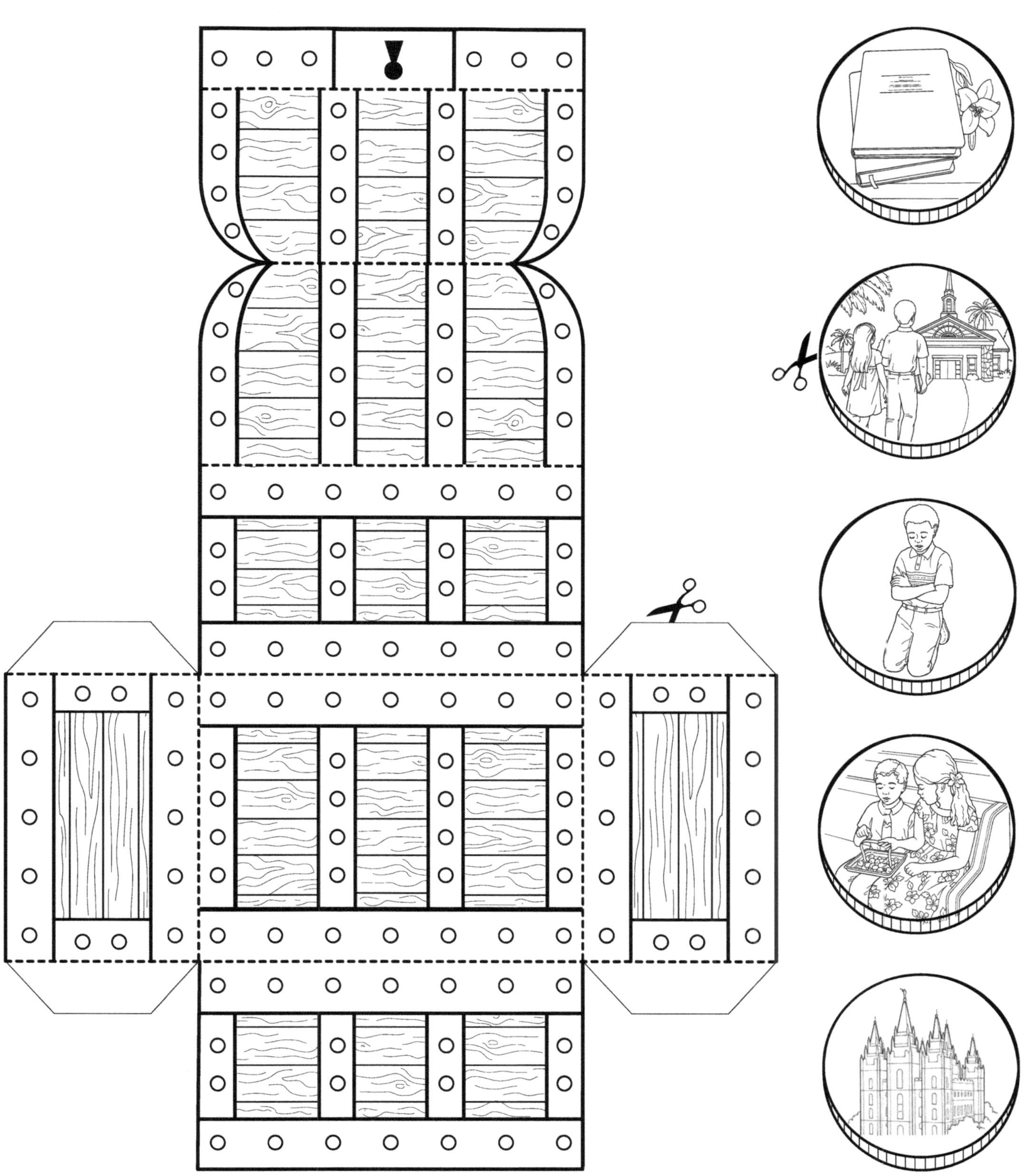

Far West, Missouri, by Al Rounds

Doctrine and Covenants 115–120

There was reason for the Saints to be optimistic about their newest gathering place, Far West, Missouri. The city was growing rapidly, the land seemed abundant, and nearby was Adam-ondi-Ahman, a place of great spiritual significance in the past and in the future (see Doctrine and Covenants 107:53–56; 116). Still, it must have been hard for the Saints not to think about what they had lost. Besides being driven from Independence, the center place of Zion, the Saints also had to flee Kirtland, leaving their beloved temple after only two years. And this time it wasn't just enemies outside the Church causing trouble—many prominent members had turned against Joseph Smith, including four members of the Quorum of the Twelve Apostles.

Instead of focusing on what they lost, the faithful just kept building Zion, this time in Far West. They made plans for a new temple. Four new Apostles were called. They understood that doing God's work doesn't mean you never fall; it means you "rise again." And though you'll have to make sacrifices, those sacrifices are sacred to God, even "more sacred . . . than [your] increase" (Doctrine and Covenants 117:13).

See *Saints*, 1:296–99.

 Ideas for Learning at Home and at Church

The name of the Church is important to the Lord.

President Russell M. Nelson said that the Church's name is "a matter of great importance" ("The Correct Name of the Church," *Ensign* or *Liahona*, Nov. 2018, 87). Think about why this is true as you read Doctrine and Covenants 115:4–6. What does the name of the Church have to do with its work and mission?

See also 3 Nephi 27:1–11.

DOCTRINE AND COVENANTS 115:5–6

Zion and her stakes offer "refuge from the storm."

As you study the powerful imagery in Doctrine and Covenants 115:5–6, consider the role the Lord wants you, as a member of His Church, to fulfill. For example, what can you do to "arise and shine forth" or "be a standard for the nations"? (verse 5). What spiritual storms do you notice around you? How do you find "refuge" through gathering? (verse 6).

See also "Brightly Beams Our Father's Mercy," *Hymns*, no. 335.

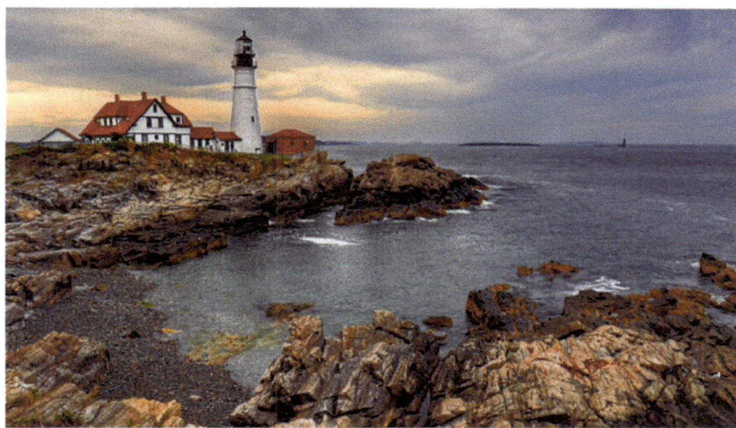

The Savior's Church can be a light and a refuge in the storm.

DOCTRINE AND COVENANTS 117

My sacrifices are sacred to the Lord.

Imagine you were Newel K. Whitney or his wife, Elizabeth, who were experiencing a prosperous life in Kirtland and then asked to leave. What do you find in Doctrine and Covenants 117:1–11 that might have helped you make this sacrifice? What sacrifices do you make for God? What do these verses teach you about who God is and what He does?

The sacrifice asked of Oliver Granger was different from the Whitneys': the Lord assigned him to stay in Kirtland and settle the Church's finances. While he represented the Church with integrity, he ultimately wasn't very successful. Consider how the Lord's words in Doctrine and Covenants 117:12–15 apply to the things He has asked of you.

See also "Far West and Adam-ondi-Ahman," in *Revelations in Context*, 239–40.

DOCTRINE AND COVENANTS 119–20

📖 My tithing helps build the kingdom of God.

The instructions in sections 119 and 120 clarify what tithing is: we contribute "one-tenth" of our interest (or income) each year (see Doctrine and Covenants 119:4). But these revelations do more than give a definition. The Lord told the Saints that tithing would "sanctify the land of Zion." And without this law, He said, "it shall not be . . . Zion unto you" (verse 6). Have you ever thought about tithing in this way? How can paying tithing help make you more sanctified, more prepared for Zion?

What do you learn from these revelations about how the Lord's servants use tithing funds? What is significant to you about the phrase "by mine own voice unto them" in Doctrine and Covenants 120?

Elder David A. Bednar has given a helpful description of how tithing is used and the blessings that come from obeying this law in "The Windows of Heaven" (*Ensign* or *Liahona*, Nov. 2013, 19–20). The following questions may help as you study his message:

- Who determines how tithing is used after it is paid to the Church?

- What is tithing used for?

- What blessings come as a result of paying tithing? For example, in what ways does paying tithing strengthen your relationship with Heavenly Father and Jesus Christ?

- What can you learn from Elder Bednar's invitation?

- How can you help others increase their faith in the Lord's law of tithing?

See also Malachi 3:8–12; "The Tithing of My People," in *Revelations in Context*, 250–55.

Help others apply what they're learning. Even when a person wants to pay tithing, sometimes they don't know how. If you're teaching your family or a class, consider taking some time to explain how to pay tithing, either online or with a Tithing and Other Offerings slip. (See *Teaching in the Savior's Way*, 27.)

For more ideas, see this month's issues of the *Liahona* and *For the Strength of Youth* magazines.

 ## Ideas for Teaching Children

DOCTRINE AND COVENANTS 115:4–5

I belong to The Church of Jesus Christ of Latter-day Saints.

- To help your children learn the name of the Church and understand why it is important, consider asking if any of them can say the Church's full name. You could then show them the name from Doctrine and Covenants 115:4 and have them repeat it with you. As you do, consider pointing out significant words and why they are important. You could also review "Chapter 43: Jesus Christ Names His Church" (in *Doctrine and Covenants Stories*, 164, or the corresponding video in Gospel Library) or sing "The Church of Jesus Christ" (*Children's Songbook*, 77).

DOCTRINE AND COVENANTS 115:4–6

My example can help others come to Christ and find safety.

- Your children may know people who are struggling and need "refuge" from the "storms of life" (verse 6). How can they help these people? Consider inviting your children to stand when you read the word *arise* in Doctrine and Covenants 115:5. They could stretch out their fingers like rays of sunlight when you read *shine forth*. Remind your children that our light comes from Jesus Christ, and help them think of ways they can "shine forth" as He does.

- Your children could draw a picture depicting Doctrine and Covenants 115:6. For example, they could draw a storm with people taking refuge in a Church building. What might the storm represent? How does the Savior's Church provide help? Help your children think of a friend, family member, or neighbor in need. How can we invite them to find help in the Church of Jesus Christ?

DOCTRINE AND COVENANTS 117

My sacrifices are sacred to the Lord.

- Invite your children to pretend that they are Newel K. Whitney. How would they feel if the Lord asked them to leave their successful job and move someplace new? (It might help to review "Chapter 41: Trouble in Kirtland," in *Doctrine and Covenants Stories*, 158–60, or the corresponding video in Gospel Library.) As you read together Doctrine and Covenants 117:1–11, ask your children to stop you when they hear something that would help them have the faith to obey the Lord. What sacrifices do we make to obey the Lord? How does He bless us?

DOCTRINE AND COVENANTS 119–20

Heavenly Father uses tithing to bless His children.

- Many of the children you teach may be too young to earn money and pay tithing, but it's good for them to understand how tithing contributes to the Lord's work throughout the world. Consider using the pictures and activity page at the end of this outline to help them understand what tithing is. (See also "Chapter 44: Tithing," in *Doctrine and Covenants Stories*, 165–66, or the corresponding video in Gospel Library.) How does Heavenly Father use tithing to bless His children? Share your feelings about the law of tithing and how it has blessed you.

When we pay tithing, we show our faith in Jesus Christ.

For more ideas, see this month's issue of the *Friend* magazine.

KITAB MORMON
HET BOEK VAN MORMON
MORMONS BOG
MORMONS BOK
IL LIBRO DI MORMON
MORMONA
TO BIBΛIO TOY MOPMON

Heavenly Father uses tithing to bless His children (Doctrine and Covenants 119–120).

Liberty Jail, by Welden Andersen

Doctrine and Covenants 121–123

The bottom level of the jail in Liberty, Missouri, was known as "the dungeon." The walls were thick, the stone floor was cold and filthy, food was scarce and rotten, and the two narrow, iron-barred windows near the ceiling allowed for very little light. This is where Joseph Smith and a few others spent four frigid months during the winter of 1838–39. During this time, Joseph was constantly receiving news about the suffering of the Saints. The peace and optimism felt in Far West had lasted only a few months, and now the Saints were without a home once again, driven into the wilderness in search of yet another place to start over—this time with their Prophet in prison.

And yet, even in that miserable jail, "knowledge from heaven" came "pouring down" (Doctrine and Covenants 121:33). Joseph's question "O God, where art thou?" was answered clearly and powerfully: "Fear not . . . , for God shall be with you forever and ever" (Doctrine and Covenants 121:1; 122:9).

See *Saints*, 1:323–96; "Within the Walls of Liberty Jail," in *Revelations in Context*, 256–63.

 Ideas for Learning at Home and at Church

DOCTRINE AND COVENANTS 121:1–10, 23–33; 122

With God, adversity can "be for [my] good."

When we or people we love are suffering, it is normal to wonder if God is aware of us. As you read Doctrine and Covenants 121:1–6, think about times when you have had questions or feelings similar to Joseph Smith's. What do you find in the Lord's response that might help you when you have these questions or feelings? For example, in verses 7–10, 26–33, notice the blessings He promises. What do you think it means to "endure . . . well"? How does the Savior help you do this?

As you read section 122, consider how the Lord wants you to view your adversities. You might ponder the experiences that have come from your trials and how they might "be for [your] good" (verse 7).

See also Quentin L. Cook, "Personal Peace in Challenging Times," *Liahona,* Nov. 2021, 89–92; "Where Can I Turn for Peace?," *Hymns*, no. 129.

True power and influence are based on "the principles of righteousness."

Worldly power forced the Saints out of Missouri and Joseph Smith into jail. But while Joseph was there, the Lord taught him about a different kind of power: His power, "the powers of heaven." Reading about that power in Doctrine and Covenants 121:34–46 could help you learn how to receive that power—and how to use it to bless others. Maybe you could record what you learn in a table with columns labeled *Powers of Heaven* and *Worldly Power*. How are these two kinds of power different? What do these descriptions of the Lord's power teach you about Him?

You might also ponder the word *influence* in verse 41. What are some situations in which you want to be an influence for good—perhaps in a family relationship, at school, at work, or in a Church assignment? What do you learn from verses 41–46 about how God influences His children? You might summarize what you learn by completing a sentence like this one: "To influence ____ for good, I will ____."

See also Jeffrey R. Holland, "Not as the World Giveth," *Liahona*, May 2021, 35–38; David A. Bednar, "The Powers of Heaven," *Ensign* or *Liahona*, May 2012, 48–51; "The Powers of Heaven" (video), Gospel Library.

Pick a phrase and study it in depth. To learn more about the wonderful blessings described in verses 45–46, you might pick a phrase that stands out to you and study it in depth. For example, what does the word *garnish* mean, and how can virtue garnish your thoughts? Or maybe you can find a picture of dew and learn about how dew forms on plants. How is this similar to the way the Lord teaches His doctrine? Share what you discover with your family or friends, including your friends at church.

Jesus Christ has descended below all things so that He can lift me up.

What do you think it means to say that Jesus Christ "descended below . . . all [things]"? Here are some additional verses that might help you understand this phrase: Isaiah 53:3–4; Hebrews 2:17–18; 1 Nephi 11:16–33; Alma 7:11–13. Based on what you learn, consider restating Doctrine and Covenants 122:8 in your own words. How can you show your gratitude to Jesus Christ for descending below all things?

Detail from *Not My Will But Thine*, by Walter Rane

"Let us cheerfully do all things that lie in our power."

In Doctrine and Covenants 123:7–8, Joseph Smith referred to false beliefs that led to suffering, including the persecution of the Saints. In March 1839, it may have seemed that there wasn't much the Saints could do about that. But in his letters written from Liberty Jail, Joseph told them what they could do: "[gather] up a knowledge of all the facts" and "stand still, with the utmost assurance, to see the salvation of God" (Doctrine and Covenants 123:1, 17). As you consider the problems in the world today, think about ways to address them that "lie in [your] power" (verses 12, 17). And don't overlook the seemingly "small things" (verse 15). Why is it important to do these things "cheerfully"? (verse 17).

For more ideas, see this month's issues of the *Liahona* and *For the Strength of Youth* magazines.

 # Ideas for Teaching Children

DOCTRINE AND COVENANTS 121:1–9; 122:7–9

With God, my trials can be for my good.

- To help your children imagine what it would have been like for Joseph Smith and his friends in Liberty Jail, you could read together "Chapter 46: Joseph Smith in Liberty Jail" (in *Doctrine and Covenants Stories*, 172–74) or "Voices of the Restoration: Liberty Jail" or watch part of the video "Joseph Smith: Prophet of the Restoration" (Gospel Library, beginning at 41:30). Then, as you read together Doctrine and Covenants 121:1–9, you could talk about how the Savior helped Joseph feel peace. How do we find peace in the Savior, even during hard times?

- To help your children recognize that our trials can "be for [our] good" (Doctrine and Covenants 122:7), you could talk with them about how our muscles grow when we carry something heavy. You could even invite them to lift a heavy object. Then you could talk about how going through hard times can help our spirits grow—as we turn to the Lord for help. Share some examples from your life.

DOCTRINE AND COVENANTS 121:34–46

Righteousness brings the "powers of heaven."

- Perhaps an analogy would help your children understand "the powers of heaven." For example, you could compare God's power to electrical power. What might prevent an electrical device from receiving power? What decreases our spiritual power? What increases it? (Look for words and phrases in Doctrine and Covenants 121:34–46; see also *General Handbook*, 3.5, 3.6, Gospel Library.)

DOCTRINE AND COVENANTS 122:7–9

Jesus Christ knows what I am going through.

- After reading Doctrine and Covenants 122:7–9 with your children, you might share an experience when you felt the Savior was with you during a difficult trial. You could also sing together a song such as "Jesus Once Was a Little Child" (*Children's Songbook*, 55) and testify that Jesus Christ can help us because He knows how we feel.

Even small things can make a big difference in God's service.

- To help your children understand Doctrine and Covenants 123:15–17, you could share with them a picture of a large ship and a small helm, or share with them Elder David A. Bednar's explanation in "The Principles of My Gospel" (*Liahona*, May 2021, 125–26). Then you could talk about small ways we can cheerfully serve our family and friends.

Like the small helm of a big ship, our small efforts can make a big difference.

For more ideas, see this month's issue of the *Friend* magazine.

Joseph Smith in Liberty Jail, by Greg Olsen

Jesus Christ knows what I am going through (Doctrine and Covenants 122:8).

Color the picture of Joseph Smith in Liberty Jail. In the space provided,
draw or write about a time the Savior comforted you.

Doctrine and Covenants 124

As difficult as the last six years had been for the Saints, things started to look better in the spring of 1839: The refugee Saints had found compassion among the citizens of Quincy, Illinois. Guards had allowed Joseph Smith and other Church leaders to escape captivity in Missouri. And the Church had just purchased land in Illinois where the Saints could gather again. Yes, it was swampy, mosquito-infested land, but compared to the challenges the Saints had already faced, this probably seemed manageable. So they drained the swamp and drafted a charter for a new city, which they named Nauvoo. It means "beautiful" in Hebrew, though it was more an expression of faith than an accurate description, at least at first. Meanwhile, the Lord was impressing His Prophet with a sense of urgency. He had more truths and ordinances to restore, and He needed a holy temple where He could "crown [His Saints] with honor, immortality, and eternal life" (Doctrine and Covenants 124:55). In many ways, these same feelings of faith and urgency are evident in the Lord's work today.

See *Saints*, 1:399–427; "Organizing the Church in Nauvoo," in *Revelations in Context*, 264–71.

 Ideas for Learning at Home and at Church

DOCTRINE AND COVENANTS 124:2–11

I can invite others to come unto Christ.

The Lord told the Prophet Joseph Smith to "make a solemn proclamation of [His] gospel" to "all the kings of the world" (see Doctrine and Covenants 124:2–11). If you received this assignment, what would your proclamation say about Jesus Christ and His restored gospel? Also ponder how you can share your witness normally and naturally with people you interact with daily.

See also "The Restoration of the Fulness of the Gospel of Jesus Christ: A Bicentennial Proclamation to the World," Gospel Library.

I can be a disciple whom the Lord trusts.

Consider sharing with others, as the Savior did in Doctrine and Covenants 124:12–21, the Christlike attributes you see in them. How has He expressed to you His love and trust?

See also Richard J. Maynes, "Earning the Trust of the Lord and Your Family," *Ensign* or *Liahona*, Nov. 2017, 75–77.

The Lord wants me to welcome and accept others.

As you ponder the Lord's instruction in Doctrine and Covenants 124:22–24, 60–61, think about how you can make your home and your ward a place like what the Lord had envisioned for Nauvoo.

See also "A Friend to All" (video), ChurchofJesusChrist.org.

Detail from *Joseph Smith at the Nauvoo Temple*, by Gary E. Smith

We build temples unto the Lord to receive sacred ordinances.

Why do you feel the Lord has "always commanded" His people "to build [temples] unto [His] holy name"? Consider making a list of reasons you find in Doctrine and Covenants 124:25–45, 55. You might find others in a hymn like "We Love Thy House, O God" (*Hymns*, no. 247) or the video "What Is a Temple?" (Gospel Library). How is the work of building temples a sign of the Lord's love for you?

See also "Why Latter-day Saints Build Temples," temples.ChurchofJesusChrist.org.

The Lord blesses people who strive to obey His commandments.

The Saints had been commanded to build a temple in Jackson County, Missouri, but were "hindered by their enemies" (Doctrine and Covenants 124:51). Verses 49–55 contain a reassuring message for people who want to obey God's commandments but are prevented from doing so because of family or other circumstances. What counsel do you find in these verses that could help someone in such a situation?

DOCTRINE AND COVENANTS 124:91–92

The Lord can guide me through my patriarchal blessing.

Shortly after the Prophet's father, Joseph Smith Sr., passed away, the Lord called Hyrum Smith to the calling that his father had held—the Patriarch to the Church. You can read about this in Doctrine and Covenants 124:91–92.

How would you describe a patriarchal blessing to someone who has never heard of it? What would you say to encourage someone to receive one? Look for answers to these questions in Elder Randall K. Bennett's message "Your Patriarchal Blessing—Inspired Direction from Heavenly Father" (*Liahona*, May 2023, 42–43) or Topics and Questions, "Patriarchal Blessings" (Gospel Library).

Based on what you've studied and experienced, consider how you would complete this sentence: "A patriarchal blessing is like _____." Why does Heavenly Father want His children to receive a patriarchal blessing?

If you have not received a patriarchal blessing, what can you do to prepare for one? If you have received a patriarchal blessing, how can you show God that you treasure this gift?

See also Kazuhiko Yamashita, "When to Receive Your Patriarchal Blessing," *Liahona*, May 2023, 88–90; *General Handbook*, 18.17, Gospel Library.

Teach from the heart. Teaching is most meaningful when it includes personal experiences and testimony. For example, if you have received a patriarchal blessing, review it as you prepare to teach about these special blessings. Why are you thankful for your blessing? How will you inspire others to prepare to receive theirs or study patriarchal blessings more frequently?

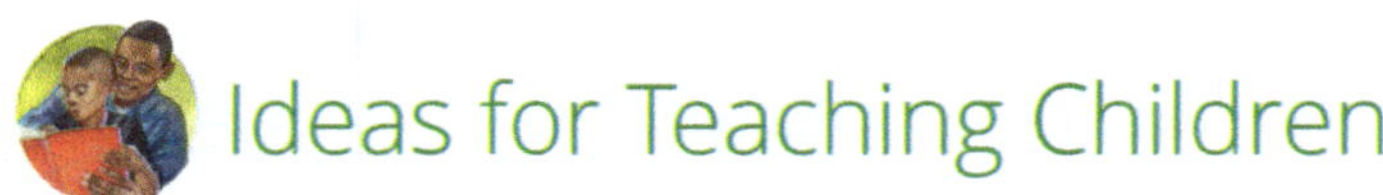# Ideas for Teaching Children

DOCTRINE AND COVENANTS 124:15, 20

Jesus Christ loves integrity.

- To help your children remember what they learn from Doctrine and Covenants 124:15, 20, you could help them draw and cut out paper hearts. On the hearts, you could help them write key phrases from these verses. A song like "Stand for the Right" (*Children's Songbook*, 159) could help reinforce the Lord's words.

- After reading together Doctrine and Covenants 124:15, 20, perhaps you could help your children find out what it means to live with integrity on page 31 of *For the Strength of Youth: A Guide to Making Choices*. What did the Lord say specifically about George Miller in verse 20 "because of the integrity of [George's] heart"? You could also share examples of children showing integrity from your own experience or from the *Friend* magazine. Invite your children to set a goal to show integrity this week and tell you how they feel when they do.

DOCTRINE AND COVENANTS 124:28–29, 39

Jesus commands His people to build temples.

- Your children might enjoy looking at pictures of temples, including an ancient temple and a temple close to where they live (see ChurchofJesusChrist.org/temples/list). You could use these pictures and Doctrine and Covenants 124:39 to explain that Jesus Christ has always commanded His people to build temples—in ancient times and in our day (see also this week's activity page).

- If you live close enough to a temple, consider taking your children there and reverently walking the temple grounds. Invite them to find the words "Holiness to the Lord—The House of the Lord" on the outside of the temple. Talk with your children about what these words mean.

- Consider using the ideas in "Being Baptized and Confirmed for Ancestors" in appendix A to help your children look forward to the day when they can enter the temple (see also "The Temple and the Plan of Happiness" in appendix B).

Solomon's Temple, by Sam Lawlor

The Lord will bless me through a patriarchal blessing.

- As you read together Doctrine and Covenants 124:91–92, help your children find what the Lord called Hyrum Smith to do. Talk about what a patriarchal blessing is: a special blessing in which the Lord teaches us about ourselves and what He wants us to do and become. Consider using the section "Receiving a Patriarchal Blessing" in appendix A to help your children prepare to receive a patriarchal blessing.

For more ideas, see this month's issue of the *Friend* magazine.

The Nauvoo Temple, by George D. Durrant

Jesus commands His people to build temples (Doctrine and Covenants 124:28–29, 39).

Color the two temples, and draw your favorite temple in the blank space.
Cut out the rectangle on the solid outer line, and fold it on the dotted lines.
Glue or tape the ends together as shown, and display it in your home.

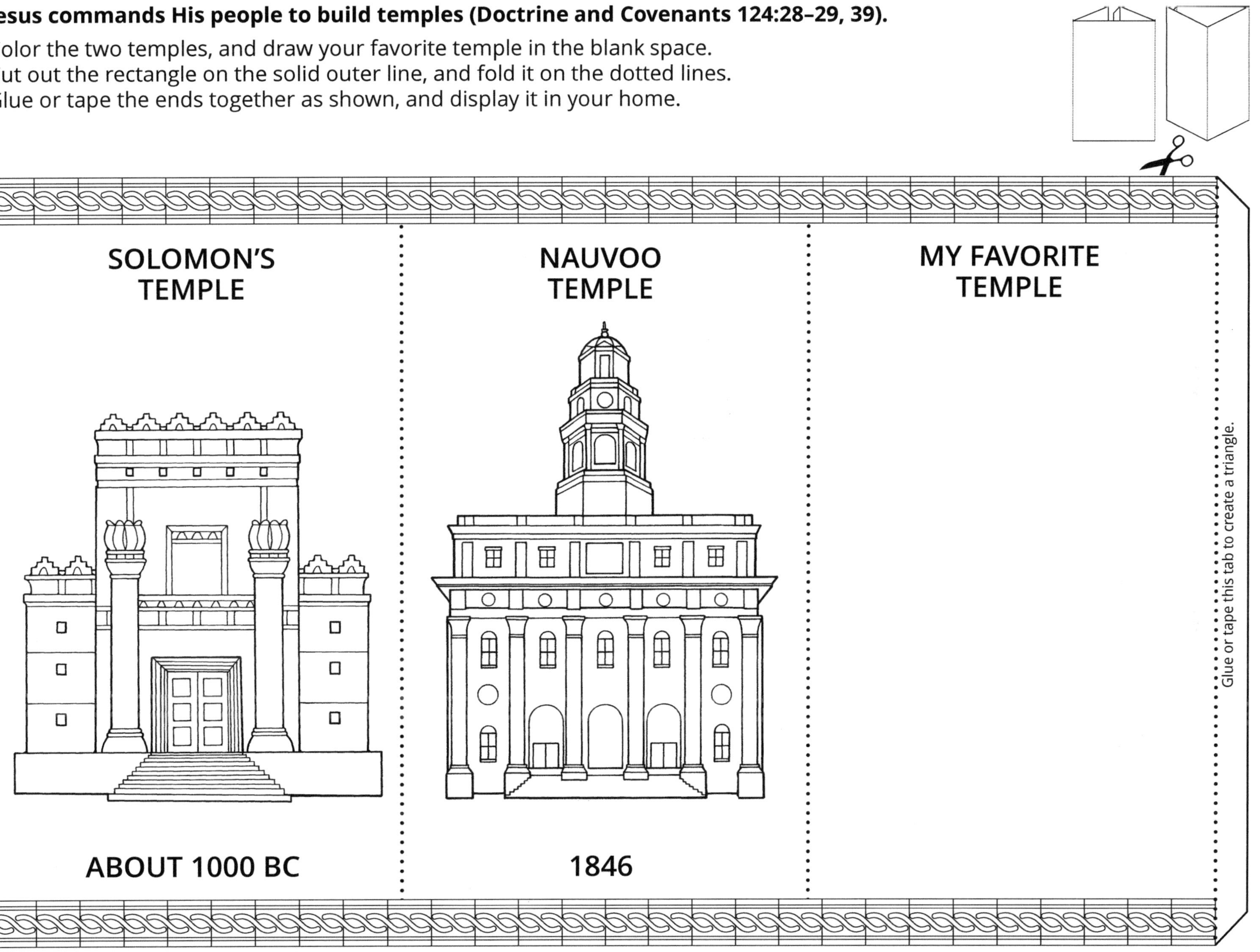

Us with Them and Them with Us, by Caitlin Connolly

Doctrine and Covenants 125–128

In August 1840, a grieving Jane Neyman listened to the Prophet Joseph speak at the funeral of his friend Seymour Brunson. Jane's own teenage son Cyrus had also recently passed away. Adding to her grief was the fact that Cyrus had never been baptized, and Jane worried what this would mean for his eternal soul. Joseph had wondered the same thing about his beloved brother Alvin, who also died before being baptized. So the Prophet decided to share with everyone at the funeral what the Lord had revealed to him about people who pass away without receiving gospel ordinances—and what we can do to help them.

The doctrine of baptism for the dead thrilled the Saints; their thoughts turned immediately to deceased family members. Now there was hope for them! Joseph shared their joy, and in a letter teaching this doctrine, he used joyful, enthusiastic language to express what the Lord taught him about the salvation of the dead: "Let the mountains shout for joy, and all ye valleys cry aloud; and all ye seas and dry lands tell the wonders of your Eternal King!" (Doctrine and Covenants 128:23).

See *Saints*, 1:415–27; "Letters on Baptism for the Dead," in *Revelations in Context*, 272–76.

 Ideas for Learning at Home and at Church

DOCTRINE AND COVENANTS 126

The Lord wants me to care for my family.

After returning from a mission to England—one of many missions he served—Brigham Young received another important calling from the Lord. He was asked to "take especial care of [his] family" (verse 3), who had suffered in his absence. As you study this section, consider why the Lord sometimes requires sacrifice in our service. What can you do to take care of your family?

See also "Take Special Care of Your Family," in *Revelations in Context*, 242–49.

I can rely on the Lord during difficult times.

False accusations and the threat of arrest had again forced Joseph Smith into hiding in August 1842. And yet the words he wrote to the Saints during this time (now Doctrine and Covenants 127) are full of optimism and joy. What do verses 2–4 teach you about God? about facing ridicule or opposition? What phrases from these verses might help you when you feel persecuted? Consider recording how the Lord is sustaining you in the "deep water" of your life.

"Whatsoever you record on earth shall be recorded in heaven."

As you read Doctrine and Covenants 127:5–8; 128:1–8, look for reasons the Lord gave Joseph Smith such specific instructions about recording baptisms for the dead. What does this teach you about the Lord and His work? How do you feel this instruction could apply to your own family records, such as personal journals?

Doing temple service for our ancestors binds our hearts to them.

📖 The salvation of my ancestors is essential to my salvation.

It's clear from what God revealed through Joseph Smith why our ancestors who weren't baptized in this life need us: we are baptized on their behalf so they can choose to accept or reject this ordinance. But the Prophet also taught that our ancestors' salvation is "necessary and essential to *our* salvation." As you read Doctrine and Covenants 128:15–18, think about why that is.

Verse 5 teaches that the ordinance of baptism for the dead was "prepared before the foundation of the world." What does this truth teach you about God and His plan? What does Elder Dale G. Renlund's message "Family History and Temple Work: Sealing and Healing" add to your understanding? (*Ensign* or *Liahona*, May 2018, 46–49).

Joseph Smith used phrases like "binding power," "welding link," and "perfect union" when teaching about priesthood ordinances and baptism for the dead. Look for these and similar phrases as you read Doctrine and Covenants 128:5–25. Can you think of objects you could use to illustrate these phrases, such as a chain or rope? Why are these good phrases to describe this doctrine?

Considering the following questions may also help your study of these verses:

- In your opinion, why could baptism for the dead be considered the "most glorious of all subjects belonging to the everlasting gospel"? (verse 17). What experiences have helped you feel this way?

- In what sense might the earth be cursed if there is no "welding link . . . between the fathers and the children"? (verse 18).

- What impresses you about Joseph Smith's words in verses 19–25? How do these verses affect the way you feel about Jesus Christ? about temple service for your ancestors? (see also "Come, Rejoice," *Hymns*, no. 9).

After studying these verses, you may feel inspired to do something for your ancestors. The ideas on FamilySearch.org could help.

The "Inspirational Videos" in the "Temple and Family History" collection of the Gospel Library can give you practical help, inspirational stories, and messages from leaders about family history.

Use related Church resources. Links in *Come, Follow Me* outlines provide easy access to helpful resources that can help you understand and apply gospel truths or act on impressions you receive. For example, the FamilySearch link above leads to activities such as building your own family tree, finding ancestors who need temple ordinances, seeing where your ancestors came from, or uploading a family story.

See also Kevin R. Duncan, "A Voice of Gladness!," *Liahona*, May 2023, 95–97.

# Ideas for Teaching Children

I can help care for my family.

- To help your children learn to serve their family members, consider sharing the information about Brigham Young in "Chapter 50: The Saints in Nauvoo" (in *Doctrine and Covenants Stories*, 184, or the corresponding video in Gospel Library) or summarize Doctrine and Covenants 126 in your own words. You might emphasize the phrase "take especial care of your family" (verse 3) and talk with your children about what it means to take special care of our families.

- It may be fun for you and your children to look at family pictures (or draw pictures) as you talk together about ways we can help "care" for family members. You could also sing a song like "Home Can Be a Heaven on Earth" (*Hymns*, no. 298).

DOCTRINE AND COVENANTS 128:5, 12

All of God's children need the chance to be baptized.

- Invite your children to find out from Doctrine and Covenants 128:1 what subject occupied Joseph Smith's mind. They could also search verse 17 to find out what subject he considered "the most glorious." Let them share what they find and talk about why this subject is so exciting.

- In addition to helping your children prepare for (and live) their own baptismal covenants, you can help them know how to help people who did not make these covenants during their lifetime. Consider telling your children about someone you know who died without being baptized. Then you could read together Doctrine and Covenants 128:5 and look at a picture of a temple baptismal font (like the one at the end of this outline). Tell your children how you feel about being baptized in temples on behalf of people who are dead so that everyone has the chance to make covenants with Heavenly Father.

DOCTRINE AND COVENANTS 128:18

Heavenly Father wants me to learn about my family history.

- It might be fun for you and your children to make a paper chain with names of parents, grandparents, great-grandparents, and so on (see this week's activity page). Then you could share with each other what you know about these ancestors. Read together Doctrine and Covenants 128:18 to find out what the "welding link" is that makes our family history "whole and complete." You could also watch the video "Courage: I Think I Get It from Him" (Gospel Library).

- Additional activities to help your children participate in family history can be found in "The Temple and the Plan of Happiness" in appendix B or at FamilySearch.org.

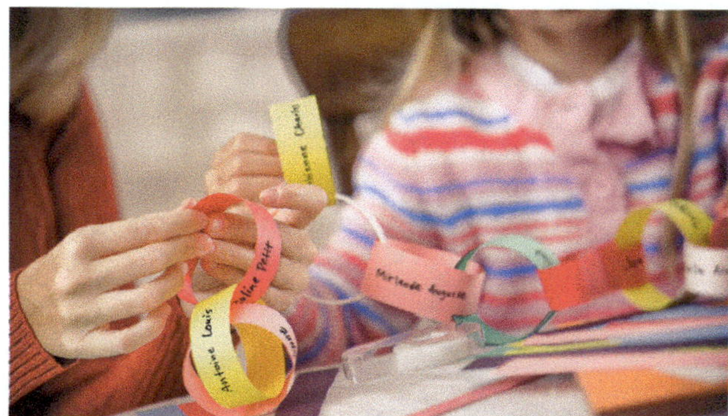

Temple ordinances help us unite families like links in a chain.

For more ideas, see this month's issue of the *Friend* magazine.

The baptismal font in the Ogden Utah Temple.

Heavenly Father wants me to learn about my family history (Doctrine and Covenants 128:18).

Cut out the strips below, and fill in the space on each one with the correct name. Draw a picture of the person's face in the circle. Make a paper chain necklace to represent your family.

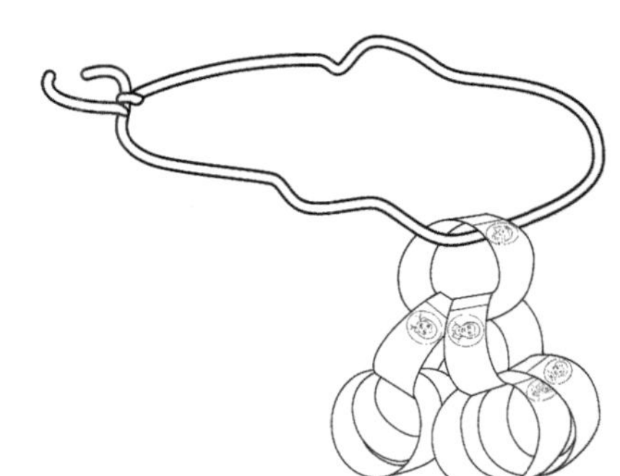

Me

My father

My mother

My grandfather (my father's father)

My grandmother (my father's mother)

My grandfather (my mother's father)

My grandmother (my mother's mother)

Doctrine and Covenants 129–132

Through Joseph Smith, the Lord took some of the mystery out of eternity. The greatness of God, the glory of heaven, and the vastness of eternity can seem almost familiar in the light of the restored gospel, even to finite minds like ours. The revelations in Doctrine and Covenants 129–32 are a good example. What is God like? He "has a body . . . as tangible as man's." What is heaven like? "That same sociality which exists among us here will exist among us there" (Doctrine and Covenants 130:22, 2). In fact, one of the most joyous truths about heaven is that it can include our cherished family relationships, if sealed by the proper authority. Truths like these can make heaven feel less distant—glorious yet reachable.

But then, sometimes God may ask us to do things that seem uncomfortable and unreachable. For many early Saints, plural marriage was one such commandment. It was a severe trial of faith for Joseph Smith, his wife Emma, and almost everyone who received it. To make it through this trial, they needed more than just favorable feelings about the restored gospel; they needed faith in God that went far deeper than that. The commandment no longer stands today, but the faithful example of people who lived it still does. And this example inspires us when we are asked to make our own "sacrifices in obedience" (Doctrine and Covenants 132:50).

 Ideas for Learning at Home and at Church

God wants to exalt His children.

There are many things we don't know about exaltation or life in the highest degree of the celestial kingdom—the kind of life God lives. Much of it may be beyond our current ability to understand. But God has revealed a few precious clues, and many of them are found in Doctrine and Covenants 130–32. You might read with questions like these in mind: What do I learn about God? What do I learn about the life after mortality? How does this information about eternal life bless my life now?

See also "Our Hearts Rejoiced to Hear Him Speak," in *Revelations in Context*, 277–80.

God blesses people who obey His laws.

How would you state, in your own words, what the Lord teaches in Doctrine and Covenants 130:20–21 and 132:5? Ponder how this principle has been demonstrated in your life.

Sometimes, even when we are obedient to God, the blessings we hope for don't come right away. How do you maintain your faith and hope when this happens? Look for insights in Elder D. Todd Christofferson's message "Our Relationship with God" (*Liahona*, May 2022, 78–80).

See also 1 Nephi 17:35; Doctrine and Covenants 82:10.

Heavenly Father made it possible for families to be eternal.

Through the Prophet Joseph Smith, the Lord restored the truth that marriage and family relationships can be eternal. As you read Doctrine and Covenants 132:13–21, look for phrases that help you understand the difference between what will "remain" eternally and what will not. What do you think it means for a marriage relationship to be "by [the Lord]"? (verse 14).

In his message "In Praise of Those Who Save," President Dieter F. Uchtdorf contrasts eternal marriage relationships with "disposable" things (*Ensign* or *Liahona*, May 2016, 77–78). What does this contrast teach you about how to nurture—or prepare for—a marriage relationship? Think about your family relationships—now and in the future—as you read Elder Uchtdorf's message. What do you find there that gives you hope in Christ for your family relationships?

President Henry B. Eyring shared this counsel he received when he was worried about his family situation: "You just live worthy of the celestial kingdom, and the family arrangements will be more wonderful than you can imagine" (in "A Home Where the Spirit of the Lord Dwells," *Ensign* or *Liahona*, May 2019, 25). How could this counsel help you or someone you know?

See also "Families Can Be Together Forever," *Hymns*, no. 300; Topics and Questions, "Marriage," Gospel Library.

A marriage can be sealed for eternity in the house of the Lord.

Plural marriage is acceptable to God only when He commands it.

Many people who read the Old Testament wonder about Abraham, Jacob, Moses, and others marrying multiple wives. Were these servants of the Lord committing adultery? Did God approve of their marriages? Joseph Smith had similar questions. Look for the answers God gave in Doctrine and Covenants 132:1–2, 29–40.

Marriage between one man and one woman is God's standard of marriage (see the section heading to Official Declaration 1; Jacob 2:27, 30). However, there have been times when God has commanded His children to practice plural marriage.

The early years of the restored Church were one of those periods of exception. If you want to learn more about plural marriage among the early Saints, see "Mercy Thompson and the Revelation on Marriage" (in *Revelations in Context*, 281–93); *Saints*, 1:290–92, 432–35, 482–92, 502–4; Topics and Questions, "Plural Marriage in The Church of Jesus Christ of Latter-day Saints," Gospel Library; "Why Was It Necessary for Joseph Smith and Others to Practice Polygamy?" (video), ChurchofJesusChrist.org.

 Ideas for Teaching Children

DOCTRINE AND COVENANTS 130:2, 18–19; 132:13, 19

Heavenly Father wants me to focus on eternal things.

- What does Doctrine and Covenants 132:13 teach us about things of the world? Maybe you and your children could pack a suitcase or backpack with items representing things that, according to Doctrine and Covenants 130:2, 18–19; 132:19, we can take with us into the next life.

DOCTRINE AND COVENANTS 130:20–21; 132:5, 21–23

God blesses me as I obey His laws.

- Perhaps a simple comparison could teach your children about obeying God's commandments. For example, you could ask them to give you directions to walk somewhere, like to a school or Church building. What happens when we don't follow the directions? Then you could read Doctrine and Covenants 130:21 and compare these directions to the commandments God has given us.

- You might also sing together a song about obedience, such as "Keep the Commandments" (*Children's Songbook*, 146–47), and look for words in Doctrine and Covenants 130:20–21 and 132:5 that are similar to those in the song. How does God bless us as we strive to keep His commandments?

DOCTRINE AND COVENANTS 130:22

Heavenly Father and Jesus Christ have immortal physical bodies.

- After reading Doctrine and Covenants 130:22 together, you and your children could look at a picture of Jesus Christ and point to His eyes, His mouth, and other parts of His body. Your children could point to those same parts of their own bodies. Tell them why it's important to you to know that our bodies look like Heavenly Father's and Jesus's bodies.

DOCTRINE AND COVENANTS 132:19

Heavenly Father made it possible for families to be together forever.

- Help your children find examples of things that do not last forever—food that spoils, flowers that wilt, and so on. Then look at Doctrine and Covenants 132:19 together and find key phrases like "everlasting covenant," "sealed," "through all eternity," and "forever and ever." (See also "Chapter 55: A Revelation about Marriage," in *Doctrine and Covenants Stories*, 198, or the corresponding video in Gospel Library.) You could also look at pictures of your family and testify that the Lord has made it possible, through the ordinances and covenants of the temple, for families to last forever.

Because of the ordinances of the Lord's house, families can be eternal.

Be sensitive to family situations. "Children today find themselves in many different and complex family configurations. . . . [We] need to reach out to [those] who feel alone, left behind, or outside the fence" (Neil L. Andersen, "Whoso Receiveth Them, Receiveth Me," *Ensign* or *Liahona*, May 2016, 49, 52).

For more ideas, see this month's issue of the *Friend* magazine.

A sealing room in the Paris France Temple

Heavenly Father made it possible for families to be together forever (Doctrine and Covenants 132:19).
Cut out enough paper dolls to represent each member of your family (make extra dolls if needed).
Draw the faces of your family members on the dolls, and color the dolls.
Put the dolls in an envelope or clip them together with a paper clip to show that your family can be sealed together for eternity.

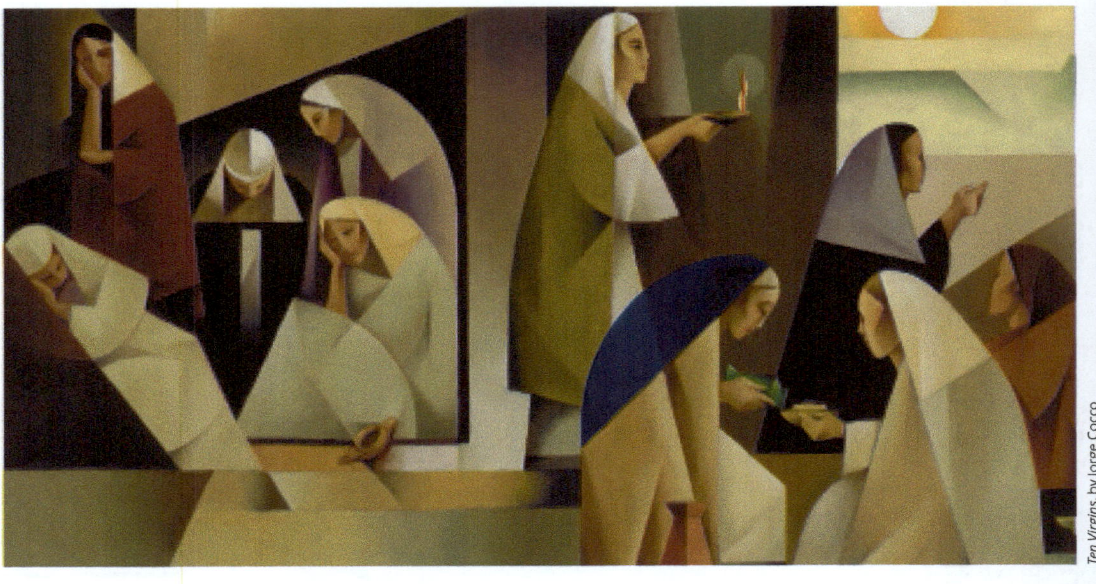

Doctrine and Covenants 133–134

In 1833, mobs attacked and destroyed the Church's printing press. Among the print jobs in progress at the time was the Book of Commandments—the Church's first attempt to compile God's latter-day revelations into one volume. The mob scattered the unbound pages, and although courageous Saints preserved some of them, only a few incomplete copies of the Book of Commandments are known to have survived.

What we now know as section 133 of the Doctrine and Covenants was meant to be the appendix to the Book of Commandments, like an exclamation point at the end of the Lord's published revelations. It warns of a coming day of judgment and repeats the call found throughout modern revelation: Flee worldliness, as symbolized by Babylon. Build Zion. Prepare for the Second Coming. And spread this message "unto every nation, and kindred, and tongue, and people" (verse 37). The original plans for the Book of Commandments were not fulfilled, but this revelation is a reminder and a witness that the Lord's work will go forward, "for he shall make bare his holy arm . . . , and all the ends of the earth shall see the salvation of their God" (verse 3).

 Ideas for Learning at Home and at Church

DOCTRINE AND COVENANTS 133:4–14

Jesus Christ calls me to reject Babylon and come to Zion.

The spiritual opposite of Zion is Babylon—an ancient city that throughout scripture symbolized wickedness and spiritual bondage. As you read Doctrine and Covenants 133:4–14, ponder how the Savior is calling you to "go . . . out from Babylon" (verse 5) and "go . . . forth unto . . . Zion" (verse 9). How are you responding to His call? What else do you learn about Zion from Elder D. Todd Christofferson's message "Come to Zion"? (*Ensign* or *Liahona*, Nov. 2008, 37–40).

DOCTRINE AND COVENANTS 133:1–19, 37–39

I can prepare now for the Savior's Second Coming.

Both section 1, the Lord's preface to the Doctrine and Covenants, and section 133, the original appendix to the Book of Commandments, begin with the same plea from the Lord: "Hearken, O ye people of my church" (Doctrine and Covenants 1:1; 133:1). Perhaps you could study

Doctrine and Covenants 133:1–19, 37–39 and list the messages the Lord invites you to "hearken" to (listen to and obey) as you prepare for His Second Coming. In particular, you might list things He wants you to do to (1) prepare yourself and (2) help prepare the world for His return. What do you learn from these lists?

President Russell M. Nelson shared important truths about what the world will be like when the Savior returns—and how to prepare. Look for these truths in his message "The Future of the Church: Preparing the World for the Savior's Second Coming" (*Liahona*, Apr. 2020, 6–11). What do you feel inspired to do—or keep doing—to "prepare the world for the Savior's return"? ("Aaronic Priesthood Quorum Theme," Gospel Library).

See also Matthew 25:1–13; Russell M. Nelson, "Embrace the Future with Faith," *Ensign* or *Liahona*, Nov. 2020, 73–76; "Come, Ye Children of the Lord," *Hymns*, no. 58; Topics and Questions, "Second Coming of Jesus Christ," Gospel Library.

DOCTRINE AND COVENANTS 133:19–56

The Second Coming of Jesus Christ will be joyful for the righteous.

As you read the description of the Savior's return in verses 19–56, what do you find that you are looking forward to? What words or phrases describe the Lord's love for His people? Consider recording your personal experiences with "the loving kindness of [your] Lord, and all that he has bestowed upon [you] according to his goodness" (verse 52).

Detail from *Healer*, by Kelsy and Jesse Lightweave

DOCTRINE AND COVENANTS 134

"Governments were instituted of God for the benefit of man."

The early Saints' relationship with government was complex. When the Saints were forced out of Jackson County, Missouri, in 1833, they asked for help from the local and national government and received none. At the same time, some people outside the Church interpreted teachings about Zion to mean that the Saints rejected the authority of earthly governments. Doctrine and Covenants 134 was written, in part, to clarify the Church's position on government. What does this section suggest about how the Lord's Saints should feel about government?

As you study section 134, consider looking for principles of government and the responsibilities of citizens. How might these ideas have been helpful to the early Saints? How are they applicable where you live?

See also Articles of Faith 1:11–12; Topics and Questions, "Religious Freedom," Gospel Library.

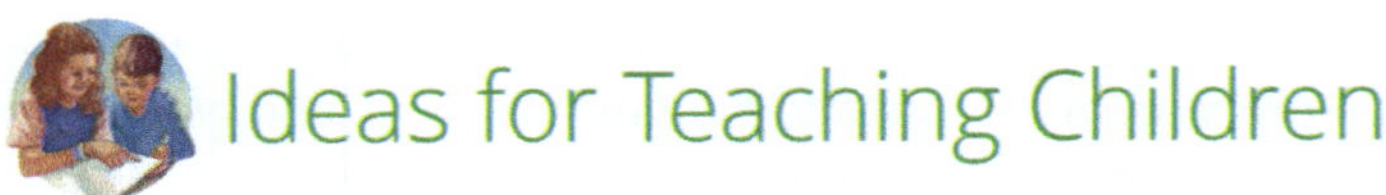

Ideas for Teaching Children

DOCTRINE AND COVENANTS 133:4–5, 14

The Lord wants me to stay away from the evil in the world.

- You and your children could list some places and situations the Lord wants us to stay away from. Then you could compare those places and situations to the definition of "Babel, Babylon" in the Guide to the Scriptures (Gospel Library). They could then read Doctrine and Covenants 133:4–5, 14. What does it mean to "go . . . out from Babylon"? (verse 5). You could also make a similar list of places and situations the Lord invites us to and compare that list to the definition of "Zion" in Guide to the Scriptures.

DOCTRINE AND COVENANTS 133:19–21, 25

Jesus Christ will come again.

- Your children might enjoy acting out what it looks like to prepare for something, like a sports tournament, an important visitor, or a favorite holiday. Why is preparation important? You could then read together Doctrine and Covenants 133:17–19, 21 and invite your children to look for what the Lord invites us to prepare for. You could show them the picture from this week's outline and ask your children what they know about Jesus Christ's Second Coming. What else do we learn from verses 19–25, 46–52? What can we do to prepare for this joyful event?

- You could hide various pictures or objects depicting things we can do to prepare for Jesus Christ's Second Coming (such as read the scriptures, share the gospel, or serve our families). Let your children find the pictures or objects and talk about how doing these things helps us get ready to meet the Savior when He returns.

- You could also sing together a song about the Second Coming, such as "When He Comes Again" (*Children's Songbook*, 82–83). Share with each other your love for the Savior and your feelings about His return.

DOCTRINE AND COVENANTS 133:52–53

Jesus Christ is loving and kind.

- You and your children could look at pictures that show that Jesus is loving and kind. (For example, see *Gospel Art Book*, nos. 42, 47.) What else has Jesus done to show His love and kindness? Read together Doctrine and Covenants 133:52, and help your children think of ways they can "mention the loving kindness of their Lord" to others.

Detail from *In His Light*, by Greg Olsen

Teach clear and simple doctrine. The Lord teaches His gospel in "plainness and simplicity" (Doctrine and Covenants 133:57). What do these words suggest to you about teaching the gospel to your family or class?

The Lord wants me to obey the law.

- Your children could list rules or laws they obey. What would life be like if no one obeyed these laws? Then you could read Doctrine and Covenants 134:1–2 with them, helping them understand any words or phrases they might not understand. Why does the Lord want us to obey the law? (see also Articles of Faith 1:12).

For more ideas, see this month's issue of the *Friend* magazine.

Christ in a Red Robe, by Minerva Teichert

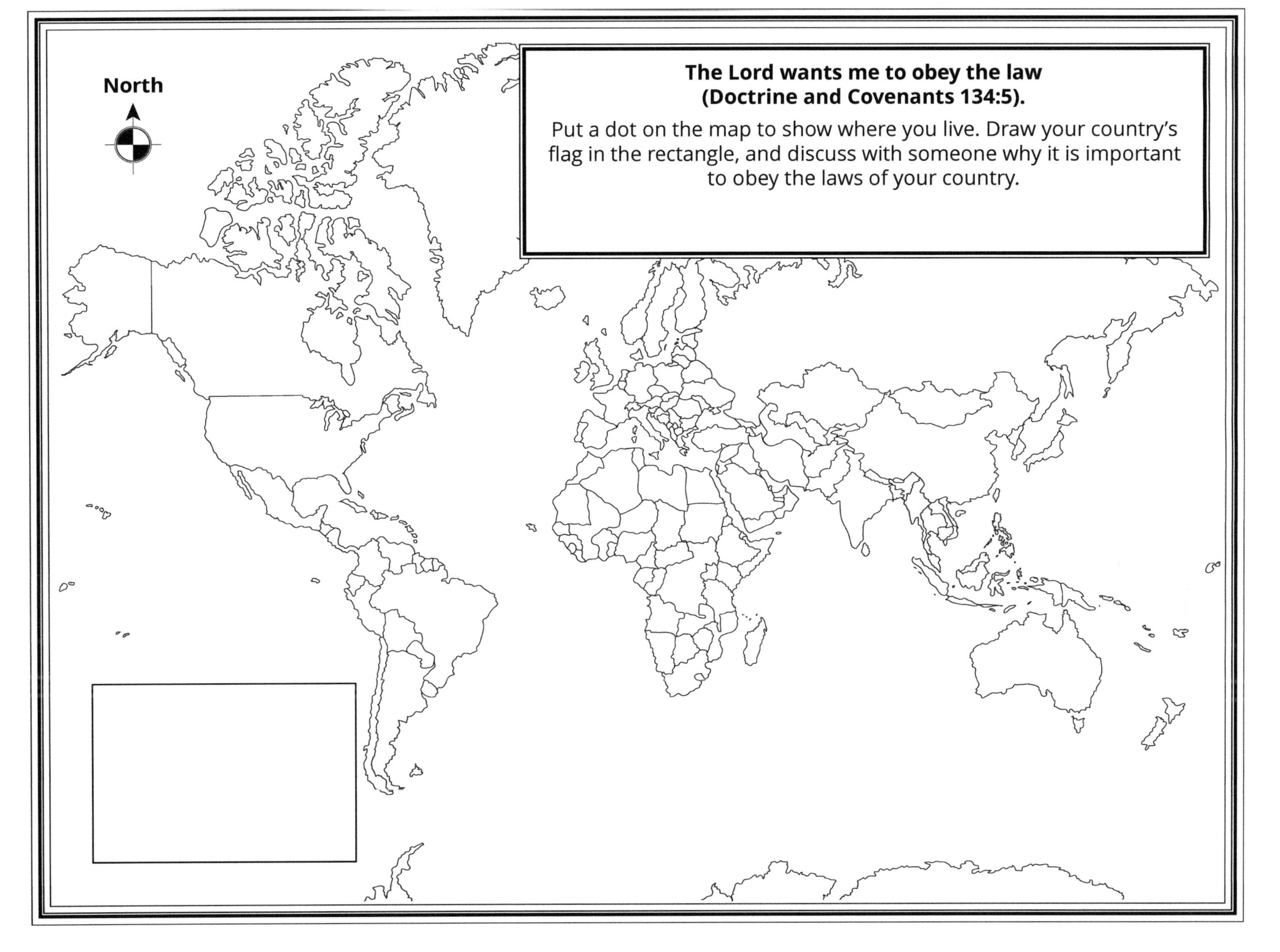

North
The Lord wants me to obey the law (Doctrine and Covenants 134:5).
Put a dot on the map to show where you live. Draw your country's flag in the rectangle, and discuss with someone why it is important to obey the laws of your country.

Carthage Jail

Doctrine and Covenants 135–136

The afternoon of June 27, 1844, found Joseph and Hyrum Smith in jail once again, accompanied by John Taylor and Willard Richards. They believed they were innocent of any crime, but they submitted to arrest, hoping to keep the Saints in Nauvoo safe. This wasn't the first time that enemies of the Church had put the Prophet Joseph in prison, but this time he seemed to know that he would not return alive. He and his friends tried to comfort each other by reading from the Book of Mormon and singing hymns. Then gunshots were heard, and within a few minutes the mortal lives of Joseph Smith and his brother Hyrum had come to an end.

And yet it was not the end of the divine cause they had embraced. And it was not the end of the Restoration of the gospel of Jesus Christ. There was more work to do and more revelation that would guide the Church forward. The end of the Prophet's life was not the end of the work of God.

See *Saints*, 1:521–52.

 Ideas for Learning at Home and at Church

Joseph and Hyrum Smith sealed their testimonies with their blood.

Imagine how you might have felt if you had been living in Nauvoo when Joseph and Hyrum Smith were killed (see *Saints*, 1:554–55). How would you have made sense of this tragic event? Doctrine and Covenants 135, published three months later, may have helped. As you search this section, consider what would have brought you understanding and reassurance. What would you say to someone who asks, "Why would God allow His Prophet to be killed?" (see Doctrine and Covenants 136:37–39).

You could also search section 135 for words or phrases that inspire you to be faithful to Christ to the end, like Joseph and Hyrum were.

See also Doctrine and Covenants 5:21–22; "Remembering the Martyrdom," in *Revelations in Context*, 299–306; *Teachings of Presidents of the Church: Joseph Smith* (2011), 522–23, 529–40; "Testimony of the Book of Mormon" (video), Gospel Library.

DOCTRINE AND COVENANTS 135:3

📖 Joseph Smith was a prophet and witness of Jesus Christ.

Doctrine and Covenants 135:3 names some of the things Joseph Smith accomplished "in the short space of twenty years." How have these things affected you and your relationship with Heavenly Father and Jesus Christ? Consider how you would complete a sentence like this one: *Because of what the Lord did through Joseph Smith, I . . .* You might also record and share your testimony of the Prophet Joseph Smith with others.

Another way to learn about Joseph Smith's mission is to try writing a brief obituary or eulogy for him. What would you say to build faith in Christ and His restored gospel? You might want to include important events or accomplishments found in Doctrine and Covenants 135 or those mentioned in the resources below.

Jesus Christ revealed many truths about Himself and His Atonement through Joseph Smith. Consider pondering the experience you have had studying the Doctrine and Covenants this year. What truths have stood out to you? You may want to share these with your family, class or quorum members, or others as you study this week. How do these truths help you understand and draw closer to the Savior?

See also "Joseph Smith: The Prophet of the Restoration" (video), Gospel Library; Tad R. Callister, "Joseph Smith—Prophet of the Restoration," *Ensign* or *Liahona*, Nov. 2009, 35–37; "Praise to the Man," *Hymns*, no. 27; Topics and Questions, "Joseph Smith," Gospel Library.

DOCTRINE AND COVENANTS 136

I can help accomplish the Lord's will as I follow His counsel.

After Joseph Smith died, the Saints were driven from Nauvoo. They now faced a 1,300-mile (2,100 km) journey through a harsh wilderness. Brigham Young, President of the Quorum of the Twelve Apostles, worried about how the Saints would survive the trek. In a temporary settlement called Winter Quarters, he pleaded for guidance. The Lord's response is recorded in section 136. "By helping the Saints remember that their conduct on the journey was as important as their destination, the revelation helped transform the westward migration from an unfortunate necessity into an important shared spiritual experience" ("This Shall Be Our Covenant," in *Revelations in Context*, 308).

Keep this in mind as you study section 136. What counsel do you find that could help turn a difficult trial in your life "into an important . . . spiritual experience"? You might ponder how this counsel can help you accomplish the Lord's will in your own life, as it helped the early Saints in their travels.

See also "This Shall Be Our Covenant," in *Revelations in Context*, 307–14; "Come, Come, Ye Saints," *Hymns*, no. 30; Church History Topics, "Succession of Church Leadership," Gospel Library.

Detail from *Winter Quarters*, by Greg Olsen

Ideas for Teaching Children

DOCTRINE AND COVENANTS 135:1–2, 4–5

Joseph and Hyrum Smith gave their lives for Jesus Christ and His gospel.

- Summarize for your children Doctrine and Covenants 135:1 or share "Chapter 57: The Prophet Is Killed" (in *Doctrine and Covenants Stories*, 201–5, or the corresponding video in Gospel Library). This could be a good opportunity for you and your children to share your feelings about the sacrifice Joseph and Hyrum made for the Savior and His gospel.

- Doctrine and Covenants 135:4–5 states that Hyrum Smith read a passage from the Book of Mormon before he went to Carthage Jail. You and your children could read this passage together (see Ether 12:36–38). How could these verses have comforted Hyrum? You could also share scriptures that bring you comfort when you are worried or sad.

- You and your children could look at pictures of prophets (see *Gospel Art Book*, nos. 7, 14, 67) and talk about some things God asks prophets to do. What did these prophets sacrifice for the Savior?

In the home, learning and living are inseparable. "The gospel takes on immediate relevance in the home. There the people with whom you are learning the gospel are the people with whom you will live it—every day. In fact, much of the time, living the gospel is how we learn the gospel" (*Teaching in the Savior's Way*, 31).

DOCTRINE AND COVENANTS 135:3

Joseph Smith was a prophet and witness of Jesus Christ.

- To help your children remember and appreciate how the Lord has blessed us through Joseph Smith's mission, you could display objects that represent things Joseph did, such as the Book of Mormon, the Doctrine and Covenants, or a picture of a temple (see also this week's activity page). Then your children could look in Doctrine and Covenants 135:3 for some things Joseph Smith did to help us come closer to Heavenly Father and Jesus Christ. Invite your children to share why they are grateful for these things.

American Prophet, by Del Parson

The Lord can bless me when I am struggling.

- Consider placing a picture of the Nauvoo Temple on one side of a room and creating a simple shelter on the other side. Invite your children to gather near the picture, and tell them about the Saints who had to leave Nauvoo after Joseph Smith died (see chapters 58, 60, and 62 in *Doctrine and Covenants Stories*, 206–8, 211–16, 222–24, or the corresponding videos in Gospel Library). Emphasize the faith these Saints had in Jesus Christ, and invite your children to walk to the shelter to represent the journey to Winter Quarters. They could sing a song like "To Be a Pioneer" (*Children's Songbook*, 218–19) as they walk.

- Explain that in Doctrine and Covenants 136, the Lord gave counsel to help the Saints on their journey to the Salt Lake Valley. Help your children find something in this revelation that could give them courage for this journey (see verses 4, 10–11, 18–30). How can this counsel help us with the trials we face today?

For more ideas, see this month's issue of the *Friend* magazine.

Greater Love Hath No Man, by Casey Childs

Joseph Smith was a prophet and witness of Jesus Christ (Doctrine and Covenants 135:3).

The Lord accomplished many things through the Prophet Joseph Smith that build our faith in Jesus Christ. Color the pictures. Match the numbered items with the pictures by writing numbers in the circles next to the related pictures.

1. Baptism
2. The priesthood
3. Missionary work
4. Temples
5. The Book of Mormon, the Doctrine and Covenants, and other scriptures

Detail from *Christ Preaching in the Spirit World,* by Robert T. Barrett

Doctrine and Covenants 137–138

The revelations recorded in Doctrine and Covenants 137 and 138 are separated by more than 80 years and 1,500 miles (2,400 km). Section 137 was received by the Prophet Joseph Smith in 1836 in the Kirtland Temple, and section 138 was received by Joseph F. Smith, sixth President of the Church, in 1918 in Salt Lake City. But doctrinally, these two visions belong side by side. They both answer questions that many people—including God's prophets—have about life after death. Joseph Smith wondered about the fate of his brother Alvin, who had died without being baptized. Joseph F. Smith, who had lost both of his parents and 13 children to untimely deaths, thought often about the spirit world and wondered about the preaching of the gospel there.

Section 137 casts some initial light on the destiny of God's children in the next life, and section 138 opens the curtains even wider. Together, both revelations testify of "the great and wonderful love made manifest by the Father and the Son" (Doctrine and Covenants 138:3).

 Ideas for Learning at Home and at Church

DOCTRINE AND COVENANTS 137; 138:30–37, 57–60

📖 All of Heavenly Father's children will have the opportunity to choose eternal life.

Alvin Smith, the Prophet Joseph's beloved brother, passed away six years before God restored the authority to baptize. The common understanding among some Christians in 1836 was that if a person died without being baptized, that person could not go to heaven. Joseph wondered about Alvin's eternal salvation for many years—until he received the revelation in Doctrine and Covenants 137.

Many people today have similar questions. Why would God require ordinances and covenants when so many people never have the opportunity to receive them? What would you say to someone who wonders this? How would you build their faith in God and His requirements for salvation? Look for truths you could share in section 137 and in section 138:30–37, 57–60. You could also look for these truths expressed in the hymn "The Glorious Gospel Light Has Shone" (*Hymns,* no. 283) and in President Henry B. Eyring's message "Gathering the Family of God" (*Ensign* or *Liahona,* May 2017, 19–22).

As you study and ponder, you might record your impressions by completing sentences like these:

- Because of these revelations, I know that Heavenly Father ______.
- Because of these revelations, I know that the Father's plan of salvation ______.
- Because of these revelations, I want to ______.

See also *Saints*, 1:232–35.

Reading and pondering the scriptures prepares me to receive revelation.

Sometimes revelation comes even though we do not seek it. But more often it comes because we diligently search and prepare for it. As you read Doctrine and Covenants 138:1–11, 25–30, note what President Joseph F. Smith was pondering when "the eyes of [his] understanding were opened." You could also compare his experience to 1 Nephi 11:1–6; Joseph Smith—History 1:12–19. Then consider how you can follow President Smith's example. For instance, what changes do you feel inspired to make to your scripture study to receive more personal revelation?

In his message "The Vision of the Redemption of the Dead" (*Ensign* or *Liahona*, Nov. 2018, 71–74), President M. Russell Ballard suggested other ways President Smith was prepared to receive this revelation. What do you learn from his experiences? Consider how the Lord has prepared you for experiences you are having—and how He might be preparing you for experiences in your future.

See also *Saints*, 3:202–5; "Ministry of Joseph F. Smith: A Vision of the Redemption of the Dead" (video), Gospel Library.

Joseph F. Smith, by Albert Salzbrenner

Invite the Spirit. "What have you observed that contributes to a spiritual environment for learning the gospel? What detracts from it?" (*Teaching in the Savior's Way*, 18). As you study President Joseph F. Smith's experience in Doctrine and Covenants 138:1–11, consider how you can encourage pondering and invite spiritual impressions for yourself and, if you are a teacher, for the people you teach.

The Savior's work continues on the other side of the veil.

President Russell M. Nelson taught, "Our message to the world is simple and sincere: we invite all of God's children on both sides of the veil to come unto their Savior, receive the blessings of the holy temple, have enduring joy, and qualify for eternal life" ("Let Us All Press On," *Ensign* or *Liahona*, May 2018, 118–19). Ponder this statement as you read Doctrine and Covenants 138:25–60. You could also consider these questions:

- What do you learn from these verses about how the Savior's work is being accomplished in the spirit world? Why is it important for you to know that this work is taking place?

- What impresses you about the Lord's messengers in the spirit world?

- How does this revelation strengthen your faith in God's plan of redemption?

If you'd like to learn more about the spirit world, you could study President Dallin H. Oaks's message "Trust in the Lord" (*Ensign* or *Liahona*, Nov. 2019, 26–29).

See also "Susa Young Gates and the Vision of the Redemption of the Dead," in *Revelations in Context*, 315–22; "A Visit from Father" (video), Gospel Library.

For more ideas, see this month's issues of the *Liahona* and *For the Strength of Youth* magazines.

 ## Ideas for Teaching Children

DOCTRINE AND COVENANTS 137:5–10; 138:18–35

All Heavenly Father's children will have the chance to hear the gospel.

- To learn about what it would have meant for Joseph Smith to see several of his family members in the celestial kingdom, your children could watch the video "Ministry of Joseph Smith: Temples" (Gospel Library), or you could share *Doctrine and Covenants Stories*, 152–53 (or the corresponding video in Gospel Library). Perhaps you could also talk about someone you know who died without the chance to be baptized. What does Doctrine and Covenants 137:5–10 teach us about that person?

- Consider using a picture of the Savior's tomb (see *Gospel Art Book*, no. 58, or Bible Photographs, no. 14) and the picture at the end of this outline to teach your children where Jesus's spirit went when His body was in the tomb. Then you could read together Doctrine and Covenants 138:18–19, 23–24, 27–30 to learn about what Jesus did while He was there. Who did He visit? What did He ask them to do? Why did He do this?

- You could also use this week's activity page to help your children compare what missionaries teach on this side of the veil (see, for example, Articles of Faith 1:4) with what missionaries teach in the spirit world (see Doctrine and Covenants 138:33). What is similar in these verses, and what is different? What does this teach us about Heavenly Father and His plan?

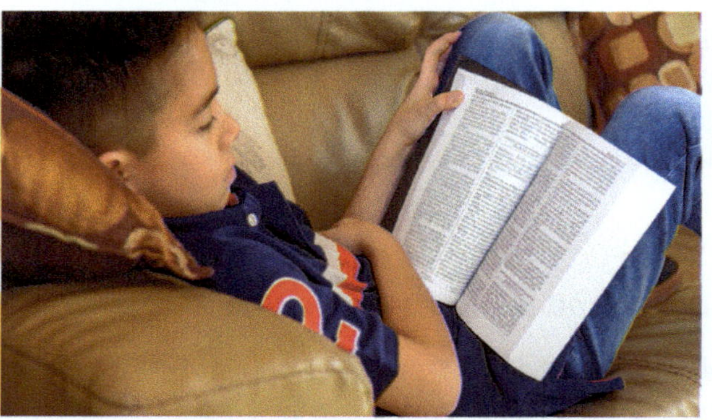

Pondering the scriptures invites the Holy Ghost.

When I ponder the scriptures, the Holy Ghost can help me understand them.

- As you and your children read Doctrine and Covenants 138:1–11 together, you could invite them to pretend they are President Joseph F. Smith and do actions that go along with the words in verses 6 and 11. You might also show them a picture of President Smith (there's one in this outline) and explain that he was the sixth President of the Church. You could also talk about a time when you pondered something in the scriptures and the Holy Ghost helped you understand it.

- Consider singing together a song about scripture study, such as "Search, Ponder, and Pray" (*Children's Songbook*, 109). What does this song say we should do to understand the scriptures?

For more ideas, see this month's issue of the *Friend* magazine.

The Commissioned, by Harold I. Hopkinson

All of Heavenly Father's children will have the chance to hear the gospel (Doctrine and Covenants 138:12–35).

Color the picture of missionaries preaching the gospel. Then draw missionaries preaching the gospel in the spirit world. If you know someone who has passed away, consider including that person in your picture.

The Articles of Faith and Official Declarations 1 and 2

Since Joseph Smith's First Vision, God has continued to guide His Church by revelation. In some cases, that revelation has included changes to the policies and practices of the Church. Official Declarations 1 and 2 announced this kind of revelation—one led to the end of plural marriage, and the other made the blessings of the priesthood available to people of all races. Changes like these are part of what it means to have a "true and living church" (Doctrine and Covenants 1:30), with a true and living prophet, led by a true and living God.

But eternal truth doesn't change, though our understanding of it does. And sometimes revelation casts additional light on truth. The Articles of Faith serve this clarifying purpose. The Church is solidly founded on eternal truth yet can grow and change "according as the Lord will, suiting his mercies according to the conditions of the children of men" (Doctrine and Covenants 46:15). In other words, "We believe all that God has revealed, all that He does now reveal, and we believe that He will yet reveal many great and important things pertaining to the Kingdom of God" (Articles of Faith 1:9).

 Ideas for Learning at Home and at Church

THE ARTICLES OF FAITH

The Articles of Faith contain foundational truths of the restored gospel.

Consider this approach to studying the Articles of Faith: For each article of faith, make a "mini-lesson" to explain what you believe. Your mini-lesson could include a related scripture, picture, hymn or children's song, or personal experience about living a truth that the article of faith teaches.

What difference do these truths make in your relationship with Heavenly Father and Jesus Christ? How have the Articles of Faith improved your gospel study or helped you share the gospel with others?

See also Guide to the Scriptures, "Articles of Faith," Gospel Library; L. Tom Perry, "The Doctrines and Principles Contained in the Articles of Faith," *Ensign* or *Liahona*, Nov. 2013,

46–48; "Chapter 38: The Wentworth Letter," in *Teachings of Presidents of the Church: Joseph Smith* (2011), 435–47.

ARTICLES OF FAITH 1:9; OFFICIAL DECLARATIONS 1 AND 2

The Church of Jesus Christ is guided by revelation.

"We believe that [God] will yet reveal many great and important things pertaining to the Kingdom of God" (Articles of Faith 1:9). With this principle in mind, review Official Declarations 1 and 2, and look for words and phrases that strengthen your faith in continuing revelation. How have these revelations affected your life? How have they helped the work of Heavenly Father's kingdom progress?

What evidence do you see that the Church is led "by the inspiration of Almighty God" today? (Official Declaration 1). Perhaps you could review one or more recent general conference messages, looking for how the Lord is guiding His Church—and your life. The most recent message from the President of the Church may be a good place to start.

What can you do if you or someone you love struggles to understand or accept what the Lord teaches through His prophets? Why are you grateful for a prophet?

See also Amos 3:7; 2 Nephi 28:30; Allen D. Haynie, "A Living Prophet for the Latter Days," *Liahona*, May 2023, 25–28; Topics and Questions, "Prophets," Gospel Library; "We Thank Thee, O God, for a Prophet," *Hymns*, no. 19.

OFFICIAL DECLARATION 1

The work of God must move forward.

In the "Excerpts from Three Addresses by President Wilford Woodruff regarding the Manifesto" (at the end of Official Declaration 1), what reasons did the prophet give for the Lord ending the practice of plural marriage? What does this teach you about God's work?

For more information about the historical background of Official Declaration 1, see *Saints*, 2:602–15; "The Messenger and the Manifesto," in *Revelations in Context*, 323–31; Topics and Questions, "Plural Marriage and Families in Early Utah," Gospel Library.

Wilford Woodruff, by H. E. Peterson

OFFICIAL DECLARATION 2

I can trust in the Lord, even when I do not have a perfect understanding.

We don't know why priesthood ordination and temple ordinances were not available to Church members of African descent for a time. Even when facing difficult unanswered questions about that policy, many Black Latter-day Saints trusted the Lord (see Proverbs 3:5) and stayed faithful to Him throughout their lives. Learning about their faith and experiences could be inspiring to you. Here are some of their accounts, found at history.ChurchofJesusChrist.org:

- "Jane Elizabeth Manning James"

- "In My Father's House Are Many Mansions" (story of Green Flake)

- "You Have Come at Last" (story of Anthony Obinna)

- "Break the Soil of Bitterness" (story of Julia Mavimbela)

- "I Will Take It in Faith" (story of George Rickford)

- "Long-Promised Day" (story of Joseph W. B. Johnson)

As you read Official Declaration 2, what do you learn about the Lord's process for guiding the policies of His Church? Ponder how you have learned to trust the Lord even when you don't have a perfect understanding.

See also 2 Nephi 26:33; "Witnessing the Faithfulness," in *Revelations in Context*, 332–41; Topics and Questions, "Race and the Priesthood," Gospel Library; Ahmad Corbitt, "A Personal Essay on Race and the Priesthood," parts 1–4, history.ChurchofJesusChrist.org; BeOne .ChurchofJesusChrist.org.

It's OK to say "I don't know." While you should try your best to help the people you teach to answer their questions about the gospel, the Lord doesn't expect you to know everything. When you don't know how to answer something, admit it. Then point learners to revealed doctrine, and bear sincere testimony of what you do know.

For more ideas, see this month's issues of the *Liahona* and *For the Strength of Youth* magazines.

 Ideas for Teaching Children

THE ARTICLES OF FAITH

I believe in the gospel of Jesus Christ.

- Consider finding and singing hymns or children's songs that can help your children understand one or more of the Articles of Faith. Perhaps they can help you choose the hymns and songs. Help your children see how the songs relate to the Articles of Faith.

- You and your children could work together to write questions people might have about the gospel of Jesus Christ or His Church. You could then work together to answer those questions using the Articles of Faith. Where else can we go when we have questions about the gospel?

ARTICLES OF FAITH 1:9; OFFICIAL DECLARATIONS 1 AND 2

The Lord guides His Church through His prophet.

- To help your children understand the ninth article of faith, perhaps you could give them a set of scriptures and a picture of the living prophet (or a recent conference issue of the *Liahona*). Ask them to hold up the scriptures as you read the words "all that God has revealed" and the picture or the magazine when you read "all that He does now reveal" (Articles of Faith 1:9). Why do we need both ancient and modern prophets?

- Your children could learn how the words of the prophets guide us by following instructions to make something, such as food or a toy. You could compare this to the instructions Jesus Christ gives us through the prophet. What are some things the Lord has taught us through His living prophet today?

God calls prophets to lead His Church.

Prophets help us know the will of Heavenly Father.

- Perhaps seeing how the ancient scriptures relate to modern revelation could help your children understand the Official Declarations. You could ask them to read Acts 10:34–35 and Jacob 2:27–30 and invite them to determine which scripture relates to Official Declaration 1 (which led to the end of plural marriage) and which relates to Official Declaration 2 (which announced that priesthood ordination and temple ordinances are available to people of all races). Bear your testimony that the Lord reveals His will to ancient and modern prophets.

For more ideas, see this month's issue of the *Friend* magazine.

THE ARTICLES OF FAITH

OF THE CHURCH OF JESUS CHRIST
OF LATTER-DAY SAINTS

We believe in God, the Eternal Father, and in His Son, Jesus Christ, and in the Holy Ghost.

2 We believe that men will be punished for their own sins, and not for Adam's transgression.

3 We believe that through the Atonement of Christ, all mankind may be saved, by obedience to the laws and ordinances of the Gospel.

4 We believe that the first principles and ordinances of the Gospel are: first, Faith in the Lord Jesus Christ; second, Repentance; third, Baptism by immersion for the remission of sins; fourth, Laying on of hands for the gift of the Holy Ghost.

5 We believe that a man must be called of God, by prophecy, and by the laying on of hands by those who are in authority, to preach the Gospel and administer in the ordinances thereof.

6 We believe in the same organization that existed in the Primitive Church, namely, apostles, prophets, pastors, teachers, evangelists, and so forth.

7 We believe in the gift of tongues, prophecy, revelation, visions, healing, interpretation of tongues, and so forth.

8 We believe the Bible to be the word of God as far as it is translated correctly; we also believe the Book of Mormon to be the word of God.

9 We believe all that God has revealed, all that He does now reveal, and we believe that He will yet reveal many great and important things pertaining to the Kingdom of God.

10 We believe in the literal gathering of Israel and in the restoration of the Ten Tribes; that Zion (the New Jerusalem) will be built upon the American continent; that Christ will reign personally upon the earth; and, that the earth will be renewed and receive its paradisiacal glory.

11 We claim the privilege of worshiping Almighty God according to the dictates of our own conscience, and allow all men the same privilege, let them worship how, where, or what they may.

12 We believe in being subject to kings, presidents, rulers, and magistrates, in obeying, honoring, and sustaining the law.

13 We believe in being honest, true, chaste, benevolent, virtuous, and in doing good to all men; indeed, we may say that we follow the admonition of Paul—We believe all things, we hope all things, we have endured many things, and hope to be able to endure all things. If there is anything virtuous, lovely, or of good report or praiseworthy, we seek after these things.

JOSEPH SMITH.

I believe in the gospel of Jesus Christ (the Articles of Faith).

Color and cut out the 13 cards, and place them in random order.
Read each article of faith, and find the card that matches it. Write the
number of the related article of faith in the circle on each card.

Godhead

Transgression

Atonement

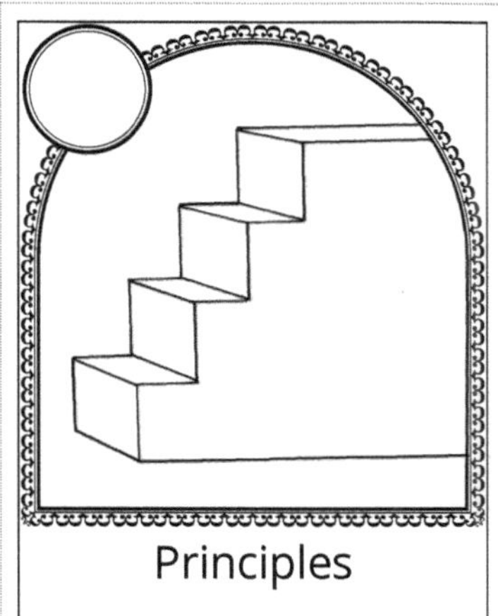

Principles

Called

Organization

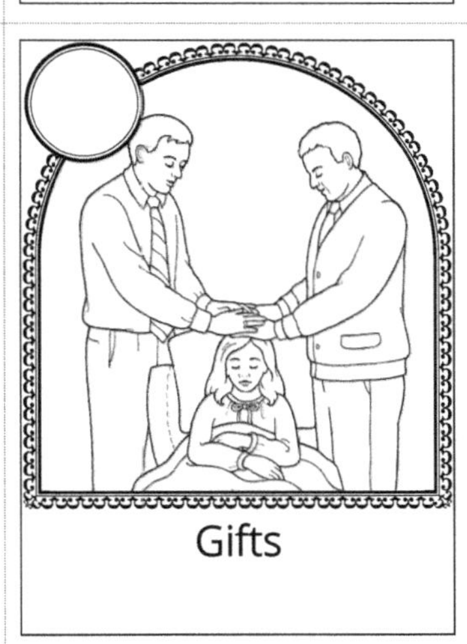

Gifts

Word

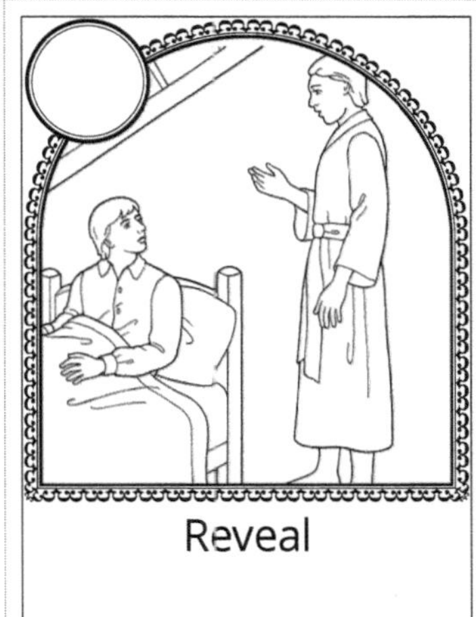

Reveal

Gathering

Worshipping

Law

Honest

The Family: A Proclamation to the World

Even before we were born, we were part of a family—the family of our heavenly parents. That pattern continues on earth. Families here, at their best, are meant to echo the perfect pattern in heaven.

Of course, there are no guarantees that earthly families will be ideal or even functional. But as President Henry B. Eyring taught, families "give God's children the best chance to be welcomed to the world with the only love on earth that comes close to what we felt in heaven—parental love" ("Gathering the Family of God," *Ensign* or *Liahona*, May 2017, 20). Knowing that families are imperfect and subject to attacks from the adversary, God sent His Beloved Son to redeem us and heal our families. And He sent latter-day prophets with a proclamation to defend and strengthen families. If we follow the prophets and put faith in the Savior, even though mortal families fall short of the divine ideal, there's hope for families—on earth and in heaven.

 Ideas for Learning at Home and at Church

"The family is central to the Creator's plan."

"The Family: A Proclamation to the World" is clearly about families. But it is equally about God's plan of salvation. One way to study the proclamation is to write the phrases *premortal life*, *mortal life*, and *postmortal life* on a piece of paper and list what the proclamation teaches about each of these topics. What do you learn when you study the proclamation this way? How does this help you understand why marriage and family are essential to God's plan? How do the truths in the proclamation influence your choices?

There are many people who, for a variety of reasons, might be fearful about marriage or raising children. If a friend said to you, "I don't ever want to get married or have a family," what would you say? Perhaps you could search the proclamation looking for something that would help your friend have hope in God's plan.

Another question you might be asked—or that you might ask yourself—is one like this: "What if my family situation does not match what's described in the family proclamation?" Here are two places you could look for prophetic counsel: the section "A Mighty Change" in Elder

Dieter F. Uchtdorf's message "Jesus Christ Is the Strength of Parents" (*Liahona*, May 2023, 55–59) and the last four paragraphs of Elder D. Todd Christofferson's message "Why Marriage, Why Family" (*Ensign* or *Liahona*, May 2015, 52).

What do you feel inspired to do because of what you have studied?

See also Dallin H. Oaks, "The Plan and the Proclamation," *Ensign* or *Liahona*, Nov. 2017, 28–31; Topics and Questions, "Family," Gospel Library.

"Each [person] is a beloved son or daughter of heavenly parents."

We often think of the family proclamation as a guide for family life. But it also teaches important truths about our heavenly family and eternal identity. Why is it important for you to know that we are all part of this family? How does this truth influence the choices you make?

See also "I Am a Child of God," *Hymns*, no. 301.

"Happiness in family life is most likely to be achieved when founded upon the teachings of the Lord Jesus Christ."

Think of paragraphs 6 and 7 of the family proclamation as a pattern for "happiness in family life." As you read these paragraphs, identify principles of "successful marriages and families." You might think about examples of these principles that you have seen in your own family or other families. How do these principles help make Jesus Christ the foundation of family life?

Then you might think about a family relationship you would like to strengthen. Make a plan, with the Savior's help, to act on impressions you receive.

See also L. Whitney Clayton, "The Finest Homes," *Ensign* or *Liahona*, May 2020, 107–9.

Parents should raise their children in love and righteousness.

"We call upon responsible citizens . . . to maintain and strengthen the family."

The last paragraph of the family proclamation includes a call to action. As you consider how you will respond to that call, it might help to study the title of the proclamation. For instance, what is a proclamation? What does that word imply to you about this document's message? What qualified the First Presidency and Council of the Twelve Apostles to issue a proclamation to the world about families? You might also make a list of what you consider to be the main messages of the proclamation. How can you promote these messages in your life, in your home, and in your community?

See also Bonnie L. Oscarson, "Defenders of the Family Proclamation," *Ensign* or *Liahona*, May 2015, 14–17; "Defenders of the Faith" (video), Gospel Library.

For more ideas, see this month's issues of the *Liahona* and *For the Strength of Youth* magazines.

 ## Ideas for Teaching Children

Families are important in Heavenly Father's plan.

- Help your children think of things that are so important that they would want to tell everyone about them. Show the children a copy of "The Family: A Proclamation to the World," and explain that prophets and apostles wrote it to tell us all how important families are to Heavenly Father. Why are families so important to Him? (see also the video "What Is the Purpose of Family?" [ChurchofJesusChrist.org]).

- Share with your children something from the proclamation that you feel we all need to know. Invite the children to share their feelings about those truths. How would our lives be different if we did not know these things? You might sing together a song that relates to truths found in the proclamation, such as "I Will Follow God's Plan" (*Children's Songbook*, 164–65).

- In section IV of his message "The Plan and the Proclamation" (*Ensign* or *Liahona*, Nov. 2017, 30), President Dallin H. Oaks described how the family proclamation was written. Perhaps you and your children could review his description together and talk about why you are grateful the Lord inspired His servants to teach us these truths about families.

- You could also show your children pictures (or invite them to draw some) portraying truths found in the family proclamation. These could be pictures of a temple, a family praying or playing together, or a couple getting married. Then your children could find sentences in the family proclamation that relate to the pictures. What does the Lord teach us about these things in the proclamation?

Heavenly Father wants families to be happy.

Be sensitive. As you teach the truths taught in the family proclamation, please be aware that many children live in families that do not match the ideals described in the proclamation. Consider how you can encourage and inspire them.

I am a "beloved spirit son or daughter of heavenly parents."

- As you sing together "I Am a Child of God" (*Children's Songbook*, 2–3), you could toss a ball to a child as you say, "I know a child of God named [child's name]." Then that child could toss the object to someone else, saying the same words and inserting that person's name. Help your children find the phrase "beloved spirit son or daughter of heavenly parents" in the family proclamation, and bear your testimony of this truth.

Families are happiest when they follow Jesus Christ.

- To begin a conversation about strengthening your family, you and your children could talk about what we do to make other things strong—such as our teeth, our bodies, or a building. You could then compare that to building a strong family. Help your children find the Christlike principles that lead to happiness in family life, found in paragraph 7 of the family proclamation (see also this week's activity page).

For more ideas, see this month's issue of the *Friend* magazine.

THE FAMILY

A PROCLAMATION TO THE WORLD

THE FIRST PRESIDENCY AND COUNCIL OF THE TWELVE APOSTLES
OF THE CHURCH OF JESUS CHRIST OF LATTER-DAY SAINTS

We, the First Presidency and the Council of the Twelve Apostles of The Church of Jesus Christ of Latter-day Saints, solemnly proclaim that marriage between a man and a woman is ordained of God and that the family is central to the Creator's plan for the eternal destiny of His children.

All human beings—male and female—are created in the image of God. Each is a beloved spirit son or daughter of heavenly parents, and, as such, each has a divine nature and destiny. Gender is an essential characteristic of individual premortal, mortal, and eternal identity and purpose.

In the premortal realm, spirit sons and daughters knew and worshipped God as their Eternal Father and accepted His plan by which His children could obtain a physical body and gain earthly experience to progress toward perfection and ultimately realize their divine destiny as heirs of eternal life. The divine plan of happiness enables family relationships to be perpetuated beyond the grave. Sacred ordinances and covenants available in holy temples make it possible for individuals to return to the presence of God and for families to be united eternally.

The first commandment that God gave to Adam and Eve pertained to their potential for parenthood as husband and wife. We declare that God's commandment for His children to multiply and replenish the earth remains in force. We further declare that God has commanded that the sacred powers of procreation are to be employed only between man and woman, lawfully wedded as husband and wife.

We declare the means by which mortal life is created to be divinely appointed. We affirm the sanctity of life and of its importance in God's eternal plan.

Husband and wife have a solemn responsibility to love and care for each other and for their children. "Children are an heritage of the Lord" (Psalm 127:3).

Parents have a sacred duty to rear their children in love and righteousness, to provide for their physical and spiritual needs, and to teach them to love and serve one another, observe the commandments of God, and be law-abiding citizens wherever they live. Husbands and wives—mothers and fathers—will be held accountable before God for the discharge of these obligations.

The family is ordained of God. Marriage between man and woman is essential to His eternal plan. Children are entitled to birth within the bonds of matrimony, and to be reared by a father and a mother who honor marital vows with complete fidelity. Happiness in family life is most likely to be achieved when founded upon the teachings of the Lord Jesus Christ. Successful marriages and families are established and maintained on principles of faith, prayer, repentance, forgiveness, respect, love, compassion, work, and wholesome recreational activities. By divine design, fathers are to preside over their families in love and righteousness and are responsible to provide the necessities of life and protection for their families. Mothers are primarily responsible for the nurture of their children. In these sacred responsibilities, fathers and mothers are obligated to help one another as equal partners. Disability, death, or other circumstances may necessitate individual adaptation. Extended families should lend support when needed.

We warn that individuals who violate covenants of chastity, who abuse spouse or offspring, or who fail to fulfill family responsibilities will one day stand accountable before God. Further, we warn that the disintegration of the family will bring upon individuals, communities, and nations the calamities foretold by ancient and modern prophets.

We call upon responsible citizens and officers of government everywhere to promote those measures designed to maintain and strengthen the family as the fundamental unit of society.

This proclamation was read by President Gordon B. Hinckley as part of his message at the General Relief Society Meeting held September 23, 1995, in Salt Lake City, Utah.

**Families are happiest when they follow Jesus Christ
("The Family: A Proclamation to the World").**

As you color each picture, discuss ways you can live that principle
to help make your family strong.

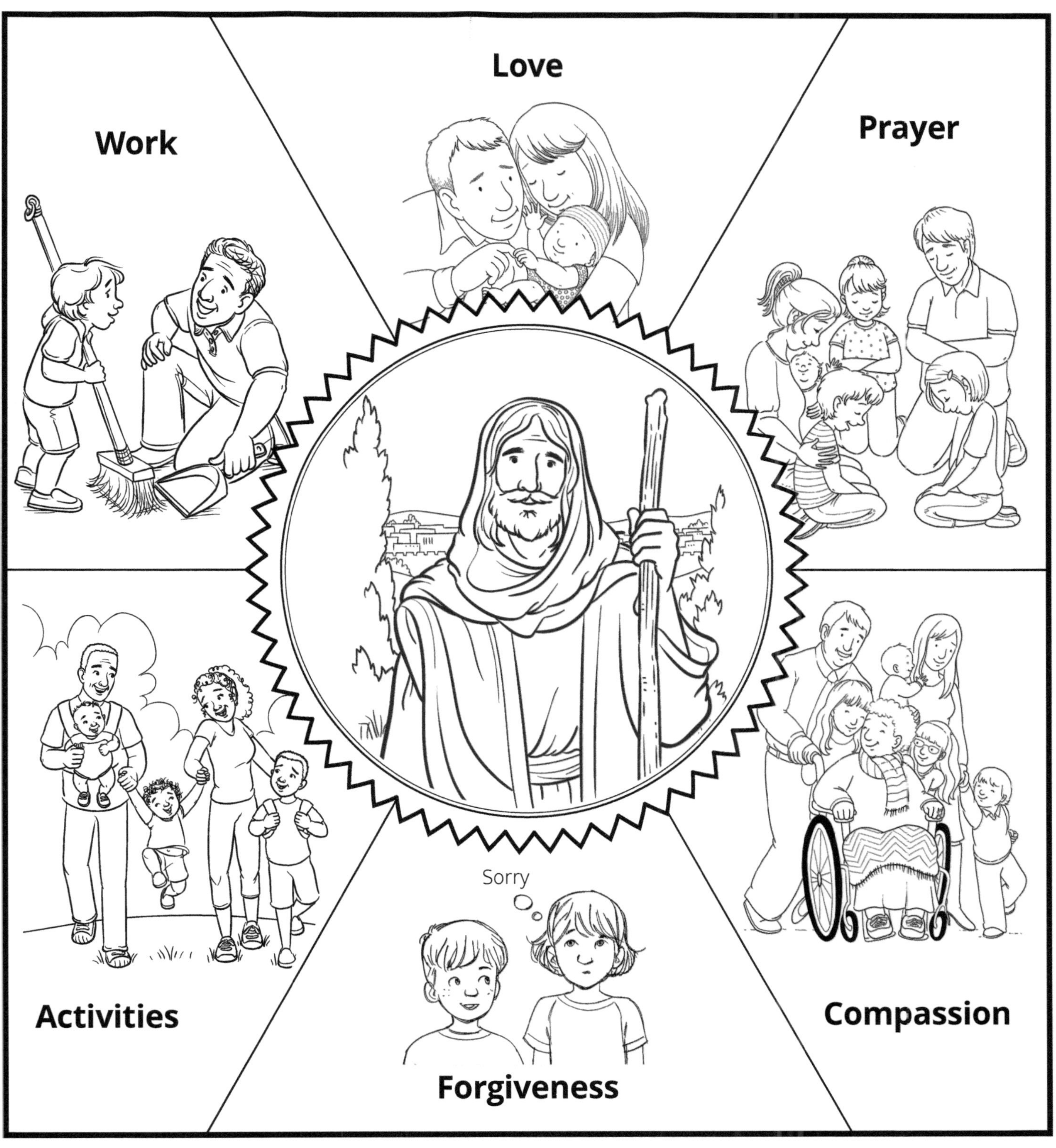

Detail from Nativity in Copper and Umber, by L. Kirk Richards

Christmas

The Prophet Joseph Smith declared, "The fundamental principles of our religion are the testimony of the Apostles and Prophets, concerning Jesus Christ, that He died, was buried, and rose again the third day, and ascended into heaven; and all other things which pertain to our religion are only appendages to it" (*Teachings of Presidents of the Church: Joseph Smith* [2011], 49). Over 160 years later, this statement inspired the First Presidency and Quorum of the Twelve Apostles to publish "The Living Christ: The Testimony of the Apostles" in honor of the 2,000th anniversary of the Savior's birth (see Russell M. Nelson, "Drawing the Power of Jesus Christ into Our Lives," *Ensign* or *Liahona*, May 2017, 40).

As Latter-day Saints, we rejoice in the blessing of continuing revelation through modern prophets and apostles. We are thankful for their inspired words of counsel, warning, and encouragement. But most of all, we are blessed by their powerful testimonies of Jesus Christ—at Christmastime and throughout the year. These are more than just stirring words of skilled writers or public speakers or insights from scriptural experts. They are the words of God's chosen, called, and authorized "special witnesses of the name of Christ in all the world" (Doctrine and Covenants 107:23).

 Ideas for Learning at Home and at Church

"None other has had so profound an influence."

What would you say in support of the statement that "none other has had so profound an influence [as Jesus Christ] upon all who have lived and will yet live upon the earth"? Look for passages in "The Living Christ" that testify of the Savior's profound influence. How has He influenced you?

Suppose someone who is unfamiliar with Christianity asked you why you celebrate Christmas. How would you respond? Review "The Living Christ" with this question in mind, and consider writing down any thoughts or impressions that come to you.

See also "Why We Need a Savior" (video), Gospel Library.

"He rose from the grave."

In "The Living Christ," the Apostles testify of the Resurrection of the Savior, mentioning three appearances of the risen Lord (see paragraph 5). Consider reading some accounts of these visits in John 20; 3 Nephi 11; and Joseph Smith—History 1:14–20. What do you learn about the Savior from His words and actions during these appearances?

Focus on the Savior. "Prayerfully reading 'The Living Christ' is like reading the testimonies of Matthew, Mark, Luke, John, and the prophets of the Book of Mormon. It will increase your faith in the Savior and help you stay focused on Him" (M. Russell Ballard, "Return and Receive," *Ensign* or *Liahona*, May 2017, 65).

"His priesthood and His Church have been restored."

During your study of the Doctrine and Covenants this year, you have had the opportunity to learn more about how the Savior's "priesthood and His Church have been restored." Which restored truths or principles have been especially meaningful to you? Consider reviewing some of the following scriptures that teach about the Restoration: Doctrine and Covenants 1:17–23; 13; 20:1–12; 65; 110; 112:30–32; 124:39–42; 128:19–21. Ponder how the truths of the restored gospel help you know and love Jesus Christ.

"He will someday return to earth."

Christmas is a time to look back on the day Jesus Christ was born and to look forward to the day He will come again. What do you learn about His return from the second-to-last paragraph of "The Living Christ"? You might also consider reading, singing, or listening to Christmas hymns that teach about the Second Coming, such as "Joy to the World" or "It Came upon the Midnight Clear" (*Hymns*, nos. 201, 207).

"He is the light, the life, and the hope of the world."

In the final paragraph of "The Living Christ," note the attributes and titles given for the Savior. Consider spending time learning about some of them. For example:

Light: How is Jesus Christ like a light to you? You might consider drawing a picture or taking a photo that, to you, represents the light He gives you. What do you feel inspired to do to share His light? (See also John 8:12; 3 Nephi 18:24; Doctrine and Covenants 50:24.)

Life: Why do you think *life* is a good word to describe Jesus Christ? In what sense does He give you life? How would your life be different without Him and His gospel? (See also John 10:10; 1 Corinthians 15:19–23; Doctrine and Covenants 66:2.)

Hope: What do you hope for because of Jesus Christ and His gospel? Do you know someone who feels hopeless about the future? Ponder how you might share with that person the hope you feel in Jesus Christ. (See also Romans 8:24–25; Ether 12:4; Moroni 7:41.)

See also Topics and Questions, "Jesus Christ," Gospel Library.

"God be thanked for [His] matchless gift."

In "The Living Christ," the Apostles refer to the Savior as a "gift" from our Heavenly Father. Based on what you find in "The Living Christ," how would you complete this sentence: "Through Jesus Christ, God gives me the gifts of . . ." Ponder what you can do to receive these gifts more fully.

How has studying "The Living Christ" affected your faith in and love for the Savior?

See also Russell M. Nelson, "Four Gifts That Jesus Christ Offers to You" (First Presidency Christmas devotional, Dec. 2, 2018), Gospel Library; "Excerpts from 'The Living Christ: The Testimony of the Apostles'" (video), ChurchofJesusChrist.org.

For more ideas, see this month's issues of the *Liahona* and *For the Strength of Youth* magazines.

 ## Ideas for Teaching Children

I can "offer [my] testimony" to celebrate Jesus's birth.

- Consider how you might introduce your children to "The Living Christ." Maybe you could help them point to the name *Christ* in the title and the signatures of the First Presidency and Twelve. You might explain that this is their testimony of Jesus Christ that they wanted to share with the world.

- You could give each child a phrase from "The Living Christ" and ask them to find or draw a picture of that phrase. Then you could help them find the phrase in "The Living Christ." You might even compile those pictures and phrases into a book.

- Share with one another how you gained your testimony of Jesus Christ. Maybe you could pass around a picture of the Savior and take turns sharing something you know about Him (including truths taught in "The Living Christ").

"He went about doing good."

- As you and your children read the second paragraph of "The Living Christ," talk with them about some of the things Jesus did. You could also look at pictures from His life (see this week's activity page and the *Gospel Art Book*). Invite your children to talk about what the

Savior is doing in the pictures. How can we serve others as He did? The "Light the World" videos in the Gospel Library could give you ideas.

"He is the light, the life, and the hope of the world."

- Help your children find Christmas hymns that tell of the light, life, and hope that the Savior's birth brought to the world, such as "O Little Town of Bethlehem" (*Hymns*, no. 208). Sing the hymns together, and let your children share how Jesus has brought light, life, and hope into their lives.

"God be thanked for the matchless gift of His divine Son."

- What gifts have we received because of Jesus Christ? Perhaps you and your children could look for these gifts in "The Living Christ" or in a song like "He Sent His Son" (*Children's Songbook*, 34–35). Then they could gift-wrap something to represent those gifts. You could suggest that your children open the gifts on Christmas Day to help them remember the Savior and His gifts to us.

For more ideas, see this month's issue of the *Friend* magazine.

THE LIVING CHRIST

THE TESTIMONY OF THE APOSTLES

THE CHURCH OF JESUS CHRIST OF LATTER-DAY SAINTS

As we commemorate the birth of Jesus Christ two millennia ago, we offer our testimony of the reality of His matchless life and the infinite virtue of His great atoning sacrifice. None other has had so profound an influence upon all who have lived and will yet live upon the earth.

He was the Great Jehovah of the Old Testament, the Messiah of the New. Under the direction of His Father, He was the creator of the earth. "All things were made by him; and without him was not any thing made that was made" (John 1:3). Though sinless, He was baptized to fulfill all righteousness. He "went about doing good" (Acts 10:38), yet was despised for it. His gospel was a message of peace and goodwill. He entreated all to follow His example. He walked the roads of Palestine, healing the sick, causing the blind to see, and raising the dead. He taught the truths of eternity, the reality of our premortal existence, the purpose of our life on earth, and the potential for the sons and daughters of God in the life to come.

He instituted the sacrament as a reminder of His great atoning sacrifice. He was arrested and condemned on spurious charges, convicted to satisfy a mob, and sentenced to die on Calvary's cross. He gave His life to atone for the sins of all mankind. His was a great vicarious gift in behalf of all who would ever live upon the earth.

We solemnly testify that His life, which is central to all human history, neither began in Bethlehem nor concluded on Calvary. He was the Firstborn of the Father, the Only Begotten Son in the flesh, the Redeemer of the world.

He rose from the grave to "become the firstfruits of them that slept" (1 Corinthians 15:20). As Risen Lord, He visited among those He had loved in life. He also ministered among His "other sheep" (John 10:16) in ancient America. In the modern world, He and His Father appeared to the boy Joseph Smith, ushering in the long-promised "dispensation of the fulness of times" (Ephesians 1:10).

Of the Living Christ, the Prophet Joseph wrote: "His eyes were as a flame of fire; the hair of his head was white like the pure snow; his countenance shone above the brightness of the sun; and his voice was as the sound of the rushing of great waters, even the voice of Jehovah, saying:

"I am the first and the last; I am he who liveth, I am he who was slain; I am your advocate with the Father" (D&C 110:3–4).

Of Him the Prophet also declared: "And now, after the many testimonies which have been given of him, this is the testimony, last of all, which we give of him: That he lives!

"For we saw him, even on the right hand of God; and we heard the voice bearing record that he is the Only Begotten of the Father—

"That by him, and through him, and of him, the worlds are and were created, and the inhabitants thereof are begotten sons and daughters unto God" (D&C 76:22–24).

We declare in words of solemnity that His priesthood and His Church have been restored upon the earth— "built upon the foundation of . . . apostles and prophets, Jesus Christ himself being the chief corner stone" (Ephesians 2:20).

We testify that He will someday return to earth. "And the glory of the Lord shall be revealed, and all flesh shall see it together" (Isaiah 40:5). He will rule as King of Kings and reign as Lord of Lords, and every knee shall bend and every tongue shall speak in worship before Him. Each of us will stand to be judged of Him according to our works and the desires of our hearts.

We bear testimony, as His duly ordained Apostles—that Jesus is the Living Christ, the immortal Son of God. He is the great King Immanuel, who stands today on the right hand of His Father. He is the light, the life, and the hope of the world. His way is the path that leads to happiness in this life and eternal life in the world to come. God be thanked for the matchless gift of His divine Son.

THE FIRST PRESIDENCY

THE QUORUM OF THE TWELVE

January 1, 2000

"He went about doing good" ("The Living Christ").

The pictures on the left show things that Jesus did to set an example. The pictures on the right show ways we can follow His example.

Draw lines to connect each picture on the left with the corresponding picture on the right.

For Parents—Preparing Your Children for a Lifetime on God's Covenant Path

Because He loves you, trusts you, and knows your potential, Heavenly Father has given you the opportunity to help your children enter and progress along His covenant path, the path to eternal life (see Doctrine and Covenants 68:25–28). This includes helping them prepare to make and keep sacred covenants, such as the covenant of baptism and the covenants made in the temple. Through these covenants, your children will be able to joyfully bind themselves to the Savior, Jesus Christ.

There are many ways to prepare your children for this journey on the covenant path, and Heavenly Father will help you discover the best way to help them. As you seek inspiration, keep in mind that not all learning happens during scheduled lessons. In fact, part of what makes learning at home so powerful is the opportunity to learn by example and through small, simple teaching moments—the kind that occur naturally in the flow of daily living. Just as following the covenant path is a consistent, lifelong process, so is learning about the covenant path. (See "Home and Family," *Teaching in the Savior's Way* [2022], 30–31.)

Below are some ideas that may lead to further inspiration. You can find additional ideas for teaching Primary-age children in "Appendix B: For Primary—Preparing Children for a Lifetime on God's Covenant Path."

Nephi taught that "the gate by which [we] should enter" the covenant path "is repentance and baptism by water" (2 Nephi 31:17).

Baptism and Confirmation

Nephi taught that "the gate by which [we] should enter" the covenant path "is repentance and baptism by water" (2 Nephi 31:17). Your efforts to help your children prepare for baptism and confirmation can set their feet firmly on that path. These efforts begin with teaching about faith in Jesus Christ and repentance. They also include teaching about how we renew our baptismal covenants by partaking of the sacrament each week.

Here are some resources that can help you: 2 Nephi 31; special issue of the *Friend* magazine about baptism; Topics and Questions, "Baptism," Gospel Library.

- Whenever you have an experience that strengthens your faith in Heavenly Father and Jesus Christ, share it with your child. Help them understand that faith is something that can grow stronger and stronger throughout life. What are some things your child can do to develop stronger faith in Christ before they are baptized?

- When your child makes a wrong choice, speak joyfully about the gift of repentance. And when you make a wrong choice, share the joy that comes when you repent. Testify that because Jesus Christ suffered and died for our sins, we can repent daily, be forgiven, and receive the power to change. When your child seeks forgiveness, forgive freely and joyfully.

- Tell your child about your baptism. Show pictures and share memories. Talk about how you felt, how keeping your baptismal covenants has helped you come to know Jesus Christ better, and how your covenants continue to bless your life. Encourage your child to ask questions.

- When there is a baptism in your family or your ward, take your child to see it. Talk together about what you and your child saw and felt. If possible, talk to the person being baptized and ask questions like the following: "How did you make this decision? How did you prepare?"

- Whenever you notice your child doing something they promised to do, give sincere praise. Point out that keeping commitments helps us prepare to keep the covenants we make when we are baptized. What do we promise God when we are baptized? What does He promise us? (See Mosiah 18:8–10, 13.)

- Talk about how being confirmed and becoming a member of The Church of Jesus Christ of Latter-day Saints has blessed you. For example, how have you come closer to Heavenly Father and Jesus Christ as you have served others and as others have served you? Help your child think of ways to serve and strengthen others as a member of the Church. Also help them experience and recognize the joy that comes from service.

- When you and your child have a sacred experience together (such as at church, while reading the scriptures, or while serving someone), tell them about the spiritual feelings or impressions you have. Invite your child to share how they feel. Note the variety of ways the Spirit can speak to people, including ways He speaks to you personally. Help your child recognize and share with you moments when they may be experiencing the influence of the Holy Ghost.

- Watch together a few of the videos in the Gospel Library collection titled "Hear Him!" Talk together about the different ways the Lord's servants hear His voice. Invite your child to draw a picture or make a video about how they hear the Savior's voice.

- Make the sacrament a sacred and joyful event in your family. Share with your child how you focus on Jesus Christ during the sacrament. Help your child make a plan to show that the sacrament is sacred to them. For example, listening to the words of the sacrament prayers can remind us of our baptismal covenants.

- Many issues of the *Friend* magazine include articles, stories, and activities to help children prepare for baptism and confirmation. Let your child choose some to read and enjoy with you. (See also the collection "Preparing for Baptism" in the children's section of the Gospel Library.)

Priesthood Power, Authority, and Keys

The priesthood is the authority and power of God by which He blesses His children. God's priesthood is on the earth today in The Church of Jesus Christ of Latter-day Saints. "All Church members who keep their covenants—women, men, and children—are blessed with God's priesthood power in their homes to strengthen themselves and their families" (*General Handbook: Serving in The Church of Jesus Christ of Latter-day Saints*, 3.6, Gospel Library). This power will assist members in doing God's work of salvation and exaltation in their personal lives and families (see *General Handbook*, 2.2).

When men and women serve in Church callings, they do so with priesthood authority, under the direction of those who hold priesthood keys. All of Heavenly Father's children—His sons and His daughters—will be blessed as they come to better understand the priesthood.

We receive ordinances by the authority of the priesthood. "Worthy male Church members receive priesthood authority through priesthood conferral and ordination to priesthood offices" (*General Handbook*, 3.4). Those who hold priesthood offices can be authorized by someone who holds priesthood keys to perform priesthood ordinances.

To learn more about the priesthood, see Russell M. Nelson, "Spiritual Treasures," *Ensign* or *Liahona*, Nov. 2019, 76–79; Russell M. Nelson, "The Price of Priesthood Power," *Ensign* or *Liahona*, May 2016, 66–69; "Priesthood Principles," chapter 3 in *General Handbook*.

- Make priesthood ordinances a consistent part of your family life. For example, help your child prepare spiritually for the sacrament each week. Encourage your child to seek priesthood blessings when they are sick or need comfort or direction. Make it a habit to point out ways the Lord is blessing your family through priesthood power.

- As you read the scriptures together, watch for opportunities to discuss how God blesses people through His power. Share your own experiences of when God has blessed you through His priesthood. For examples of blessings we receive from God through the priesthood, see *General Handbook*, 3.2, 3.5.

- Teach your child that after baptism, they can receive priesthood power by keeping the baptismal covenant. Review together President Russell M. Nelson's message "Spiritual Treasures" (*Ensign* or *Liahona*, Nov. 2019, 76–79). Tell your child how priesthood ordinances have brought God's power into your life. For a list of some of the ways we are blessed by priesthood power, see *General Handbook*, 3.5.

- Discuss the question "What is a servant of the Lord like?" Read together Doctrine and Covenants 121:36–42, and look for answers. Whenever you notice your child (or someone else) applying one of the principles or attributes in these verses, point it out.

- When you or your child uses keys to unlock a door or start a car, take a moment to compare those keys to the keys that priesthood leaders hold. (For a definition of priesthood keys, see *General Handbook*, 3.4.1). What do priesthood keys "unlock" or "start" for us? See also Gary E. Stevenson, "Where Are the Keys and Authority of the Priesthood?," *Ensign* or *Liahona*, May 2016, 29–32; "Where Are the Keys?" (video), Gospel Library.

- When you are set apart for a calling, invite your child to be present, if possible. Let your child see you fulfilling your calling. You might even look for appropriate ways they can help you. Describe how you feel the Lord's power in your calling.

Being Baptized and Confirmed for Ancestors

Temples are a part of Heavenly Father's plan for His children. In the house of the Lord, we make sacred covenants with Heavenly Father as we participate in sacred ordinances, all of which point to Jesus Christ. Heavenly Father has provided a way for all His children to make covenants and participate in ordinances, including people who did not receive them in this life. At the beginning of the year your child turns 12, they are old enough to be baptized and confirmed in the temple for deceased ancestors (see also 1 Corinthians 15:29).

- Go to the house of the Lord as often as your circumstances allow. Talk to your child about why you are going and how the temple helps you feel closer to Heavenly Father and Jesus Christ.

- Review and discuss the temple recommend questions together. You can find them on pages 36–37 of *For the Strength of Youth: A Guide for Making Choices* (2022). Talk to your child about what happens in a temple recommend interview. Share why having a temple recommend is important to you.

- Read together Malachi 4:6. Talk about how your hearts could turn to your ancestors. Learn more about your ancestors by exploring your family history together on FamilySearch.org. Look for ancestors who need to be baptized and confirmed. A ward temple and family history consultant can help you.

- Review together some of the resources in the collection titled "Temple" in the children's section of the Gospel Library. (See also "Preparing Your Child for Temple Baptisms and Confirmations" on ChurchofJesusChrist.org.)

Receiving a Patriarchal Blessing

A patriarchal blessing can be a source of guidance, comfort, and inspiration. It contains personal counsel to us from Heavenly Father and helps us understand our eternal identity and purpose. Help your child prepare to receive a patriarchal blessing by teaching them the significance and sacred nature of patriarchal blessings.

To learn more, see Topics and Questions, "Patriarchal Blessings," Gospel Library; Julie B. Beck, "You Have a Noble Birthright," *Ensign* or *Liahona*, May 2006, 106–8.

- Share with your child your experience of receiving a patriarchal blessing. You could share things like how you prepared to receive it, how it has helped you come closer to God, and how He continues to guide you through this blessing. You could also invite your child to talk to other family members who have received their patriarchal blessings.

- Review together Elder Randall K. Bennett's message "Your Patriarchal Blessing—Inspired Direction from Heavenly Father" and Elder Kazuhiko Yamashita's message "When to Receive Your Patriarchal Blessing" (*Liahona*, May 2023, 42–43, 88–90). Share with each other what you learn from these messages about why Heavenly Father wants us to receive a patriarchal blessing. To learn about the process of receiving a patriarchal blessing, see *General Handbook*, 18.17.

- If you have ancestors who received patriarchal blessings, it might be inspiring to read some of them with your child. To request the blessings of ancestors who have died, log in to ChurchofJesusChrist.org, click **Tools** at the top right corner of the screen, and select **Patriarchal Blessing**.

- After your child has received a patriarchal blessing, invite any family members who were present to record their feelings and share them with your child.

Receiving the Endowment

God wants to endow, or bless, all His children with "power from on high" (Doctrine and Covenants 95:8). We go to the temple to receive our own endowment only once, but the covenants we make with God and the spiritual power He gives us as part of the endowment can bless us every day of our lives.

- Display a picture of the temple in your home. Tell your child about the feelings you experience in the house of the Lord. Talk often about your love for the Lord and His house and the covenants you have made there. Look for opportunities to go to the temple with your child to perform baptisms and confirmations for their ancestors.

- Explore together temples.ChurchofJesusChrist.org. Read together articles like "About the Temple Endowment" and "Prepare for the House of the Lord." Let your child ask any questions they have about the temple. For guidance about what you can talk about outside the temple, see Elder David A. Bednar's message "Prepared to Obtain Every Needful Thing" (*Ensign* or *Liahona*, May 2019, 101–4; see especially the section titled "Home-Centered and Church-Supported Learning and Temple Preparation").

- As you and your child participate in or witness other ordinances (such as the sacrament or a blessing of healing), take a moment to discuss the symbolism involved in the ordinance. What do the symbols represent? How do they testify of Jesus Christ? This can help your child prepare to ponder the symbolic meaning of temple ordinances, which also testify of Jesus Christ.

- Help your child notice how they are keeping the baptismal covenant described in Mosiah 18:8–10, 13. Also help your child notice how the Lord is blessing them. Build your child's confidence in their ability to keep covenants.

- Talk openly and frequently about how your temple covenants guide your choices and help you grow closer to Jesus Christ. You could use *General Handbook*, 27.2, to review the covenants we make in the temple. If you have received the endowment, tell your children about how the temple garment helps you remember your covenants with Jesus Christ (see "Sacred Temple Clothing" [video], Gospel Library).

Serving a Mission

Elder David A. Bednar taught: "The single most important thing you can do to prepare for a call to serve is to become a missionary long before you go on a mission. . . . The issue is not going on a mission; rather, the issue is becoming a missionary and serving throughout our entire life with all of our heart, might, mind, and strength. . . . You are preparing for a lifetime of missionary work" ("Becoming a Missionary," *Ensign* or *Liahona*, Nov. 2005, 45–46). The experiences your child has becoming a missionary will bless them eternally, not just for the period of time they may serve as a missionary.

To learn more, see Russell M. Nelson, "Preaching the Gospel of Peace," *Liahona*, May 2022, 6–7; M. Russell Ballard, "Missionary Service Blessed My Life Forever," *Liahona*, May 2022, 8–10; "Missionary Preparation: Adjusting to Missionary Life," Gospel Library.

- Model how to share the gospel in natural ways. Always be alert to opportunities to share with others your feelings about Heavenly Father and the Savior and the blessings you receive from the Savior's restored gospel and as a member of His Church. Invite others to join your family in Church- and family-related activities.

- Look for opportunities for your family to interact with missionaries. Invite them to teach your friends, or offer to let them teach people in your home. Ask the missionaries about the experiences they're having and how missionary service is helping them draw closer to Jesus Christ. Also ask what they did (or wish they had done) to prepare to be missionaries.

- If you served a mission, talk openly and often about your experiences. Or invite friends or family members who served missions to talk about theirs. You could also talk about ways you've shared the gospel with others throughout your life. Help your child think of ways they can share the gospel.

- Give your child opportunities to teach your family principles of the gospel. Your child could also practice sharing their beliefs with others. For example, you could discuss questions like "How would we introduce the Book of Mormon to someone who has never heard of it?" or "How would we describe the need for the Savior to someone who is not a Christian?"

- Help your child become comfortable talking to people. What are some good ways to start a conversation? Encourage your child to learn how to listen to what others say, understand what is in their hearts, and share truths of the gospel that could bless their lives.

- Look for opportunities for your child to learn about other cultures and faiths. Help them recognize and respect the good and true principles in others' beliefs.

Receiving the Sealing Ordinance

In the temple, a husband and wife can be married for eternity. This occurs in an ordinance called "sealing." Even though this ordinance may be many years away for your daughter or son, the small, simple, consistent things you do together during those years can help them prepare for this wonderful blessing.

- Read together "The Family: A Proclamation to the World" (Gospel Library). What does this proclamation teach about happiness in family life and about successful marriages? With your child, choose one of the principles listed in the proclamation to study. You could look up scriptures related to that principle in the Guide to the Scriptures. You could also set goals to apply that principle more fully in your family. As you work on your goals, discuss together the effect that living that principle has on family life.

- With your child, read President Dieter F. Uchtdorf's message "In Praise of Those Who Save" (*Ensign* or *Liahona*, May 2016, 77–80). When you get to the section titled "A Society of Disposables," you might look for things in your home that are disposable and other things that are not. Talk about how you treat things differently when you want them to last a long time. What does this suggest about how we should treat marriage and family relationships? What else do we learn from President Uchtdorf's message about how the Savior can help us build strong marriages and families?

- Be open with your child about the things you and your spouse are learning about having a Christ-centered eternal marriage and the ways you're trying to improve. If you and your spouse have been sealed in the temple, show your child by example how you strive to keep your covenants with the Lord. Tell your child how you strive to make Heavenly Father and the Savior the center of your relationship and how They are helping you (see also Ulisses Soares, "In Partnership with the Lord," *Liahona*, Nov. 2022, 42–45).

- When family decisions need to be made, hold family councils and discussions. Make sure that all family members' opinions are heard and valued. Use these discussions as an opportunity to model healthy communication and kindness in family relationships, even when not everyone sees things the same way. (See M. Russell Ballard, "Family Councils," *Ensign* or *Liahona*, May 2016, 63–65.)

- When there is disagreement or conflict in the family, demonstrate patience and compassion. Help your child see how handling conflict in Christlike ways can help them prepare for a happy marriage. Read together Doctrine and Covenants 121:41–42, and talk about how the principles in these verses can be applied to marriage.

For Primary—Preparing Children for a Lifetime on God's Covenant Path

In months that have five Sundays, Primary teachers are encouraged to replace the scheduled *Come, Follow Me* outline on the fifth Sunday with one or more of these learning activities.

Principles and Ordinances of the Gospel of Jesus Christ

The doctrine of Christ teaches us how to return to God.

When Jesus Christ appeared to the people in the Americas, He taught them His doctrine. He said that we can enter the kingdom of God if we have faith, repent, are baptized, receive the Holy Ghost, and endure to the end (see 3 Nephi 11:31–40; see also Doctrine and Covenants 20:29). The activities below can help you teach the children that these principles and ordinances will help us draw closer to the Savior throughout our lives.

To learn more about the doctrine of Christ, see 2 Nephi 31.

Possible Activities

- Give the children pictures that represent faith in Jesus Christ, repentance, baptism, and confirmation (see *Gospel Art Book*, nos. 1, 111, 103, and 105). Read or recite with the children the fourth article of faith, and ask them to hold up their pictures when that principle or ordinance is mentioned. Help the children understand how each of these principles and ordinances helps us become more like Heavenly Father and Jesus Christ.

- How can you help the children understand that faith, repentance, baptism, and confirmation are not one-time events but influence our spiritual growth throughout our lives? For instance, you could show them a picture of a seed and a large tree (or draw these things on the board). Help them think of things that help the seed grow into a large tree, such as water, soil, and sunlight. Help them see that these are like the things we do to grow closer to God throughout our lives—building our faith in Jesus Christ, repenting each day, living our baptismal covenants, partaking of the sacrament, and listening to the Holy Ghost.

- Share with the children the story about the firecracker from Elder Dale G. Renlund's message "How Can Repenting Help Me Feel Happy?" (*Friend*, Dec. 2017, 12–13, or *Liahona*, Dec. 2017, 70–71; see also the video "Repentance: A Joyful Choice" [Gospel Library]). At various points during the story, invite the children to think about how Elder Renlund might have felt. Why do we feel joy when we repent? Share with the children the joy and love you have felt when you have asked Heavenly Father to forgive you.

Baptism

Jesus Christ set an example for me when He was baptized.

Even though Jesus was without sin, He was baptized to set a perfect example of obedience to Heavenly Father (see 2 Nephi 31:6–10).

To learn more about baptism, see Doctrine and Covenants 20:37; Topics and Questions, "Baptism," Gospel Library.

Possible Activities

- Show a picture of the Savior's baptism and another person's baptism (or see *Gospel Art Book*, no. 35 and either no. 103 or no. 104). Ask the children to share what is different and what is the same between the two pictures. Read together Matthew 3:13–17 or "Chapter 10: Jesus Is Baptized" in *New Testament Stories*, 26–29 (or the corresponding video in Gospel Library). Let the children point to things in the pictures that are mentioned in the reading or the video. Tell the children about your love for the Savior and your desire to follow Him.

- Listen to or sing a song about baptism, such as "When Jesus Christ Was Baptized" (*Children's Songbook*, 102). What do we learn about baptism from the song? Read 2 Nephi 31:9–10, and invite the children to listen for why Jesus Christ was baptized. Invite them to draw a picture of themselves on their baptism day.

I can choose to make a covenant with God and be baptized.

Preparing for baptism means much more than preparing for an event. It means preparing to make a covenant and then keeping that covenant for a lifetime. Ponder how you can help the children understand the covenant they will make with Heavenly Father when they are baptized, which includes the promises He makes to them and the promises they make to Him.

Possible Activities

- Explain that a covenant is a promise between a person and Heavenly Father. As we strive to keep our promises to God, God promises to bless us. Write on the board *My Promises to God* and *God's Promises to Me*. Read together Mosiah 18:10, 13 and Doctrine and Covenants 20:37, and help the children make a list of the promises they find under the appropriate headings (see also Dallin H. Oaks, "Your Baptism Covenant," *Friend*, Feb. 2021, 2–3). Share how Heavenly Father has blessed you as you strive to keep your baptismal covenant.

- Show the children pictures of things Jesus Christ did during His ministry (for some examples, see *Gospel Art Book*, nos. 33–49). Let the children talk about what Jesus is doing in each picture. Read Mosiah 18:8–10, 13, and invite the children to listen for things they promise to do when they are baptized (see also "The Baptism Covenant," *Friend*, Feb. 2019, 7, or *Liahona*, Feb. 2019, F3). How will these promises influence our actions every day? Invite the children to draw a picture of themselves helping someone the way Jesus would.

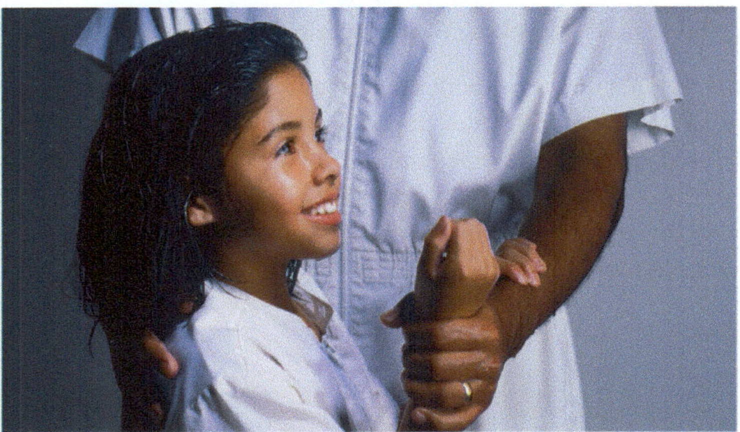

When we are baptized, we make promises to God and He makes promises to us.

Confirmation

When I am confirmed, I become a member of The Church of Jesus Christ of Latter-day Saints.

Becoming a member of The Church of Jesus Christ of Latter-day Saints brings many blessings, including opportunities for the children to be active participants in God's work.

To learn more about confirmation and the gift of the Holy Ghost, see Gary E. Stevenson, "How Does the Holy Ghost Help You?," *Ensign* or *Liahona*, May 2017, 117–20; Topics and Questions, "Holy Ghost," Gospel Library.

Possible Activities

- Invite someone who was recently baptized and confirmed to come to class and share what it was like to be confirmed. Ask this person to talk about what it means to him or her to become a member of The Church of Jesus Christ of Latter-day Saints. Help the children think of ways they can keep their baptismal covenant as members of the Church (such as serving others, inviting others to learn more about Jesus, saying prayers in meetings, and so on). Share how doing these things has helped you feel the joy of being a member of Christ's Church.

- Show a picture of the people at the Waters of Mormon (see *Gospel Art Book*, no. 76), and ask the children to describe what they see in the picture. Tell the story of Alma and his people being baptized there (see Mosiah 18:1–17; "Chapter 15: Alma Teaches and Baptizes," in *Book of Mormon Stories*, 43–44, or the corresponding video in Gospel Library). Review Mosiah 18:8–9 and invite the children to do actions to help them remember the things the people were willing to do as members of Christ's Church. For example, how can we help others "take a step toward making covenants with God"? (Russell M. Nelson, "Hope of Israel" [worldwide youth devotional, June 3, 2018], Gospel Library). Share an experience of when you have witnessed members of the Church serving in these ways.

When I am confirmed, I receive the gift of the Holy Ghost.

When we are baptized and confirmed, Heavenly Father promises that we "may always have his Spirit to be with [us]" (Doctrine and Covenants 20:77). This wonderful gift from God is called the gift of the Holy Ghost.

Possible Activities

- Read Doctrine and Covenants 33:15, and ask the children to listen for the special gift that Heavenly Father gives us when we are baptized and confirmed. To help them learn more about how the gift of the Holy Ghost will help them, review together John 14:26; Galatians 5:22–23; 2 Nephi 32:5; 3 Nephi 27:20. You could also review the article "The Holy Ghost Is . . ." (*Friend*, June 2019, 24–25, or *Liahona*, June 2019, F12–F13).

- Before class, ask the parents of one or more of the children to share how they have been blessed because they have the gift of the Holy Ghost. How does He help them? How do they hear His voice?

- Sing together a song about the Holy Ghost, such as "The Holy Ghost" (*Children's Songbook*, 105). Help the children understand what the song teaches us about how the Holy Ghost can help us.

The Holy Ghost can speak to me in many ways.

Children who can recognize the voice of the Spirit will be prepared to receive personal revelation to guide them throughout their lives. Help them understand that there are many ways the Holy Ghost can speak to us.

Possible Activities

- Help the children think of different ways we could talk to a friend who lives far away, such as writing a letter, sending an email, or talking on the phone. Teach them that Heavenly Father can speak to us in different ways through the Holy Ghost. Use President Dallin H. Oaks's message "How Does Heavenly Father Speak to Us?" to help the children understand the different ways the Holy Ghost can speak to our minds and hearts (*Friend*, Mar. 2020, 2–3, or *Liahona*, Mar. 2020, F2–F3).

- Share an experience when the Holy Ghost communicated with you, either through thoughts in your mind or through a feeling in your heart (see Doctrine and Covenants 6:22–23; 8:2–3; see also Henry B. Eyring, "Open Your Heart to the Holy Ghost," *Friend*, Aug. 2019, 2–3, or *Liahona*, Aug. 2019, F2–F3). Testify to the children that the Holy Ghost can help them in similar ways.

- Help the children recognize times when they are feeling the Spirit—for example, when singing a song about the Savior or when doing something kind for others. Help them recognize the spiritual feelings that the Holy Ghost brings, especially His promptings to act. Why do you think the Holy Ghost gives us these feelings? Help the children think of things that we need to do to hear the Holy Ghost speak to us. Talk about what you do to hear the Spirit more clearly.

The Sacrament

When I take the sacrament, I remember the Savior's sacrifice and renew my covenants.

The Savior gave us the sacrament to help us remember His sacrifice for us and renew our covenants.

To learn more, see Matthew 26:26–30; 3 Nephi 18:1–12; Doctrine and Covenants 20:77, 79.

Possible Activities

- Invite the children to color "Jesus Introduced the Sacrament to the Nephites" in *Scripture Stories Coloring Book: Book of Mormon* (2019), 26. Ask them to point to what the people are thinking about in the picture. Read to the children portions of 3 Nephi 18:1–12 or "Chapter 45: Jesus Christ Teaches about the Sacrament and Prayer," in *Book of Mormon Stories*, 126–27 (or watch the corresponding video in Gospel Library). What can we do to remember Jesus Christ during the sacrament?

- Ask the children to tell you some things they should always remember to do, such as tying their shoes or washing their hands before they eat. Why is it important to remember these things? Read Moroni 4:3 to the children, and invite them to listen for what we promise to always remember when we take the sacrament. Why is it important to remember Jesus Christ? Help the children understand how the bread and water of the sacrament help us remember what Jesus has done for us (see Moroni 4:3; 5:2).

- Write on the board "I promise to . . ." Read the sacrament prayers to the children (see Doctrine and Covenants 20:77, 79). When they hear a promise we make to God, pause and help them complete the sentence on the board with the promise they heard. Help them understand that when we take the sacrament, we are making the same promises we made at baptism.

- What does it mean to take upon ourselves the name of Jesus Christ? To help the children answer this question, share an example of something that we put our names on. Why do we put our names on these things? Why would Jesus Christ want to put His name upon us? Consider sharing this explanation from President Russell M. Nelson: "Taking the Savior's name upon us includes declaring and witnessing to others—through our actions and our words—that Jesus is the Christ" ("The Correct Name of the Church," *Ensign* or *Liahona*, Nov. 2018, 88).

Priesthood Power, Authority, and Keys

God blesses His children through priesthood power.

All of God's children—female and male, young and old—receive God's power as they keep the covenants they have made with Him. We make these covenants when we receive priesthood ordinances such as baptism (see *General Handbook: Serving in The Church of Jesus Christ of Latter-day Saints*, 3.5, 3.6, Gospel Library). To learn more, see Russell M. Nelson, "Spiritual Treasures," *Ensign* or *Liahona*, Nov. 2019, 76–79; "Priesthood Principles," chapter 3 in *General Handbook*.

Possible Activities

- Help the children notice the blessings they receive because of the priesthood. To give them some ideas, you could show the video "Blessings of the Priesthood" (Gospel Library). Consider listing these blessings on the board. Why are these blessings important to us? Testify that these blessings come to us because of Jesus Christ and His priesthood power.

- Help the children find pictures that illustrate how God uses His power to bless us. For example, they could find a picture of the world He created for us, examples of healing the sick, and sacred ordinances He has provided for us (see *Gospel Art Book*, nos. 3, 46, 104, 105, 107, 120). Share why you are grateful for the priesthood and the blessings it brings. Help the children think of experiences when they were blessed by God's priesthood power.

- One of the main ways we receive the blessings of God's power in our lives is through priesthood ordinances (see Doctrine and Covenants 84:20). To help the children learn this truth, you could list the following scriptures on the board: 3 Nephi 11:21–26, 33 (baptism); Moroni 2 (confirmation); Moroni 4–5 (sacrament). The children could each choose one of these passages and identify the ordinance it describes. Invite the children to share how they have been personally blessed by receiving priesthood ordinances.

- Help the children understand that they will receive power from God as they are baptized and keep their baptismal covenant. Ask the children how this power could help them.

God's work is directed by priesthood keys and accomplished by priesthood authority.

Whenever a person is set apart for a calling or assigned to help in God's work, she or he can exercise delegated priesthood authority. In addition, worthy male Church members can be ordained to an office in the priesthood. The use of all priesthood authority in the Church is directed by individuals who hold priesthood keys, such as the stake president, the bishop, and quorum presidents. Priesthood keys are the authority to direct the use of the priesthood in doing the work of the Lord.

Possible Activities

- Read with the children Mark 3:14–15, and show them a picture of the event described there (such as *Gospel Art Book*, no. 38). Ask the children if they have ever seen someone be set apart for a calling or ordained to a priesthood office (or tell them about experiences you have had). How is that similar to what the Savior did with His Apostles? Help the children list on the board callings or priesthood offices that can be given to members of the Church, such as a teacher or leader in an organization. Next to each calling or office, you could write what someone with that calling or office has the authority to do. Tell the children how being set apart by someone with the direction of priesthood keys has helped you serve.

- Invite the children to think of something that you need a key for, such as a car or a door. What happens if you don't have the key? Read together Doctrine and Covenants 65:2, and share your testimony about the importance of having priesthood keys. You could also watch the video "Where Are the Keys?" (Gospel Library) and look for what Elder Gary E. Stevenson teaches about priesthood keys.

The Temple and the Plan of Happiness

The temple is the house of the Lord.

Temples are a part of Heavenly Father's plan for His children. In temples, we make sacred covenants with Him, are endowed with priesthood power, receive revelation, perform ordinances for our deceased ancestors, and are sealed to our families for eternity. All of this is possible because of Jesus Christ and His atoning sacrifice.

How can you help the children you teach recognize the sacredness of the Lord's house and prepare themselves to be worthy to participate in temple ordinances? Consider reviewing these resources: Doctrine and Covenants 97:15–17; Russell M. Nelson, "Closing Remarks," *Ensign* or *Liahona*, Nov. 2019, 120–22; "Why Latter-day Saints Build Temples," temples. ChurchofJesusChrist.org.

Temples are a part of Heavenly Father's plan for His children.

Possible Activities

- Display one or more pictures of temples. Ask the children what makes the temple a special place. Point out that on each temple is this inscription: "Holiness to the Lord—The House of the Lord." Ask the children what they think "Holiness to the Lord" might mean. Why is the temple called the house of the Lord? What does this teach us about the temple? If any of the children have been to a temple, they could also share how they felt when they were there. If you have been to the temple, share how you have felt the Lord's presence there, and talk about why the temple is a sacred place to you.

- Read together Doctrine and Covenants 97:15–17. Ask the children to look for what the Lord expects of people who enter His holy house. Why do we need to be worthy to enter His house? As part of this conversation, talk to the children about temple recommends, including how to receive one. You could invite a member of the bishopric to share with them what a temple recommend interview is like and the questions that are asked in one.

In the temple, we make covenants with God.

President Russell M. Nelson taught, "Jesus Christ invites us to take the covenant path back home to our Heavenly Parents and be with those we love" ("Come, Follow Me," *Ensign* or *Liahona*, May 2019, 91). Help the children understand that the covenant path includes baptism, confirmation, and the temple endowment and sealing.

Possible Activities

- Ask the children to help you review the covenant that we make with God when we are baptized and that we renew when we partake of the sacrament (see Mosiah 18:10; Doctrine and Covenants 20:77, 79). Show a picture of the temple, and explain that Heavenly Father has more blessings He wants to give us in the temple.

- Draw a gate leading to a path. Ask the children why they think it is helpful to have a path to walk on. Read together 2 Nephi 31:17–20, where Nephi compares the covenant of baptism to a gate and invites us to continue on the path after baptism. There are more covenants to make after baptism, including covenants made in the temple. Explain that President Nelson has called this path the "covenant path."

In the temple, we can be baptized and confirmed for ancestors who have died.

The gospel of Jesus Christ makes it possible for all of God's children to return to live with Him, even if they die without knowing the gospel. In the temple, we can be baptized and confirmed members of the Church of Jesus Christ on their behalf.

Possible Activities

- Talk about a time when someone did something for you that you could not do for yourself. Invite the children to share similar experiences. Explain that when we go to the temple, we can receive sacred ordinances such as baptism for others who have died. How are we being like Jesus when we are doing work for the dead? What has He done for us that we couldn't do for ourselves?

- Invite one or more youth who have been baptized for their ancestors to share their experience. Ask them what it was like in the temple. Encourage them to share how they felt doing this work for their ancestors.

- Draw a tree on the board, including the roots and branches. Ask the children to think of how a family is like a tree. Label the roots *Ancestors*, label the branches *Descendants*, and label the trunk of the tree *You*. Read together this sentence from Doctrine and Covenants 128:18: "For we without them [our ancestors] cannot be made perfect; neither can they without us be made perfect." Ask questions like the following: "Why do we need our ancestors? Why do our ancestors need us? How have our parents, grandparents, and other ancestors helped us?" Invite the children to search the rest of Doctrine and Covenants 128:18 for a phrase that describes how we can help our ancestors.

- Consider working with the parents of each child to find the name of an ancestor who needs ordinances in the temple (see FamilySearch.org).

For Primary—Instructions for Singing Time and the Children's Sacrament Meeting Presentation

Sacred music is a powerful tool to help children learn about Heavenly Father's plan of happiness and the foundational truths of the gospel of Jesus Christ. As children sing about gospel principles, the Holy Ghost will testify of their truthfulness. The words and music will stay in the children's minds and hearts throughout their lives.

Seek the help of the Spirit as you prepare to teach the gospel through music. Share your testimony of the truths you sing about. Help the children see how the music relates to what they are learning and experiencing at home and in Primary classes.

Guidelines for the Sacrament Meeting Presentation

With the direction of the bishop, the children's sacrament meeting presentation is normally held during the fourth quarter of the year. As the Primary presidency and music leader, work with the counselor in the bishopric who oversees Primary to plan the presentation.

The presentation should allow the children to present what they and their families have learned from the Doctrine and Covenants at home and in Primary, including the Primary songs they have sung during the year. As you plan the presentation, think of ways it can help the congregation focus on the Savior and His teachings.

Units with small numbers of children may consider ways in which family members can participate with their children. A member of the bishopric may conclude the meeting with brief remarks.

As you prepare the presentation, remember the following guidelines:

- Practices should not take unnecessary time away from Primary classes or families.

- Visuals, costumes, and media presentations are not appropriate for sacrament meeting.

See *General Handbook: Serving in The Church of Jesus Christ of Latter-day Saints*, 12.2.1.2, Gospel Library.

Instructions for Singing Time

5 minutes (Primary presidency): Opening prayer, scripture or article of faith, and one talk

20 minutes (music leader): Singing time

The Primary presidency and music leader select songs for each month to reinforce principles the children are learning in their classes and at home. A list of songs that reinforce these principles is included in this guide.

As you teach songs to the children, invite them to share what they have already learned about the stories and doctrinal principles the songs teach. Invite the children to share their thoughts and feelings about the truths found in the songs.

The *Children's Songbook* is the basic resource for music in Primary. Hymns from the hymnbook and songs from the *Friend* are also appropriate. The use of any other music in Primary must be approved by the bishopric (see *General Handbook*, 12.3.4).

Music for Singing Time

January
- "Follow the Prophet," *Children's Songbook*, 110–11

- "Search, Ponder, and Pray," *Children's Songbook*, 109

February
- "Dare to Do Right," *Children's Songbook*, 158

- "A Child's Prayer," *Children's Songbook*, 12–13

March
- "Every Star Is Different," *Children's Songbook*, 142

- "When I Am Baptized," *Children's Songbook*, 103

April
- "When He Comes Again," *Children's Songbook*, 82–83

- "Did Jesus Really Live Again?," *Children's Songbook*, 64

May

- "'Give,' Said the Little Stream," *Children's Songbook*, 236

- "Shine On," *Children's Songbook*, 144

June

- "The Holy Ghost," *Children's Songbook*, 105

- "I Want to Be a Missionary Now," *Children's Songbook*, 168

July

- "Stand for the Right," *Children's Songbook*, 159

- "He Sent His Son," *Children's Songbook*, 34–35

August

- "I'm Trying to Be like Jesus," *Children's Songbook*, 78–79

- "I Feel My Savior's Love," *Children's Songbook*, 74–75

September

- "I Love to See the Temple," *Children's Songbook*, 95

- "To Think about Jesus," *Children's Songbook*, 71

October

- "Family History—I Am Doing It," *Children's Songbook*, 94

- "The Church of Jesus Christ," *Children's Songbook*, 77

November

- "Keep the Commandments," *Children's Songbook*, 146

- "To Be a Pioneer," *Children's Songbook*, 218–19

December

- "I Am a Child of God," *Children's Songbook*, 2–3

- "O Little Town of Bethlehem," *Hymns*, no. 208

Using Music to Teach Doctrine

Singing time is intended to help the children learn the truths of the gospel. The following ideas can inspire you as you plan ways to teach the gospel principles found in hymns and Primary songs.

Read related scriptures. For many of the songs in the *Children's Songbook* and the hymnbook, references to related scriptures are listed. Help the children read some of these passages, and talk about how the scriptures are related to the song. You could also list a few scripture references on the board and invite the children to match each reference to a song or a verse from a song.

Fill in the blank. Write a verse of the song on the board with several key words missing. Then ask the children to sing the song, listening for the words that fill in the blanks. As they fill in each blank, discuss what gospel principles you learn from the missing words.

Testify. Bear brief testimony to the children of gospel truths found in the Primary song. Help the children understand that singing is one way they can bear testimony and feel the Spirit.

Stand as a witness. Invite children to take turns standing and sharing what they learn from the song they are singing or how they feel about the truths taught in the song. Ask them how they feel as they sing the song, and help them identify the influence of the Holy Ghost.

Use pictures. Ask the children to help you find or create pictures that go with important words or phrases in the song. Invite them to share how the pictures relate to the song and what the song teaches. For example, if you are teaching the song "When He Comes Again" (*Children's Songbook*, 82–83), you could place pictures throughout the room that depict important words from the song (such as *angels*, *snow*, and *star*). Ask the children to gather the pictures and hold them up in the correct order as you sing the song together.

Share an object lesson. You could use an object to inspire discussion about a song. For example, when singing the song "'Give,' Said the Little Stream" (*Children's Songbook*, 236), you could show the children a picture of things like a stream, grass, rain, and flowers. This could lead to a discussion about how even small acts of service can bless others in important ways.

Invite sharing of personal experiences. Help the children connect the principles taught in the song with experiences they have had with these principles. For example, before singing "I Love to See the Temple" (*Children's Songbook*, 95), you could ask the children to raise their hands if they have seen a temple. Invite them, as they sing, to think about how they feel when they see a temple.

Ask questions. There are many questions you can ask as you sing songs. For example, you can ask the children what they learn from each verse in the song. You can also ask them to think of questions that the song answers. This can lead to a discussion about the truths taught in the song.

Use simple hand actions. Invite the children to think of simple hand actions to help them remember the words and messages of a song. For example, when you sing "Search, Ponder, and Pray" (*Children's Songbook*, 109), you could invite the children to point to their eyes as they sing about searching the scriptures, point to their heads as they sing about pondering, and fold their arms as they sing about praying.

For Aaronic Priesthood Quorums and Young Women Classes—Meeting Agenda

Meeting date:

Conducting (member of the class or quorum presidency):

Opening

Hymn (optional):

Prayer:

Repeat the Young Women Theme or the Aaronic Priesthood Quorum Theme.

Counsel together

Led by the person conducting the meeting, the class or quorum spends 5 to 10 minutes counseling together about their responsibilities in God's work of salvation and exaltation. This is an opportunity for the class or quorum presidency to follow up on items discussed in presidency meetings or ward youth council meetings.

The person conducting could also use one or more of these questions:

Living the gospel

- What recent experiences have strengthened our testimonies of Jesus Christ and His gospel?

- What are we doing to draw closer to the Savior? How are we trying to be more like Him?

- How have we felt the Lord's guidance in our lives?

Caring for people in need

- Who have we felt guided to help or serve? What assignments have we received from the bishopric to help someone in need?

- What challenges are the members of our class or quorum facing? How can we support each other in the things we are going through?

- Has someone recently moved into our ward or joined the Church? How can we help them feel welcome?

Inviting all to receive the gospel

- What can we do to help others feel God's love?

- What activities are coming up that we can invite our friends to attend?

- What plans to share the gospel have been discussed in ward youth council meetings? How can our class or quorum get involved?

Uniting families for eternity

- What are some ways we can better connect with family members, including grandparents and cousins?

- What are we doing to find names of our ancestors who need temple ordinances? What can we do to help others find the names of their ancestors?

- How can we participate more in temple work—individually and as a class or quorum?

Learn together

An adult leader or a member of the quorum or class leads instruction about this week's *Come, Follow Me* reading. They use the study ideas in *Come, Follow Me—For Home and Church*. The study idea with this icon is aligned with seminary and is especially relevant to youth. However, any of the study ideas may be used. This portion of the meeting usually takes about 35 to 40 minutes.

Closing

The person conducting the meeting:

- Bears testimony of the principles taught.

- Discusses how the class or quorum will act on what they learned—as a group or individually.

Prayer:

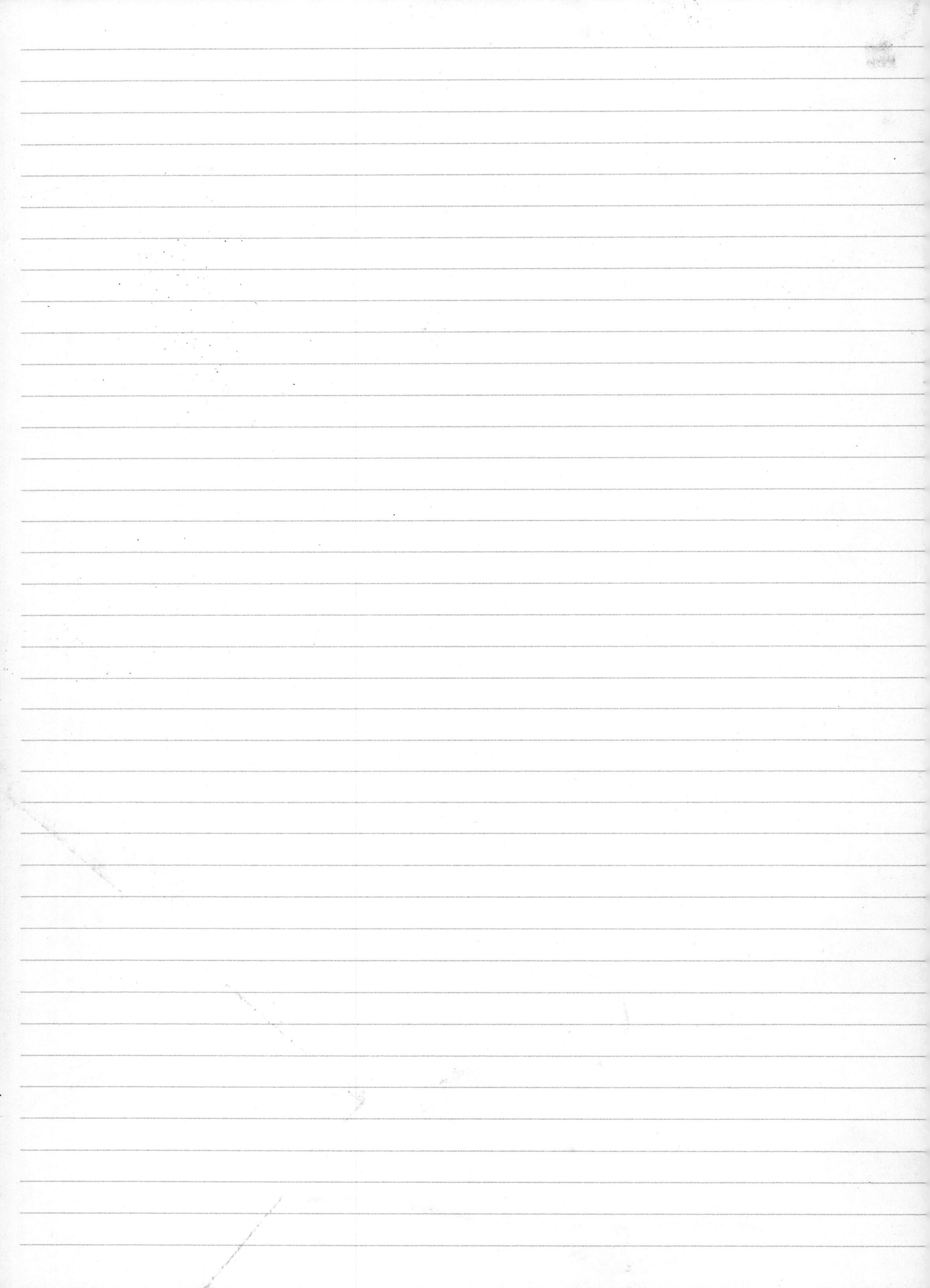